Life in the Classroom and Playground

The Accounts of Primary School Children

Social Worlds of Childhood

General Editor: Rom Harré

Life in the Classroom and Playground

The Accounts of Primary School Children

Bronwyn Davies

Illustrated by Paul, Jacob and Daniel Davies

Routledge & Kegan Paul
London, Melbourne, Boston and Henley

First published in 1982
by Routledge & Kegan Paul Ltd
39 Store Street, London WC1E 7DD,
296 Beaconsfield Parade, Middle Park,
Melbourne, 3206, Australia,
9 Park Street, Boston, Mass. 02108, USA, and
Broadway House, Newtown Road,
Henley-on-Thames, Oxon RG9 1EN
Set in IBM Press Roman by
Thames Typesetting, Abingdon
and printed in Great Britain by
Redwood Burn Ltd, Trowbridge, Wiltshire

Library of Congress Cataloging in Publication Data

Davies, Bronwyn, 1945-
Primary school children's accounts of life in the
classroom and playground.
(Social worlds of childhood)
Bibliography: p.
Includes index.
1. School children — Attitudes. 2. Socialization.
I. Title. II. Series.
LC191.D354 1982   372.18'1   82–11297

ISBN 0–7100–9210–5

Contents

General Editor's Preface

For most of us childhood is a forgotten and even a rejected time. The aim of this series is to recover the flavour of childhood and adolescence in a systematic and sympathetic way. The frame of mind cultivated by the authors as investigators is that of anthropologists who glimpse a strange tribe across a space of forest and millennia of time. The huddled group on the other side of the school playground and the thumping of feet in the upstairs rooms mark the presence of a strange tribe. This frame of mind is deliberately different from that of the classical investigators of child psychology, who have brought adult concepts to bear upon the understanding of children's thoughts and actions, and have looked at childhood primarily as a passage towards the skills and accomplishments and distortions of adults. In these studies the authors try to look upon the activities of children as autonomous and complete in themselves. Of course, not all the activities of childhood could be treated in this way. Rather than being in opposition to the traditional kind of study, the work upon which this series is based aims to amplify our understanding by bringing to light aspects of childhood which usually remain invisible when it is looked at in the traditional way. The ethogenic method is in use throughout the studies represented in this series, that is the children themselves are the prime sources of theories about their actions and thoughts and of explanations of the inwardness of their otherwise mysterious activities.

Acknowledgments

The author and publishers gratefully acknowledge permission to reprint the following material: Peter L. Berger and Thomas Luckmann: *The Social Construction of Reality*, pp. 53–4, 71, 79. Copyright © Peter L. Berger and Thomas Luckmann, 1966. Permission granted by Penguin Books Ltd and Doubleday & Company Inc. J. Britton: 'What's the use? A schematic account of language functions', in A. Cashdan (ed.): *Language in Education* (1972), p. 246, Routledge & Kegan Paul. Permission granted by the Editors of *Educational Review*. W. Damon: *The Social World of the Child* (1977), pp. 157–8, 159, Jossey-Bass. 'Aspects of the problem of common sense knowledge of common sense structures', quoted by H. Mehan in A. Cicourel *et al.* (eds): *Language Use and School Performance* (1975), Academic Press. H. H. Gerth and C. Wright Mills: *Character and Social Structure* (1954), p. 300, Routledge & Kegan Paul and Harcourt Brace Jovanovich. Jules Henry: *Culture Against Man* (1965), pp. 289, 290, 291, Random House Inc. Koestler: *The Act of Creation* (1966). Permission granted by the Hutchinson Publishing Group. C. Wright Mills: *The Sociological Imagination* (1959), pp. 220–1, and *Power, Politics and People: The Collected Essays of C. Wright Mills*, ed. I. L. Horowitz, copyright © 1963 by the Estate of C. Wright Mills. Reprinted by permission of Oxford University Press Inc. I. Opie and P. Opie: *The Lore and Language of Schoolchildren* (1959), p. 324, Oxford University Press. A. Schutz: *The Phenomenology of the Social World* (1972), pp. 73, 74, 99, 127, 128, 133, 171, Heinemann Educational Books and Northwestern University Press. A. Schutz: *Collected Papers vol. 1 The Problem of Social Reality* (1973), pp. xxix, 7, 326, 327, Martinus Nijhoff. M. Speier: 'The Child as Conversationalist', in M. Hammersley and P. Woods (eds): *The Process of Schooling* (1976), Routledge &

Kegan Paul. A. L. Strauss: 'Language and Identity', in A. Cashdan (ed.): *Language in Education* (1972), p. 72, Routledge & Kegan Paul and the Free Press. D. H. Zimmerman and D. L. Wieder: 'Ethnomethodology and the Problem of Social Order', in J. Douglas (ed.): *Understanding Everyday Life* (1971), Routledge & Kegan Paul and Aldine Publishing.

1
Introduction

How does the world look to children?

Overview

Children have been written about from many perspectives, and for a multitude of purposes. Rarely have they been asked to speak for themselves, though their written work is sometimes taken seriously enough (see, for example, Dunkle and the Children's Panel, 1979, and for their traditional literature see Opie and Opie, 1959, and Turner, 1969). But children are generally not asked to make an account of the social world as they perceive it. To approach children from an ethogenic orientation, and to ask them to give an account of their world, involves taking children more seriously than we have been used to doing, as people with a perspective of their own and strategies of their own for dealing with the social world that they perceive; as people who have, in fact, a culture of their own.

A variety of social scientists, in various parts of the world, have commenced this task of gathering accounts from children concerning their particular perspectives and strategies in relation to the social world.*

---

*Some of the social scientists who have actually begun asking children to make an account of their social world include, for example, Baker, 1980; Corrigan, 1979; Damon, 1977; Furlong, 1976; Kitwood, 1980; Lambart, 1976; Marsh, Rosser and Harré, 1978; Meyenn, 1980; Morgan, O'Neill and Harré, 1979; Rosser and Harré, 1976; Silvers, 1977a; Werthman, 1971; Willis, 1977; and Woods, 1976, 1979, 1980.

Others have begun making detailed observations of children in interaction with each other, and with adults, in an attempt to gain a clearer understanding of the social world of children. These include, for example, Byers and Byers, 1972; Cicourel and Boese, 1972; Cottle, 1967; Cusick, 1973; Denzin, 1977; Dumont and Wax, 1971; Edwards and Furlong, 1978; Goodnow, 1976; Gracey, 1975; Griffin and Mehan, forthcoming; Hammersley, 1976, 1977; Henry, 1965, 1968; Holt,

A common thread running through the work of each of these authors is the idea that children interpret the world differently from adults, not because they have not yet learned to see the world 'properly', but because they are viewing it in their own terms, terms which some of these authors have come to view as the culture of childhood.

This study seeks to extend the insights developed by these various authors and to do so in the Australian context with children of upper primary school age. That the children of the study are Australian and of an age group different from any of the children in the cited studies makes them, on the surface of things, quite different. Yet it will be apparent, as the work progresses, that there are many parallels in children's culture in Australia, Britain and North America, and that *being a child* is more significant than belonging to a particular country or a particular age group, or even a particular social class.

The study is based on understandings derived from conversations that I had over a period of one year with a group of 10- and 11-year-old children. Our talk covered a wide range of topics. Amongst other things we talked about the people who mattered to them – friends, family and teachers, each of these becoming topics of conversation when they were problematic in the ongoing lives of the children, and slipping into the background taken-for-granted world when interactions with them flowed smoothly and needed no thought or attention. In this manner I discovered through the children's accounts what was important to them, from their point of view.

This study has thus capitalised on the ability children have to make an account of their experiences. It has moved from children's interpretations of their experiences in school to adult interpretations of that talk and those experiences.

But the study does not deal solely with children's *talk about* their experiences. Because they came into the interview in groups they brought their social world with them and that social world became an observable part of the talk. They talked to me about their interactions and they interacted with each other and with me at the same time. The interviews were, in an important sense, not separate from life as the children knew it; they were life, brought into the interview room from the classroom and the playground. My own children further provided an interactional forum for the development of my thinking about the children at school.

My research experience was one of listening, observing, and interacting with children, of developing through these experiences with

1969; Leiter, 1976; Malcolm, 1977; Mehan, 1974, 1979a, 1979b; Sharp and Green, 1975; Shields, 1978; Silvers, 1977b, 1979; and Speier, 1976.

children an understanding of the particular perspectives children bring to their interactions with each other and with adults. Chapter 2 deals with the methodology which makes such a study possible.

In Chapter 3 I look at the social location of children and the contextual framework of their accounts. I will examine the interactions I had with them in terms of how we each cued into the other's world and found an appropriate and workable system of interaction.

In Chapter 4 I use the discussions I had with the children about friendship to demonstrate the centrality and power of childhood culture as it applies to the children's interactions with one another. Why they are so important to one another, how they influence one another and why and how they interact in the ways they do are the central themes of this chapter. In many ways, this is the most challenging piece of analysis, for it involves understanding those aspects of the children's world to which I am not privy and yet which, I feel, are central to their construction of the world. Here there are no adults to call the tune and no dominant adult culture to which they must react. This is the world of children where their own cultural meanings, standards, rules and beliefs are established and maintained.

In Chapter 5 I analyse the strategies the children use for making sense of and coping with the adult world. The children's world is presented in this chapter as one with its own pragmatic philosophy. The integrity of children's culture, often difficult for outsiders to comprehend, is comprehensible if studied from the insiders' point of view. The effects of continued contact with the more powerful adult culture, and the forces which maintain the separate children's culture are discussed. One of the purposes of this chapter is to throw some light on classroom processes by looking at these processes from the children's point of view. The knowledge children bring to adult-child interactions is different from that brought to their shared culture, and it is different again from the knowledge adults bring to adult-child interactions. Though adults may assume a reciprocity of perspectives when they interact with children, it is clear if one listens to children that this is a somewhat fallacious assumption. The tasks which face children in the classroom, as Hargreaves (1975, p.144) has pointed out, are different from the tasks facing adults. Where tasks differ, perceptions, understandings and strategies will differ also. School for children, then, need not necessarily be about teachers and how to cope with them. That was an early assumption *I* had to overcome. The following conversation is an amusing example of questions asked from my adult perspective (which assumes that school is about teaching and learning), and answers given from the children's point of view:

*Transcript 1.1: Henry, Sally and Garry**

B.D.:   OK now Henry, tell me what you think of the class you're in.

Henry: Oh, I like it better than any other school. Except for X School.

Sally: Erh — that's awful.

B.D.:   Did you go to X School for a while?

Henry: No, I never went there but my brother went there.

B.D.:   What do you think would be good about X School?

Henry: 'Cos they buy icecreams, lollies, scrummos.

Garry: Not scrummos!

B.D.:   Don't you have those at the tuckshop here?

Sally: But you've got to eat them before you go to class!
          (*indignant — in ref. to X School*)

B.D.:   What do you like about this school, Henry?

Henry: You can just about do anything.

Garry: Oh/

Sally: You get more things here.

B.D.:   Let Henry tell me will you?

Henry: You know them iced coffee, strawberry milk and new packets of chips, nut chew, oranges and apples.
          (*Other children interject or amend this food list, all talking at once and with great enthusiasm*)

In the year of my study, however, teachers did become problematic because the children had to learn to cope with a succession of very different teachers whose views of the teaching-learning process differed quite markedly from one to another. The children found themselves continually stressed by their inability to get on with their teachers, and so teachers were often the subject of our talk. Under more 'normal' circumstances the children may have found little to say about the class-room and the teaching-learning enterprise since not only is this aspect of schooling generally considered by children to be part of the teacher's rather than the pupils' responsibility, but most of what happens in the classrooms is taken-for-granted, unproblematic and not in need, there-fore, of further attention and analysis.

In the Conclusion I look at what is to be gained by studying children from their own perspective. The study of children's culture has direct implications for adult-child interaction and for teacher-pupil inter-action in particular. I suggest that teachers who can take the pupils'

---

* The names of the children, staff and the school are pseudonyms. Since much of what we said was in confidence I wish to uphold that confidence through granting anonymity to the protagonists.

perspective into account will more successfully interact with these
pupils in the process of passing their adult knowledge on to their
pupils.

Autobiographical Note

C. Wright Mills declares that the authors of the best social science
present themselves as people rather than as depersonalised automatons
whose heavy style depends on some reified knowledge of 'how it is
done'. He says:

> We must distinguish two ways of presenting the work of social
> science according to the idea the writer has of himself, and the voice
> with which he speaks. One way results from the idea that he is a
> man who may shout, whisper, or chuckle – but who is always there.
> It is also clear what sort of man he is: whether confident or
> neurotic, direct or involuted he *is* a centre of experience and
> reasoning; now he has found out something, and he is telling us
> about it, and how he found it out. This is the voice behind the best
> expositions available in the English language.
>
> The other way of presenting work does not use any voice of
> any man. Such writing is not a 'voice' at all. It is an autonomous
> sound. It is a prose manufactured by a machine. That it is full of
> jargon is not as noteworthy as that it is strongly mannered: it is
> not only impersonal; it is pretentiously impersonal. Government
> bulletins are sometimes written in this way. Business letters also.
> And a great deal of social science. Any writing – perhaps apart
> from that of certain truly great stylists – that is not imaginable as
> human speech is bad writing. (1970, p.242)

My reasons for presenting myself as 'I' rather than as 'the author'
stem not just from a stylistic preference, but from a recognition of the
fact that the pragmatic nature of this study necessarily involves me as
a person.*

To present the data as if I had not been involved would be to tell
only part of the story.

In reading similar research, but without personal knowledge of the
author, I have sometimes been bothered by lack of such knowledge
and found myself turning continually to the dust jacket and the front
pages of the book hoping to pick up some glimmer of information
about the person writing that I may have missed on first perusal. The

---

* James (1978), pp. 11–13, for instance, claims that ideas are
largely influenced by the temperament of the writer.

few biographical sentences which are sometimes to be found (aided by the occasional photograph) go some way to filling the vacuum, though rarely far enough.

Much about an author can be guessed at from the written style and from the content of the work. It is my wish to reduce the guesswork on this occasion by telling you something of myself and my background, such that I am clearly present in what follows.

I was born on 10 January 1945, the third child of a well-to-do solicitor in an Australian country town. I was raised partly by my mother, a quiet, shy, gentle woman of some 'breeding' though little education and by the succession of 'maids' who lived in and helped my mother manage our large and rowdy household. There were four of us: my older sister, much like Hartley's Hilda in *The Shrimp and the Anemone*, powerfully stamped her model of the world on whoever would listen, and persecuted somewhat mercilessly those who would not; my older brother who attempted to solve his problems through systematic persecution of those he would love; and my younger brother who was a sometime delightful companion.

The most vivid feeling attached to my childhood was one of freedom. My father was rarely present. My mother believed that the old style of strict upbringing was wrong but could find nothing definite to take its place. She fairly steadfastly steered a course of non-interference and non-intervention in our lives and pursued her own interests instead. We were free to wander all day through the country-side, to read curled up in bed late into the night, to explore and develop close relationships with people outside and unknown to the family. Free to be quiet and to think, free to make mistakes, free to fight, and free to make reconciliation if we could. Sometimes I experienced freedom as lonely and frightening, since I seemed to be accountable only to myself. It grew upon me none the less as the only conceivable state of being, to be alone with my own consciousness yet open to close enduring relationships of my own making.

I was educated in a small Church of England private school for girls which was staffed by English, Australian and New Zealander women whose main function was to create in us a love of all that was good in English history and literature and in the manners of the Australian upper middle class. In speech, manners, and understanding of the world we were gently tutored (gently, that is, with a few ogreish exceptions), gently, because we showed little resistance. There were some rebels, but these were to be succoured and embraced in a spirit of acceptance and understanding. They were definitely not to be rejected for their differences. Again the primary message, through the religious teaching of the school, was that we must strive for our own personal answers to life's mysteries. These were not something anyone else could provide for us. We must find them for ourselves.

Out of this somewhat rarefied existence I was ejected at the age of 16 and made my way to the university to become a teacher, modelling myself on those who had attended to my education. Youthful in the extreme and with a somewhat shaky educational background I struggled through the three years necessary to gain a BA in psychology and English. At the end of those three years excited by vaguely apprehended new horizons and no longer prepared to fit old models, I took myself off to the city to gain employment and to discover something of the world beyond what schools and small country towns had to offer. I tried several different jobs, but found no satisfying direction for myself. Age-old patterns reasserted themselves and marriage presented itself as an obvious direction for my life.

Three small sons and five painful years later, at the tender age of 25 I found myself a widow with no clear means of financial support. I returned to the private school system which had nurtured me once, this time as a teacher. Whilst I welcomed the warm familiar supportive environment, I no longer found it compatible with the person I had become. I continued teaching, but enrolled in a DipEd course at the same time. Further qualifications seemed necessary for the sort of freedom I wanted. I discovered, then, in the study of sociology the key to a more coherent and useful construction of the world than I had heretofore been able to find. Much that I had not been able to explain in myself and others began to make sense. My life began to take a more coherent shape and direction as I pursued further studies. An incidental and unexpected (though much appreciated) reward for my studies came in the form of a tutorship, then a lectureship (albeit temporary) in the education faculty of the University of New England.

Looking after three babies, working and studying made for a demanding and exhilarating existence. The children, Paul, Jacob and Daniel, now aged 16, 14 and 13, still at the hub of my existence, are in many ways also the authors of this book. They it is who have patiently (and sometimes not so patiently) explained to me the workings of their own minds, related to me the details of their experiences at school as they perceived them and defended the integrity and logic of their own position and their own view of things, in spite of anything I might say.

Currently I am still lecturing in the education faculty and as this project draws to a close, I am initiating a video study of primary classrooms.

The project

In 1975 I enrolled in a PhD programme. My wish was to extend an earlier study that I had undertaken of Aboriginal children in open classrooms to a study of Aboriginal children's world views. I contemplated a variety of approaches during that first year, but continually bumped up against the fact that I knew and could find nothing about the way the world looked to children in general, let alone Aboriginal children.* An entire year slipped by while I thought and read and dreamed up one impossible research design after another. Novels for children and about children seemed to be the most insightful material I could find relating to the children's world. It occurred to me that these authors must have spent a good deal of time with children, talking to them and listening to them. And that seemed to me a vital clue. So simple and obvious, and yet so difficult to discover in the first place. Why not, I asked myself, ask them? Simply ask the children to tell me what the world looks like from their perspective.

Having come to such a conclusion, two nagging questions needed to be resolved.

Would the children want to talk to me? And where would I find a group of children to start with?

My second question was resolved when Mr Bell of 'the New School' agreed to have me in his school. My first question remained unanswered until my first morning of interviewing, (following two weeks of observation) when, armed with tape recorder, plasticine, textas and paper I set myself up in the school library and waited anxiously for the children to appear. While waiting I modelled several little people out of plasticine to while away the time. When Mr Bell finally got around to asking for volunteers from his class I was amazed at the enthusiasm with which his request was greeted. The children had, the previous week, been introduced to me as 'Mrs Davies, from the university, come to study open-plan education' (wording insisted on by Mr Bell as far more acceptable to children than my notion of telling them that I was interested in how they thought about themselves in relation to the world).

Three children were chosen by Mr Bell from the mass of waving arms. Somewhat nervously the four of us retreated to the library to begin. The plasticine models were an instant success. I handed over the remainder of the plasticine for them to play with, explained my purpose in my words, asked if they minded the tape recorder and began. That beginning is analysed in detail in Chapter 3.

During 1976 I alternated between spending my time talking to the children and continuing with my teaching duties at the university. At first I tried to transcribe the conversations each night but found myself unable to keep up the effort. (Transcribing did not take place in any consistent way until the following year when I was fortunate enough to

---

* This was, at least in part, because most of the relevant research (as cited in the Introduction) appeared after 1975, and is all British or North American.

be granted a small amount of research money to be used in paying transcribers.)

During the year, then, I made many hours of tapes, as I followed the continuing saga of the New School from the children's perspective. I also talked at considerable length to the teachers, but did not feel that taping conversations with them was feasible since most of these conversations happened informally in the staff room at morning tea break. Further, to have brought them into the library for interviews would have destroyed the feeling that the children and I had developed that that was *our* place (cf. Corrigan, 1979, p.12).

When I commenced work with Mr Bell's class I had imagined that this would be one group of children amongst many that I should study, since my interest was not confined to a particular age group in a particular type of classroom. It did not take long for me to realise, however, that it would take me all my time to work with and come to understand this one group of fifth-graders.

That one year of data collection was followed by several fairly arduous years of working through the tapes, analysing and reanalysing, writing and rewriting, alternating still with teaching duties. There is a true sense in which this second stage is never complete, since there is always room for further clarification and revision. As I put the finishing touches to the final draft there are six new books sitting on my desk which I should read, and which I am sure are relevant. In putting into print my thoughts at this point I am momentarily halting the progression of thought. Yet in publishing my work at this point, I am in a sense opening myself to the possibility of yet further conversations, which will lead to further thoughts, which in turn will lead to further revisions.

The School*

The New School is to be found in a large country town in northern New South Wales. The school was conceived of and designed as a result of a partial commitment on the part of the New South Wales Education Department to open education in its primary schools (partial in the sense that it endorsed the philosophy of openness but felt uncertain of its workability.) The department planned therefore to have a sprinkling of open-plan schools throughout New South Wales as a cautious first (and perhaps final) step towards openness. The New School, the first of its kind to be built in the area, was opened in 1974, two years before

---

* Information for this section comes from conversations with the Head and the Deputy Head of the school and with the then Director of Primary Education in New South Wales.

my research began.

The school, conceived in line with the new and radical ideas emerging in educational thought, found itself squarely in the middle of a poorer area of town where the population it was built for had little or no experience of, or wish for, open-plan education. Due to departmental policy the school could not 'de-zone' itself and open its doors to people who wished for open education for their children. Instead it had to try to sell itself to a populace who had no choice about whether they bought it. Further, due to departmental policy, the teachers assigned to teach in the New School were not (with the exception of the headmaster) chosen on the basis of experience of, or interest in, open schooling. Nevertheless the school 'plant' was designed for openness and the charter given to the headmaster, Mr Bell, was to run an open-plan school.

Mr Bell commenced his task with energy, idealism and excitement. He recognised that he needed to educate his staff, his parents and his pupils to accept and put into practice a new form of education. Not daunted by the immediate setbacks, Mr Bell recognised that the processes involved in learning new forms of interaction were lengthy processes. He also recognised that to push his captive population into accepting his ideals would run counter to his philosophy.

At the beginning of the 1976 school year, when I began my research, Mr Bell had accepted partial defeat in his task since half the school had become 'teacher-directed' due to increasing parental pressure. Mr Bell had felt it necessary to provide parents and children with a choice, such that each child could be placed in an 'open-plan' or a 'teacher-directed' class. Mr Bell's hope at the beginning of 1976 was that at least open education could work with those children who had chosen it. Unfortunately, to balance numbers, some children who had not chosen open plan were placed in the open-plan classrooms. Further, the school, along with its zoned area, was expanding and the number of pupils increasing. As a result the school was almost certain to be reclassified and Mr Bell thereby relieved of teaching duties, to become a full-time headmaster. His class (containing the children of my study) was therefore in a state of uncertainty as to who was to teach them. Officially they were 'Mr Bell's class', but in fact they were being taught by a 'relief' teacher.

The education department's policy for coping with this beginning of year uncertainty over pupil numbers is to have floating or relief teachers who are used as stopgaps in whichever school they are needed most. Mr Bell's class was taken over temporarily by Mr Droop in this relief capacity. Neither Mr Bell nor Mr Droop knew whether Mr Droop was to stay and Mr Bell did not know whether his school was to be reclassified, thereby taking him away from 'his class'. It was during this period of uncertainty that I first made my entrance to the school.

The Children

In attempting to describe the children, I have had much of the difficulty I experienced in writing my own autobiographical note. What does one choose to tell? What is relevant? If I count as relevant the fact that they are generally from poorer homes and that they are considered to be average or below average on school performance, I am not describing them in terms that they would choose in describing themselves. What I have finally chosen to do is describe each child briefly, in some of the terms that they might choose themselves. In doing so I run the risk of placing them in categories which are too limited to encompass the complexity and variety that each of them displayed. What follows, then, must be taken as a brief introduction which serves to give the reader a first glimpse of each of the children. Their characters will emerge more fully as the work unfolds.

Boys group no.1 (see Figure 1.1) The five boys in this group were seen by the others as a powerful and dominating group. Each had a memorable and impressive personality of his own.

> *Warwick* tall, quiet, good-looking Aboriginal boy from the Reserve.*
> Known to be a good fighter though rarely involved in fights,
> much fancied by the girls, and generally thought of as a leader
> amongst the boys.
> *Henry* skinny, tough Aboriginal boy, also from the Reserve, with
> a ready wit and very ready fists. Henry was well liked by the
> children. He was regarded as leader of the group when he was
> around but more usually he was at a home for sick children
> because he had 'trouble with his ears'.
> *Roddie* close friend of Warwick's. Small, tough, charming and
> witty with a cocky self-assured manner which endeared him to
> some and outraged others.
> *Roy* good-looking Aboriginal boy from the Reserve with a
> reputation as the class funny boy. Well liked by boys and girls
> though not a romantic figure.
> *Simon* small, tough and wiry, very fair skin and hair though of
> Aboriginal descent. A shy manner with adults but apparently
> assertive amongst peers. Close friend of Warwick's but deadly
> enemies with Roddie.

Boys group no.2 Boys group no.2 was by no means as stable as group no.1. Many of the boys in this group were peripheral in the sense that they were friends to everyone and no one in particular.

---

* The Reserve is an Aboriginal settlement on the edge of town.

Terry a marginal member to the group, drifting in and out of friendships. Terry was tall and slim and quite attractive, with an endless
stream of chatter.

James big blue eyes, fair hair, a pretty, baby-faced boy with glasses,
picked on by others for his father's anti-social behaviour in the
community and his own proclivities towards theft and petty
crime.

Garry scrawny, slightly unkempt, softly spoken, with an endless
wish to talk.

Patrick slow drawling voice, high-pitched giggle — little interest in
conversation except where it touched on tales of misdeeds and
exploits of others.

Grahame and Ian nondescript children who tagged along and joined
in occasionally, but left little lasting impression of themselves.

Girls Two girls who spent a lot of time with the boys on the pretext
that they like playing the sports the boys played — but who were
suspected by the others to have interests beyond the sporting:

Suzie slim, attractive, with long brown hair, fun-loving and full of
chatter, with a gentle concern for others and their needs.

Mandy also slim, attractive with freckled nose and long blonde hair,
immensely aware of her presence and its effect on others.
Wavered between presenting herself as a freckleface tomboy and
a stylish hippie.

Another pair, also inseparable, sought out by the boys but only
passingly interested in their company:

Anne sister to Simon, tall, extremely attractive, clear olive skin and
short curly fair hair, endless love of anything funny.

Adrienne short, pretty, long fair hair, full of giggles and pranks.

Another pair of girls who had not been together for the whole
year were:

Vanessa and Jane both somewhat plain, envious of the others,
constantly indulging in petty disagreements with each other,
interspersed with giggles.

One girl, a peripheral member of girls' groupings, was:

Betty tall, blonde, athletic, quite nice-looking with an abrupt,
somewhat abrasive manner. An only child. Did well in class but
was believed to cheat.

Two Aboriginal girls:

> *Sally and Teresa* spent all their time together separate from the
> rest except when playing sport, which constituted their only
> real participation in school activities. Their friendship group was
> made up of Aboriginal girls in other classes.

BOYS

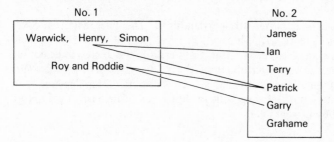

GIRLS

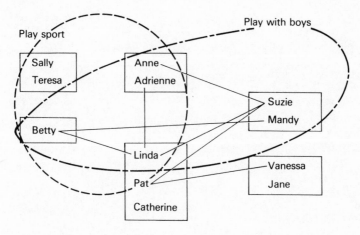

Figure 1.1 Friendships

A group of somewhat peripheral members of the class were Linda,
Pat and Catherine.

> *Catherine* shy, plump and pretty, enjoyed gossiping and giggling
> with the other two. Good at school work.
> *Pat* overweight, very shy and unsure of herself but a fiercely loyal
> friend.

Linda plump and pretty, occasionally grew tired of the giggling and chatting of the other two and sought more adventurous and lively play with the other groups.

The friendship groups were fairly durable, there being two large boys' groups and several smaller diadic and triadic groups among the girls. (The frictions within and across these groups is described in the chapter on friendship.) Figure 1.1 is an attempt to portray these groupings.

The boxes indicate strong friendships. The lines between boxes indicate secondary friendships which I have described as 'contingency' friendships in Chapter 4. The numbers on the boxes indicate the perceived relative powerfulness of the groups. The girls' groups sometimes form into larger friendship groups whose friendship depends upon the activity (sport, playing with the boys, etc.). These larger groups are indicated by broken lines.

2
The Research Act

Ethogeny

In coming to the decision simply to ask children how the world looked to them, I was, in terms of the academic world, being both radical and ambitious. According to some fellow academics working within the old paradigm, my decision was incomprehensible. According to new paradigm research, I was buying into complex theoretical problems, so involuted and involved that they seemed to necessitate a separate study in themselves. The tangles of thought I experienced in this complex interface between various theories and my data, where each influences perception of the other, are illustrated in Appendix 1.

Out of the multiplicity of potential approaches I have chosen the ethogenic perspective (Harré and Secord, 1972, and Harré, 1979), as one which provides a framework for my data which is at once constructive, and yet productive of freedoms not present in other perspectives. Other perspectives seemed to catch me up and push me in a variety of directions with my data analysis. The ethogenic paradigm provided, in contrast, a philosophical framework which legitimated the use of actors' abilities to reflect upon and give meaning to their experiences. At the same time, the degree of closure in other paradigms about the way social science should be done, did not seem to be present in the ethogenic paradigm. As Harré says, he hopes he is 'modest enough to recognise the provisional and historically conditioned character' of what he has to say (1979, p.3).

This freedom arises, too, because ethogeny attempts to provide a theory of social being in which we can recognise ourselves, and in which our common-sense knowledge of everyday life is not negated. At the same time it attempts to clearly articulate that common-sense knowledge, such a task being made necessary by the extensive theorising about social being which ignores the knowledge and competencies which social actors bring to their everyday lives. As Harré says, in his introduction to *Social Being*,

> I began this work in an attempt to clear from my mind the confusion and uncertainty I experienced when trying to reconcile my experience of social life with the representations of the process by which that life is created that are to be found in the writings of social scientists. (1979, p.2)

Ethogeny gives force to the intuitive being of the researcher and of the researched, in their attempts to understand the social processes in which they are each caught up. It seeks to explore the processes whereby social actors articulate their meanings and display those meanings coherently to others (such that they are received as they are intended). Such articulation is not viewed as separate from observable life, but as part of the process of living in and making sense of the various social worlds we live in.

The ethogenic perspective emphasises the fact that we are aware of what we do and that in making an account of our actions we create the acts by giving meaning to them. In looking at accounts, ethogenists are aware of the subtle influences of social and institutional contexts on the accounts that are made and of the multiplicity of potential accounts of any one event. Ethogeny is interested in the way individuals struggle to present themselves coherently as worthwhile people, and in the power of social contexts which facilitate or detract from each individual's attempts. Ethogeny seeks to strengthen our understanding of the process of meaning-making, recognising at the same time the complex interplay between the meanings individuals give to their social worlds, and the identities made available to those people by their social worlds. The process of meaning-making is examined in Appendix 2.

Ethogeny thus views human consciousness as a critical but neglected element in research in social behaviour. In this respect the ethogenic paradigm is similar to the interpretive or phenomenological sociology of Schutz (1972, 1973). The particular strength of the ethogenic paradigm lies in its theoretical recognition and empirical use of the understandings we have as researchers, and as people being researched, about what we do.*

---

* Earlier ethogenic research has placed some emphasis on observational work which provides triangulation of data. My research places less emphasis on independent, separate observation, because the children came to the interviews in a social group. They were, in their interactions with me, and with each other, making accounts of their actions which were not separate from the actions that were ongoing in the interview situation itself.

Discovering the Children's World

It was not an easy task for me to comprehend the children's perceived world. Though they were more than willing to pour out their thoughts to me, and squabbled each day about whose turn it was to come and talk to me, to understand these outpourings was not as easy as one might assume. (That teachers sometimes do not or cannot take the pupils' perspective into account is not surprising in light of the difficulties I experienced in this regard, even though I was free to listen endlessly, and had no teaching responsibility to distract me from my central purpose.) In fact, the difficulties I had in comprehending the children's world, at times, amounted to culture shock. An excerpt from field notes written during the year illustrates this point:

An interesting note. The kids like to replay what they have said. As it is replayed they listen for two things: 1 their own grammatical mistakes which they pick up and correct. This is a group effort. They all agree over the error and no offence is taken, though they may laugh over it; 2 anything clever or amusing that was said is listened for, played back, repeated and then apparently forgotten. They seem to be developing competence with language, ad libbing or playing on themes – a ceaseless flow of chatter that has little lasting significance (except where the topic of friendship is touched on which is taken very seriously). Time seems to have little meaning. My adult mind is always prompting me to ask 'When?', 'How long?' and 'Why?' Most often these are answered with 'I don't know' since they are not important questions.

My adult mind must know these things in order to put shape and meaning and continuity to it all. I want a total picture. I want to take all the details and put them in a pattern that I understand. Not so the children. Extemporise. Like jazz. Find a time, find a theme, get lost in it, leave it if it doesn't work, play with it a little, no lasting pattern is necessary, best of all, find music that makes you run hot, high, takes you outside of time and place but don't worry if you don't see it again. When do they start to want the things I want? Are there signs of some of them wanting it already? Why do I want it? Why don't they want it?

According to Cottle (1967) children who have uncertain backgrounds want the safety and protection of known patterns. What are the safeties sought in the lives of these children? Do they seek safeties? Their friends? Is running hot safety? Is that what Cottle meant in relation to drugs?

After time off to contemplate the apparent purposelessness of this morning's effort, I should perhaps modify what I have said. There was some purpose in the squabble (unrecorded) between

Roddie and Suzie Monday, where Roddie was accusing Suzie of messing with his toy cars. Suzie denied this. Roddie claimed that some of his friends had reported seeing her messing with them. Suzie claimed she had been with Mrs . . . all of break so he should ask her. Roddie asked why his friends would tell him she was messing with them if she wasn't. Then Suzie pointed to him and yelled 'sucked in'. Roddie knew he had lost the game, retorted, 'Well you should get some new undies Mond'y' and walked out. The latest game seems to be to get someone 'sucked in' to getting angry or believing something which isn't true and then laughing at them.*

So that was a game with a recognisable structure. Playing back the tapes and correcting grammar and admiring the witty bits was a recognisable pastime — an appreciation of the best pieces of extemporary conversation. For the rest, except where they are telling of something traumatic that has occurred which they haven't been able to tell anyone else, or a fantasy of symbolic value, or documenting a series of events which has occurred recently, it is a mistake for the adult to even try to impose meaning or structure on what is going on. From our adult point of view it seems impossible that there not be a purpose or a meaning. If we can't see it, it must be hidden. We busily impute meanings wherever we can. This is where we go wrong. They are simply extemporising, kidding around (bullshitting?).

Further analysis of the tapes has brought me beyond this point of culture shock to a point where I can more readily comprehend the children's perceived world. There is always the danger that in the process of recovering from culture shock researchers unwittingly impose their perceptions on their data.† I am aware of this danger, and have constantly returned to the children's words to check whether what I say makes sense in the light of what they say. In other words, I look for the meanings they intended via the interpretive schemes they used (as revealed in their words), rather than assume at any point that the

---

* This 'game' is analysed in Chapter 4.

† Schutz goes so far as to say '"Intended meaning" is ... essentially subjective and is in principle confined to the self-interpretation of the person who lives through the experience to be interpreted. Constituted as it is within the unique stream of consciousness of each individual, *it is essentially inaccessible to every other individual.*' He goes on to say, however, 'We are asserting neither that your lived experiences remain inaccessible to me nor that they are meaningless to me. Rather, the point is that the meaning I give to your experiences cannot be precisely the same meaning you give to them when you proceed to interpret them.' (1972, p.99, emphasis in original)

interpretive scheme I am using is necessarily correct. Schutz refers to this as looking for the subjective meanings of the other, rather than searching for some 'objective' meaning to attach to the words:

> The problematic of subjective and objective meanings includes evidences of all sorts. That is to say, anyone who encounters a given product can proceed to interpret it in two different ways. First, he can focus his attention on its status as an object, either real or ideal, but at any rate independent of its maker. Second, he can look upon it as evidence for what went on in the mind of its makers at the moment it was being made. In the former case the interpreter is subsuming his own experiences (*erfahrende Akte*) of the object under the interpretive schemes which he has at hand. In the latter case, however, his attention directs itself to the constituting Acts of consciousness of the producer (these might be his own as well as those of another person).

He goes on to say:

> *We speak, then, of the subjective meaning of the product* ['product' in this context meaning 'utterance'] *if we have in view the meaning-context within which the product stands or stood in the mind of the producer. To know the subjective meaning of the product means that we are able to run over in our own minds in simultaneity or quasi-simultaneity the polythetic Acts which constituted the experience of the producer.* (1972, p.133, emphasis in original)

This transition from non-understanding to understanding of what the children say is still of course a claim made by an adult to other adults about a world we each shared once and, strictly speaking, share no longer. It is important to try to spell out, first, what this transition to so-called understanding is, and what claims I am prepared to make about the extent of my understanding.

During the actual conversations I had with the children, in seeking to understand their perspective, I was learning to recognise their intended meanings, and their interpretive schemes. The way in which I, as 'interpreter', do this, is analysed by Schutz:

> The interpreter puts himself in the place of the other person and imagines that he himself is selecting and using the signs. He interprets the other person's subjective meaning as if it were his own. In the process he draws upon his whole personal knowledge of the speaker, especially the latter's ways and habits of expressing himself. Such personal knowledge continues to build itself up in the course of a conversation. (1972, p.127)

Not only does one increasingly 'understand' the other, but the conversants are continually taking into account the needs of the other in this process of coming to understand:

> To illustrate what we mean, consider the fact that, in a conversation, thoughts like the following may run through the heads of the participants. The person about to speak will say to himself, 'Assuming that this fellow speaks my kind of language, I must use such and such words'. A moment later his listener will be saying to himself, 'If this other fellow is using words the way I understand them, then he must be telling me such and such'. The first statement shows how the speaker always chooses his words with the listener's interpretation in mind. The second statement shows how the listener always interprets with the speaker's subjective meaning in mind. In either case an intentional reference to the other person's scheme is involved, regardless of whether the scheme is interpretive or expressive. (Schutz, 1972, p.128)

Through this attention to the other's conceptual framework, we learn to selectively attend to what the other attends to in interpreting his environment. In this manner a *We-relationship* is built and consequently an understanding of each other's interpretive schemes:

> The world of the We is not private to either of us, but is our world, the one common intersubjective world which is right there in front of us. It is only from the face-to-face relationship, from the common lived experience of the world in the We, that the intersubjective world can be constituted . . . .
>
> I can constantly check my interpretations of what is going on in other people's minds, due to the fact that, in the We-relationship, I share a common environment with them. In principle, it is only in the face-to-face situation that I can address a question to you. But I can ask you not only about the interpretive schemes which you are applying to our common environment. I can also ask you how you are interpreting your lived experiences and, in the process, I can correct, expand and enrich my own understanding of you. This becoming-aware of the correctness or incorrectness of my under-standing of you is a higher level of the We-experience. On this level I enrich not only my experience of you but of other people generally.
>
> If I know that you and I are in a face-to-face relationship, I also know something about the manner in which each of us is attuned to his conscious experiences, in other words, the 'attentional modifications' of each of us. This means that the way we attend to our conscious experiences is actually modified by our relationship

to each other. (Schutz, 1972, p.171)

During my conversations with the children (the first level of the research act), my aim was to move into their world and discover their interpretive schemes, to enter into a We-relationship. That We-relationship was, of course, not achieved simply by my discovery of their conceptual framework, but also by *their* discovery of *my* conceptual framework. Part of my conceptual framework that they accommodated to, however, related to my purpose in being there, namely, to understand their conceptual framework. The idea that I was there to listen to them and learn from them how they perceived the world, in order, ultimately, to write a book about children, impressed them immensely. They were very keen, therefore, that I get it right. They were interested in the process of recording their conversations, and of replaying these conversations so that they could, amongst other things, draw my attention to those aspects of the conversation which they thought were noteworthy; so they could *teach me to interpret social scenes from their point of view*. An insight into the importance the children attached to my research occurred when we realised I had neglected to turn the tape over when it finished its first side. They insisted that we recreate the missing scene including the actions (who walked in the door when) and the talk (who had said what to whom), so that that part of the act, that scene, would not be missing from my data.

From Data to Theory

The reflexive nature of ethogenic research makes the description of the path from data to theory a complex task. I went into the study with some ideas about children and schools. These ideas were refined, changed, developed and modified through my participation in the We-relationship with the children. That developing We-relationship changed the way that I heard what they were saying and it also changed the lenses with which I read the related research literature; and this literature in its turn suggested new ways of understanding what it was the children were saying to me. A written description of the research process is in danger of suggesting a quality of linearity which that process did not have. So, in the present account, I try to reveal the reflexive, folding-back nature of the research act. In Figure 2.1 I show graphically this reflexive folding-back quality, where each arrow represents the process of meaning-making.

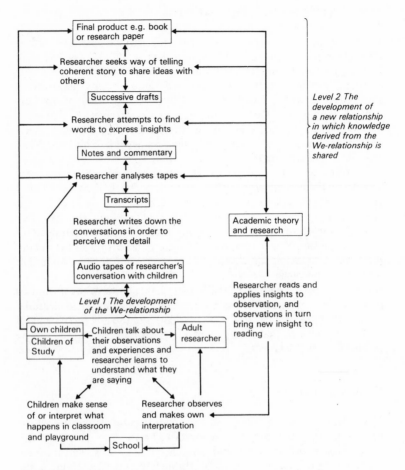

Figure 2.1 A diagrammatic presentation of the research act

The development of the We-relationship

This took place at the school with the children of my study, and also at home with my own children. (At first, I regarded the We-relationship with my own children as an informal aid to the 'real' study. It was not until I was writing up my data that I recognised the importance of the role they too had played in the development of my understanding and in the grounding of my theory.) Within the We-relationship that I developed with the children of my study, the children actively sought to help me see things their way. They enjoyed being listened to, they enjoyed the opportunity to clarify and make sense of their social world. The conversations I had with them provided them with an opportunity to review and rehearse their 'social scripts'; to examine these scripts, in all their complexity and with their inherent tendency to break down or go wrong, as they were played out in day-to-day interactions. Through talk, the children could clarify how they thought social interactions should normally go, and also what sense was to be made of the complications which inevitably arose. In this sense their talk was akin to many of the conversations that some of us adults have much of the time. What set them apart from other 'normal' conversations was the primacy of *their* point of view in the conversation. As well, because the conversations were recorded, the We-relationship could be more rapidly developed through a shared listening to the tapes after they were made, where the children could comment on various aspects of the conversation, drawing attention, both mine and each other's to what they thought was noteworthy in what had been said.

Transcribing

This process took place partly in parallel with the recording, but mostly afterwards. The transcribing *slowed down* the conversation. It made available aspects which otherwise were not noticed in the ebb and flow of the conversational act itself, and even in the act of listening to its recorded form. The written form, along with the sound of the words, facilitated a detailed analysis of what was said. This analysis enabled me to pay more careful attention to what I had learned in the We-relationship. It also enabled me to extend my understanding beyond that which I had learned within the We-relationship, towards a theoretical statement about the children's social construction of reality.

Analysis

Each tape was transcribed, and summarised. As well, I developed the technique of writing running commentaries alongside each conversation. These commentaries were continually revised as further conversations indicated possible prior misinterpretations. The commentaries, too, sometimes prompted more careful listening to particular passages and a consequent revision of the transcript, the original mis-hearing being pointed up by the inconsistent interpretation derived from the mistake.

Further development of my understanding of what the children told me was actually helped at this stage by those aspects of their conversations that I could not readily understand, that I had to stop and puzzle over. This is because such elements of their conversation provided, on closer analysis, novel and unexpected ways of seeing the world. It was in searching for answers to the puzzles thus presented that I slowly moved from the understandings I had developed within the We-relationship to a formulation of children's culture that could make sense of what, on the surface, was not sensible. This process of clarification began *within* the We-relationship itself, in the questions I asked *at the time* about aspects of their accounts that I could not understand. Parallel with this were questions I asked of my own children, as I puzzled over something that had been said that day or some element of my analysis that I could not understand. As well, in *interacting* with my own children on a day-to-day basis I was able to explore the practical dimension of each new insight. (My own children provided a comparative element, being of different class backgrounds and attending a different school. The fact that they shared many of the perceptions of the children of my study I took as strong evidence for the existence of 'a children's culture'.)

As each puzzle presented itself for consideration, I went through all the transcripts seeking all the statements that had been made on the topic. Piecing these statements together I was able to develop an idea about the particular sense the children were giving to that topic (for example, what it is to be a 'pose'). I would then take this idea back to the transcripts as a whole to see whether the understanding I was developing helped my understanding of the children's accounts. At the same time I would call on my own children to test my developing understanding against their understanding. One such conversation with my son Jacob went as follows:

B.D.:　What's a pose?

Jacob:　Someone who reckons they're real great and better than everyone.

B.D.:　What do you think about posing?

Jacob:　If somebody poses you feel snotty. You feel like bashing them up because they're trying to put you down. They're trying to make you feel weak. If you use the right words you can make somebody who poses feel piss weak.

B.D.:　What words?

Jacob:　'Ah, you big pose, you reckon you're great. All you are is a big lump of shit.' And then he might say, 'I'm dobbing on you for swearing.'

B.D.:　And then what would you say?

Jacob:　'Ah you little dobber.'

B.D.:　What happens then?

Jacob:　Sixth-grade kids would say, 'All right, I won't dob.' Fourth-grade kids would say, 'well I'm still dobbing' or 'well now I'm

dobbing on you again.'
(*reconstructed from notes taken during an impromptu conversation*)

In this conversation Jacob added an element to 'posing' that the children of the study had not clearly articulated, namely, the feeling of being put down when others put themselves up. This element helped to make sense of the negative reactions the children of the study described themselves as having when they perceived other children posing.

A further extension of my understanding occurred in each stage of writing up the 'findings', each stage being an attempt to tell a more coherent story. Multiple drafts of each chapter involved rethinking my explanation. Reorganisation of material under different chapter headings drew in different elements of the story to be told, and each new telling involved a return to the transcripts for new material and new insights. Each new draft required, too, a further search for the most apt concepts to describe what the children were telling me (the trying, for example, of terms like 'existentialist' and 'pragmatist' to capture the essence of the children's underlying philosophies), and a return to the literature to search out better ways of construing what the children were saying to me.

Each attempt to write a coherent story I gave to others to read. This invariably brought comments from those others on aspects of what the children were saying. These comments were invaluable in bringing my attention to elements that I had not fully focused on, or elements of my own commentary that needed further thought. In this way the coherence for *others* of my developing understanding was facilitated. I was thus entering into a new relationship, one with other adults, in which I shared the understandings I had developed within the We-relationship with the children.

In the very late stages of the write-up, where the major focus was on explaining rather than understanding, the underlying interactional rules of children's culture (those of reciprocity, facticity of events and plasticity of people), emerged as simple conceptual devices for giving a clearer pattern to the children's social constructions of reality. I used them as devices for explaining what the children were saying. Through these conceptualisations I was also providing myself with a clearer understanding of what the children were saying. I thus reflexively moved from participation in a We-relationship to a theoretical statement about the knowledge derived from the We-relationship. I moved from an understanding of the children's readings of their social scripts and their accounts of the breakdowns in those scripts, to a theory which sets out to explain *why* they regard these breakdowns as such, and why they go through the processes they describe themselves as going through to recreate the orderliness of their social world. That is, I have arrived at a theory which begins to explain the data, a patterning device which allows others to key into what it is these children understand about their social worlds.

3
The Social Context of Children

The purpose of this chapter is to analyse the social context in which the children made their accounts. The children's words, on the tapes or transcribed onto paper could simply be presented as they stand, i.e., the first level of the research act could be allowed to stand on its own. The idea that the children's words presented without comment or analysis might be truer to the children's world is at first glance an appealing one. But those words were spoken in a particular institutional context to a particular person. That context, and the person they were talking to were an integral though not always explicit part of the talk. The transcribed conversations themselves are 'evidence', not of the children's world as such, but of the We-relationship developing between the children and myself. Within that relationship I was in process of correcting, developing and expanding my intersubjective understandings of the children. This particular knowledge of each other, built up and built upon in the talk, must be opaque to observers. (The brief auto-biographical note and my descriptions of the children have introduced you as reader to us as actors, but have not brought you into the play.) The second level of analysis, my attempt to go *beyond* what I understood as a member of the We-relationship at the time of that relationship attempts to bring you as observer into that We-relationship.

In this chapter I will discuss the social location of children which shapes the context of the talk. In particular here I will discuss those aspects of the children's world which keep them separate from the adult world and the effect of this separateness on adult-child interaction. Following this discussion of the setting, I will examine the ways in which people cue into each other's worlds, such that a We-relationship can develop. Through the early conversations I had with the children I will show the manner in which we took each other into account in the early stages of the relationship. The purpose of these sections is twofold, since I will show the social skills and understandings that the children brought to bear on, first, the We-relationship itself,* and second, their analysis of, or talk about their interactions with other people in their everyday world.

The Social Location of Children: The Contextual Framework for Children's Accounts

Children have little choice about adopting some elements of the adult world. Adults structure the world in ways that appear external and inevitable to children. Though children bring their own interpretations to bear upon these structures, and thus have a different view of them than adults do, they nevertheless experience those structures as external and inevitable, and indeed, in some cases, necessary for survival. Examples of such external and inevitable structures are:

language;† and
social skills necessary for getting about as a socially competent person.

Additional structures which may not have the same degree of inevitability but which bind children to the adults' conceptual framework are:

schools and school attendance; and
the curriculum and basic skills, such as reading and writing useful for future occupation.

For knowledge of these, children rely totally on the adult world. These are the 'givens' in the children's world which appear to be inevitable. Words have specific meanings, school is compulsory, social interaction is disrupted if you don't follow certain basic rules, and finally, teachers tell you certain things and then test you on them. These are the 'facts', external facts that must be incorporated into the world of children and which give them partial membership in the adults' world.

In the following discussion with Roddie, Garry and Patrick, relating to a traumatic episode with Mr Bell where they were punished for 'no good reason', the power of adults to define reality for children is demonstrated. The boys have been engaging in some harmless cuddling with the girls under some blankets in the music room. When Mr Bell sees the children under the blankets, he reads the riot act. The boys are angry with him, not because they disagree with him, but because they

---

* Cf. Baker (1980) who, using an interpretive framework, illustrates how adolescents, while being interviewed, *display* to the adult interviewer their knowledge of adult-adolescent interaction.

† Cf. Cook-Gumperz (1975) who says 'The child's understanding of the normative structure of a shared world is gained through the acquisition of language. . . .' (p.145)

could not have predicted his response when he had not previously defined what they were doing as wrong. In other words they accept his right to define correct and incorrect behaviour, though they do not accept his right to react before he does his defining, since this contravenes normal practice.

Transcript 3.1: Garry and Roddie

B.D.: Do you think he was wrong to get mad?

Garry: Yeah.

Roddie: He had no right to get mad at us. He could've given us a warning first, but ah no! straight to the office!

Garry: We've had warnings before, tons of warnings.

B.D.: About what?

Garry: About five warnings we get in the class before we go out.

Roddie: But not about going under the blankets.

B.D.: So you're saying that Mr Bell normally warns you but this time he didn't.

Garry: No. (*in agreement, i.e., no he didn't warn us*)

B.D.: So that's a bit tough you reckon?

Roddie: Yeah!

B.D.: But do you reckon if he'd come in and warned you that it was the wrong thing to do that you'd have accepted that it was the wrong thing to do?

All: Yeah!

B.D.: So even if you think it's just a good fun thing to do and Mr Bell tells you that it's not allowed here, then you would agree with him and not do it?

Roddie: Yeah! But he didn't have to blow us up first.

So what Roddie and his friends see as harmless good fun, becomes, within the confines of the school at least, bad behaviour. There is an absoluteness about the adult world which appears to children to be unquestionable, at least for the duration of their interactions with these powerful adults.

Transcript 3.2: Roddie and Garry

Roddie: I don't think it's wrong 'cos we wasn't doing nothin'! Just listenin' to a tape. We was! We didn't have nothin'. I was sittin' near Warwick.

Garry: Yeah, the girls were up one end and the boys up the other!

B.D.: But just say you were doing something, would there be anything

wrong with that?
Garry and Roddie: Yeah.
B.D.:   Why?
Roddie: Dunno. 'Cos you're not meant to do that at school.

Yet despite the power of adults to define reality, in this way children do develop their own manner of construing the world, which I will elaborate in later chapters. Before I do so, however, I would like to examine those elements of the social context of children which make possible this separation between adults' and children's culture.

There are several fairly powerful reasons both from the adults' and from the children's perspective for the development of a separate world.

Adults have their own private life and expect children not to intrude on this. As a result children spend more time with their peers who, because of their similar placement in the social world, are more likely to perceive similar problems. That is, problems that arise out of the nature of the institutions of family and school and their positions or roles within those institutions.

And like-situated people will help formulate workable solutions, based on similar perspectives, perspectives that may well be incommensurate with parents' and teachers' perspectives.

Adults are not always available for these definition-solution sessions. When they are available they often provide information when its relevance or usefulness is not apparent, since it bears no relation to currently experienced problems.

Further, adults may provide 'solutions' that are unworkable for children because the children do not have certain powers or the necessary skills to carry out adult solutions. Often, for example, when my children were younger, they squabbled over the rules of the latest fantasy games (usually with toy cars). On one such occasion, when Jacob was becoming infuriated with Daniel for lifting his car off the ground to move it from one place to another (and anyone *knows* that cars can't fly), I asked Jacob (aged 9) why he could not do as I would do, and calmly and quietly explain the rules of the game to Daniel (aged 8) so that the friction would cease. He explained that there was no point, since Daniel *would not listen to him*, i.e., he did not have the power to make Daniel stop and listen in the way an adult might.

Alternatively, adults provide solutions which require the child to act in ways that conflict with what he and his peers define as acceptable behaviour. For example, when Paul (aged 13) was going through a lonely and miserable time at school I suggested that he start his own group. 'Start a chess club,' I suggested, 'or start a school newspaper.' Paul refrained from answering, and simply smiled quietly. Jacob (aged 11) with a slightly disbelieving and amused grin explained, 'kids don't do that, Mum.'

A further, and perhaps more compelling reason for the development of a separate culture is that the balance of power between children, particularly of the same age and size, is more handleable. Here the adult rules of unquestioned deference, politeness, respect for elders, can be dropped and a basis for relating in terms of equality worked out – or power differentials *won* through fighting or prowess clearly demonstrated, the rules being closer to what they can manage for themselves without adult interference. Moreover, since the rules are established through experience, they have greater immediacy and convincingness as rules to be followed. Resorting to adult authority can rob the children of their own power to make decisions and to control the situation.

The adults' perception of reality which they, as adults, assume to be superior, does not always appear so to children. Because of the taken-for-granted knowledge which informs their world, they do not or cannot spell out to children why they think as they do. When children ask adults questions, the adults may produce what for them are hard-won solutions to earlier problems, and yet are, for the children, meaningless riddles because even where the adults are aware of the links they have made, the children can't trace the steps from the first viewing of the problem to the ultimate solution. So too Roddie, in relation to his 'misdemeanours' under the blankets, found Mr Bell's thinking about what had happened quite opaque. When I asked what Mr Bell had said when he found them he said, 'Nothin'. He just said, "What are you doin' under there?" Ravin' on.' And adults may not even answer children's questions at all. Children's questions can be irritating, embarrassing and awkward, and they may on occasion appear to be futile and pointless. Adults sometimes find the perspective from which children's questions arise quite beyond them.

And yet, if children behave like mini-adults (as Roddie and his friends were in fact attempting to do) or converse in an adult manner (as Aries, 1962, has shown children of the past were wont to do), they are seen as inappropriate, even immoral. This ambivalence towards children – wanting them to be like adults and wanting them to be like children is an interestingly inconsistent feature of adults' attitudes towards children.

Children, to be acceptable, must act like children. Yet the credibility that adults are prepared to give to the associated world view that goes with acting like or being a child is somewhat lacking. Children's views which differ markedly from adult views may be seen simply as a result of incomplete socialisation or even failed socialisation, rather than the legitimate products of another culture – the culture of childhood (cf. Denzin, 1977, p.4).

There is a further barrier that exists between the child's and the adult's reality which stems from the fact that the *roles* each are required to play within the school system lead to differing perceptions of what is relevant or meaningful.

Mr Bell's anger with the children under the blankets was in fact related to anxiety about public opinion if it were ever thought that he allowed sexual activity in his school. This anxiety related to his role as headmaster and was not something he felt he could explain to the children. For teachers, responsibility for discipline and for teaching create the central tasks relating to their role. What the teachers perceive in their day-to-day carrying out of their roles will be closely related to these central tasks. Though teachers may wish that children would take on these tasks as their own, they cannot escape from the fact that school is an adult-imposed institution and the curriculum and many of the requirements made of children in school are adult-imposed. From the children's perspective, the aspects of their environment that they may feel they have some say in will more likely be how to avoid trouble with teachers, how to make and keep friends, and how to survive in the system.

These are the topics of conversation often touched on by the children. (The handbook which deals with these topics is of course *Down with Skool!*) In looking at the children's accounts, it is clear that they have little interest in tasks related to the teachers' role. Those aspects of their lives that the children can most easily give accounts of are ones which they feel are related to their tasks rather than teacher-initiated tasks. For example, when I first started talking to the children, I perceived the oft-used phrase 'I don't know' as an easy way out of not answering my questions, or as evasion. I began to realise, however, that 'I don't know' just as often signalled 'I don't know and I don't think I could or should know, since that is to do with the adult world.'

In other words, children develop the capacity to see clearly from their own position within the social structure, and do not worry unduly about what it looks like to the adults. It is enough to learn to successfully play the role of child without having to know more about adults than is necessary to interact with them. Yet the adults perceive their task, in socialising the children, as helping them to see the world correctly, i.e., as adults do, and as teaching them to become adults. Children are caught in a world where they must balance on the one hand the convincingness of their own world and on the other the powerful and convincing world of adults. In this latter world of the adults, moreover, there is no real recognition of the former world as experienced and developed by the children. Adults provide structures which children are dependent on and legitimate these very structures in the process of socialising their children. Yet adults do not want children to share this adult world or to *be* adults. Holt has some fairly angry words to say about the powerlessness this position creates for children in his *Escape from Childhood*. But even without the rights enjoyed by adults, and despite the expectations placed on them as members of the institution of childhood, children busily get on with the business of constructing their own reality with each other, as well as making sense of and developing strategies to cope with the adult world as and when it impinges on their world. This reality and its related strategies I refer to as the culture of childhood.

Cueing into the Other's World

Learning to interact with adults involves learning what the adults want. In the school context this *can* involve putting aside one's own know-ledge derived from experience within the culture of childhood and attempting to tap into the relevant adult knowledge. This process is documented by Henry (1968) who notes the strong desire that children have to please the teacher by giving her what she wants (though he also notes that they fail to do so). Gracey (1975) describes the process whereby children learn that this is what school is about. Holt (1969) has elaborated the many skills children develop which help them to detect the right answer. Hammersley (1977) has analysed the resources required by the children to answer teachers' questions. In other words, a strong element in the teacher-pupil communication system is indeed the capacity of the pupil to figure out what he *should* say and do in relation to adults. An important question for me as adult researcher, working with children, then becomes to what extent does this teacher-pupil communication system carry over to the conversations I had with the children? What I have found is that some conversations I had with the children can be compared to this classroom 'game' of finding out what teacher wants. For the purposes of gathering *substantive* infor-mation about the children's social world outside the interview these are obviously 'failed' interviews, and it is important to be able to identify this kind of failure and to show how it differs from those conversations where the children are more intent on the exploration and analysis of their own perspective. The transcript I have chosen is from a con-versation with Betty and Linda where I am asking them to tell me about friendship. Although it does not start off that way, the conver-sation rapidly degenerates into the game of looking for 'the right answers'. Betty, who starts by giving me her own answer, then switches to looking for what I want because I inadvertently cue her that her answer is not acceptable. (Betty and Linda are both regarded by their teachers as 'good pupils'. That good pupils are often also cue-seekers has been demonstrated by Miller and Parlett (1976).)

Transcript 3.3: Betty and Linda

1 *B.D.:*   What makes a good friend?

2 *Betty:*   Someone that plays with you all the time and you can trust and all.

    2   This first part of the answer, 'someone that plays with you all the time', is repeated by many of the children on different occasions as a critical defining feature of friendship (see Chapter 4).

3 *B.D.:*   How do you know if you can trust somebody?

4 *Betty:*   By telling them a secret and finding out if they've told anyone about it.

    4   Betty's answer is 'correct' in the sense that that is indeed how one *could* find out.

5 *B.D.:*   Mmhm. And what else makes a good friend? (*long pause*)

    5   By repeating the original question I cue Betty that her answer is not acceptable and that I am asking closed questions.

6 *Betty:*   (*holds mike up to Linda and says in an 'interview voice'*) What else makes a good friend, Linda?

    6   Betty, after a long pause, resolves the stalemate by introducing Linda into the conversation.

7 *Linda:*   I don't know. (*embarrassed tone of voice*)

8 *B.D.:*   Don't put that in front of her, she'll get embarrassed. (*both giggle*)

9 *B.D.:*   Um, just think for a minute, try and think what it is that would make a really good friend to you.

    9   'Just think for a minute' – a typical teacher phrase. Again without intending to do so, I prompt children to keep looking for the 'right' answer.

10 *Betty:*   Oh, if she invited us out to her place and all, and to birthdays and Christmas parties and all? (*Betty and Linda promise each other invitations to birthdays. Betty has claimed Linda as her best friend but later in the conversation Linda mentions the fact that she has*

    10   Betty now produces an answer in a questioning tone of voice further away from her own experience (though still with some basis in a general understanding of friendship).

never been to Betty's place.)

11 *Betty:* Um, what's a real good friend?

12 *B.D.:* Well, we'll leave that for a while.

13 *Linda:* Helping you in Maths and that, and your problems.

14 *Betty:* Yeah, helping with problems and all.

15 *B.D.:* Mmhm, so a friend is someone who plays with you?

16 *Betty:* Yes.

17 *B.D.:* Who helps you with your work?

18 *Betty:* Trust, who you can trust?

11-14 Having their own answer put aside for an adult's hidden but preferred answer is not unusual.
They take it on willingly as their own search, even when I cue them (12) that they can stop.

18 As I sum up what they have told me, Betty adds to the list in a questioning tone of voice, *asking* if I want to include trust as part of the answer.

19 *B.D.:* And one you can trust who won't, well, somebody you can trust would be somebody who wouldn't go and be better friends with somebody else then.

20 *Betty:* Yeah.

21 *Linda:* Yeah, like this/ (*disturbance from other kids*)

22 *Linda:* Like this morning we were in, oh sorry.

23 *B.D.:* Yeah, go on.

24 *Linda:* This morning, about trusting each other, this morning Mr Bell, some kids got in trouble for mucking round in here and we were just sitting, Mr Bell said, 'Show us how much you've done in your contract' and in our busy books, so, I said, 'I'll go and get your busy book if you like, Betty' and she said, 'Right it's in my case' just like that, so that's sort of trusting

21-24 Linda justifies the addition of trust to the answer by giving an example.

each other isn't it? To go and
get things out of their case?

25   *B.D.:*   Mmhm.

26   *Betty:*   Yeah, if you could
trust someone to get something out of your case, 'cos
you might have something
valuable in there.

27   *B.D.:*   Mmhm.

28   *Betty:*   If you can trust 'em   28   Betty shows a certain lack of
and know they won't pinch it,   trust here which illustrates
hey? She didn't pinch nothing   the fact that trust is not high
I don't think. *(laughs)*   in this particular friendship.

29   *Linda:*   I know I didn't!

30   *Betty:*   Mandy did!

Betty suggests trust as basic to friendship but indicates by her
words that her level of trust (28) is not in fact high. She also suggests
invitations to play as important but has extended no invitations to date
though she claimed earlier that Linda was her friend. Betty's first
answer, 'Someone that plays with you all the time and you can trust
and all' was, in all the children's terms, critical for friendship. The
action of being with someone and playing with them was to be a friend.
When I pursue the question further (5) with 'What else makes a good
friend?', the pattern for the children changes from open to closed
questioning. They have given the answer they know and apparently
that is not acceptable or else I would cease questioning. I must therefore be looking for an answer that I know and their job is to guess the
answer. Subsequent answers tend to come in a questioning tone of
voice (10, 18) as they seek out the 'correct' answers. But this conversation is only a failure if we think of it in these substantive terms. In
interactional terms it is interesting since it reveals the cue-seeking
strategies children adopt in relation to adults, in some contexts and
under certain conditions.

Cue-seeking does not only occur in this kind of 'closed' conversation, since in any conversation the participants must be aware of a
multiplicity of facets of the conversation (though this may be taken-
for-granted or tacit awareness). They must:

1   ascertain how the other defines the situation (i.e., what does he
know, what does he accept, what does he assume about the situation?);

2   ascertain what role the other is playing and what role therefore is
appropriate in response (i.e., what rules are operating in this
situation?);

3 know, following from 1 and 2, what types of behaviours are appropriate for that type of person and that type of situation (what style
of speech in terms of accent, vocabulary, sequencing, initiating and
formulating responses etc., or in other words, given previous knowledge of such situations, what rules need to be adhered to and what
rules can be ignored?);

4 endeavour to establish the sense that they are worth talking to, i.e.,
their own credibility, trustworthiness and value;

5 maintain an involvement in the content of the talk or maintain at
least a sense of interest and comprehension of the topic in hand;
and

6 following an awareness of the other person they must know where
their own world will seem obscure and will therefore need illus-
tration, clarification, or elaboration.

The extreme form of cue-seeking conversation, whose aim involves
finding out what the other wants, may be generated in two ways; first,
through an anxiety related to those facets of conversation (1-6)
mentioned above which is generated through an insufficient knowledge
of the other and one's role in relation to the other in the particular
situation; and second, where cues are given (or read) which suggest that
the rules to be followed are those of closed question-and-answer
sequences. These are two conditions under which the major focus of
the child, in the adult-child interaction, is on reading or cueing into
what the adult believes. In contrast, where neither of these conditions
is operating, the child, while following the rules appropriate to the
particular interaction, may attend primarily to what it is that he wants
to say (as does Henry in transcript 1.1, Roddie in transcript 3.1 and
Betty at the beginning of transcript 3.3).

The former of these conditions, involving heightened attention to
the form of the interaction, is normally the case in any new interaction
setting. As participants move into any new interaction there is a certain
amount of strain involved as they give and receive cues on the nature of
themselves and the other and the type of interaction appropriate
between them. It is difficult to say just how these first cues are given,
since our knowledge of them is, in part, tacit. Smooth, flowing interactions may be established without either of the participants paying
conscious attention to how they were achieved.* Cicourel (1973)
claims that there is a dearth of information on these procedures and

---

* Schutz (1971) analyses the situation of the stranger whose background expectancies differ in such a way that he cannot establish
smooth flowing interactions with the people to whom he is stranger.

that they are very much in need of study.*

The mode in which the children and I cued into each other's world and established the dimensions of our relationship with each other, and discovered the type of talk that was appropriate can be shown through some of the early taped conversations.

Cicourel suggests that people, on first contact, act according to socially ascribed status and role positions. That is, in my first interactions with the children, our relative statuses were those of adult and child and our roles were those of interviewer and interviewees. Gender of both children and adult probably also influenced perceived status and role. Later, Cicourel suggests, information gained about the other should lead to a different, more informal basis for interaction. In the following excerpts from early conversations with the children, I will demonstrate how they 'played' early conversations and what information was sought by each of us in order to move beyond the formal status/role-based talk.

Before the conversations with the children began I had imaginatively constructed that beginning in terms of information I should seek from them. I was not sure that this information was important, but felt that my imagined constructions would form a structure to fall back on if the conversation did not flow easily. With the benefit now of hindsight (or second level of analysis) I can see that many of the questions I thought to ask were related to establishing details of the status and role of each child, thereby facilitating my early interactions with them, i.e., the questions can be interpreted not only in terms of the substantive information they might *lead to*, but also in terms of the interactional process whereby the children and I move into a We-relationship. These preconceived questions, as I wrote them at the time, were as follows:

Name
Age
Class – response to class organisation
Success in class – reading, number work, sport, other?
Response to teacher
Friends
Role with teacher – enjoy/not enjoy?
Role with friends
Home address, mother's and father's occupation
Role at home – enjoy/not enjoy?
Difference? Conflict?

---

* Edwards and Furlong (1978) have taken up Cicourel's challenge in terms of teacher-pupil interactions in a secondary school humanities class and Mehan (1979b) has done the same in a study of infants' classrooms.

Are other people like that?
Language – describe first day at school
Language problems?
Language problems now?
Racial identity – how describe self.

These questions reveal a variety of elements which need 'unpacking'. In what follows I will outline what I see as the *interactional* purpose of gathering each item of information. Where the purpose appears to be clearly 'adult' or 'social scientific', I will clarify its purpose with reference to the contrasting point of view – child or lay person. It will become clear that the very questions I chose to ask reveal *my* initial status and role as presented to the children.

'Name' One of the first elements needed in an introduction between adults is a verbal symbol to attach to the person. Whilst these may seem essential to adults it is noteworthy that pre-school and infants' school children do not share the assumption that knowing a person's name is prior to knowing the person. My own children have often announced that they have a 'new friend', but when asked what his or her name is declare that they don't know. By requesting name at the outset I clearly set myself in an adult role. Or rather, I confirm appearances – I look like an adult and I commence my interactions like an adult.

'Age' Since so many rites of passage are associated with age, even for small children, age is a significant denoter of role and status in western society. This importance is further increased for the social scientist who cannot fail in some sense to be influenced by the writing of Freud (e.g., 1963), Erikson (e.g., 1965), Piaget (e.g., 1977), Kohlberg (e.g., 1969), etc., i.e., authors who have associated modes of action and thought with the various ages and stages of childhood through to adulthood. Within the culture of the school, age is a highly significant characteristic of persons since entrance to each stage of schooling, entrance into particular sports teams,* and grouping of children all depend on age. In asking age then, I tap into the 'knowledge' shared by adults and children in the school system. This question tells little about my role and potentially reveals much about the children's perceived role.

---

* The children had a curious way of saying how old they were, which had developed directly from sports team membership. Instead of stating how old they were at the present moment, they tended to say 'ten this year' or 'eleven this year', which indicated the age they would turn that year (and therefore which sports team they were eligible for).

'Class'   Class, i.e., grade level, has much of the same significance as age though perhaps is not as far-reaching in its implications. Teachers, pupils and educationists are those most likely to feel that the class you are in signifies something about you, i.e., it is a significant variable within the culture of the school. 'Response to class organisation' and 'success in class', however, are aimed at discriminating amongst the conformists, colonisers, rebels and intransigents.* These may be significant variables (though perhaps by other names) within the culture of the school (see, for example, Woods, 1980) but my labelling of them in this way indicates my separateness from school culture. The following questions are also aimed at discovering the type of adaptation being made to the school: 'response to teacher', 'friends', 'role with teacher – enjoy/not enjoy', 'role with friends'.

'Home address, mother's and father's occupation'   These are clearly aimed at discovering something of the class (SES) background of each child. These not only lead to status-oriented information (at least in terms of the wider society) but for the social scientist (and perhaps the social snob) they provide a potential interpretive framework from which it is possible to predict something of the other's beliefs, understandings and practices. The significance of home address and parental occupation for the children is clearly different from this. Where you live is relevant only in terms of whether it is possible to go there to play (cf. Lambart, 1976), and the occupation of others' parents seems to hold no significance for them whatsoever. Some of the children did not even know their own parents' jobs. Again this question places my role firmly as adult, perhaps similar to teacher, since this, along with name and age, is a question frequently asked by teachers at the beginning of the year. What served to set me somewhat apart from teachers in such a question is that I took time after asking this question to discuss home, who lived there, what it was like, etc. For some of the children, however the difference between the role of teacher and my role was not marked.

   'Role at home – enjoy/not enjoy?'; 'Difference? conflict?'; 'Are other people like that?'; 'Language – describe first day at school' etc.; *'Racial identity'*. These various questions were prompted by the extensive literature which suggests that it is a problem for children to switch from home roles to school roles if these are significantly different (see, for example, Bullivant, 1973). School is thought to be a problem for children who are not white and middle-class. Because my original

---

* Goffman (1968a) has made the best known use of these terms in his analysis of the modes of adaptation adopted by inmates of mental asylums.

interest was in Aboriginal children, I was interested to know whether the switch from home to school was experienced as difficult by all children, or simply by those who were culturally different. These last questions then are not status and role-oriented but related to gathering information concerning a long-standing problem of my own in relation to my own study and thinking.

Beyond these questions, however, (which I must stress I did not see as mandatory) I simply wished to let the children talk. In examining the transcripts, it is possible to see how they gathered their own information to facilitate their part in the conversation, whilst the talk was going on. Many issues were raised almost in passing and without, apparently, being paid particular attention at the time. In slowing down the conversations (which in effect one is doing by writing them down) many features can be pinpointed as part of this process of establishing the nature of the interaction.

In this very first conversation there is a careful, slightly hesitant quality as we get under way. Several points are noteworthy:

1 Where mention is made of problems the children are having (17, 18), or themes of interest to them (20) they are skated over lightly by all participants. It is not until later in the conversation that these themes are picked up and dealt with seriously.
2 The flow of conversation is maintained through this 'agreement' to skate carefully on the surface. A delicate balance between being *agreeable* and saying what they think is maintained by the children.
3 The initiative for talk is left entirely to me. Though suggestions of themes which later become central topics of conversation are made, the children adhere to a strict regime of polite answers to my questions, followed by careful listening for my next point. It is not until I pick up these points injected by the children into the conversation that enthusiastic child-initiated and maintained conversation gets under way.

When I was ready to begin interviewing after my period of observation, Mr Bell asked for volunteers. Many children were keen to come and talk and the three who did come were selected by Mr Bell out of the sea of waving arms and eager faces. The library was a small room with small wooden desks and chairs. In the middle of the room were four desks pushed together, with chairs all round. This library was set aside for our interview room for the days I was to be at school. We sat around the tables and after learning their names and establishing that the tape recorder did not bother them, the interview began.

Transcript 3.4: Garry, Roy and Warwick

1 *B.D.:*   How old are you,
   Warwick?
2 *Warwick:*   Ten.
3 *B.D.:*   Roy?
4 *Roy:*   Ten.
5 *B.D.:*   Garry?
6 *Garry:*   Eleven.
7 *B.D.:*   Are you all in Mr
   Bell's class? Right.

8 *All:*   Yes.
   (*five second pause*)
9 *B.D.:*   Who else do you have
   for your teacher in that class?
10 *Garry:*   Mr Droop and Mr
   Cooley.
11 *B.D.:*   Which one is the prac.
   teacher?

12 *Garry:*   Mr Droop.

13 *B.D.:*   Ah, how do you like
   being in Mr Bell's class?

7   Confirmation sought for what
    I know already. Signal I am
    interested in their school life.

9-11 I read the pause as an indi-
    cation that I should again
    take the initiative. I genuinely
    do not know the answers to
    these questions, and so right
    from the beginning I am
    seeking knowledge which
    they have and which I do
    not have.

12 In actual fact, as I discovered
    later, Mr Cooley was the
    prac. teacher and Mr Droop
    was a relief teacher. But both
    were new to the class, so the
    children had not sorted out
    these details for themselves
    yet.

13 I had met Mr Bell and ob-
    served his teaching and was
    quite impressed. If at this
    point the children are attend-
    ing primarily to what I want
    rather than what they think,
    then the fact that I like Mr
    Bell may influence their
    answer if they become aware
    of this fact through my tone
    of voice and facial expression.
    Certainly the answer I get is
    what I would have expected
    at this point.

14 *Greg:*   Ah, good.
15 *Warwick:*   It's good.
16 *B.D.:*   Good?

14-16 Though it may well be that the children are simply being agreeable here, I would suggest that they can select information from their experience to be agreeable in this way *only if such information exists.* They may choose, for the time being, to ignore any less pleasant associations with him as irrelevant in the present context. It is worth pointing out that later, when they are angry with Mr Bell (as with the incident under the blankets) they cease attending to his positive features (which are no longer relevant) and attend to those negative features relevant to their current feeling toward him. In other words, as in any conversation, the feeling may sway in accord with feelings of the other. But *where an event or feeling is sufficiently important to reduce or negate the importance of agreeing with the other*, or where one has lost any wish to be agreeable with the other, one's own views will be put forward.

17 *Greg:*   With Mr Bell it is.
18 *Warwick:*   Yes, with Mr Bell it is.

17,18 This implied suggestion that Mr Bell *in contrast with the other teachers* is good, brings into the conversation an aspect of their point of view that I had not anticipated, namely problems with the other teachers. (This theme I do not become aware of until later, because what I am focusing on at the time of the conversation is the goodness

(of Mr Bell, whilst they, it turns out, are more conscious of problems with the other teachers.)

19 *B.D.:*   Why with Mr Bell is it good?

20 *Garry:*   Ah, get out of doing work.

20 In a later conversation on the same day the girls are very critical of this approach which they see as a misguided view of open plan.

21 *B.D.:*   (*laughs*)

21 My laughter is in response to the unexpectedness of the response.

22 *Garry:*   You have to learn things.

22 Garry now states the opposite. My surprised laughter cues Garry that the answer though honest, was inappropriate. Both statements (20, 22) however, are true of Mr Bell's class, since the children have fun and time to muck around *and* learn quite a lot.

23 *B.D.:*   What sort of things do you like to learn?

24 *Garry:*   Um/

24 Now this is more difficult, since my purpose in asking is not clear.

25 *Warwick:*   I like to learn Maths.

25 Warwick answers in terms of subject categories.

26 *Garry:*   I like to do research.

26 This enables Garry to classify my question and answer appropriately.

27 *B.D.:*   Do you?

28 *Roy:*   Yes, so do I.

29 *B.D.:*   When you chose to be in Mr Bell's class, did you or your parents choose which class you would be in, Warwick? (*etc.*)

28-29 First time Roy has said anything, and this is in an enthusiastic voice. His silence has not been due to non-participation.
They claim they like these aspects of learning but they do not choose to develop a conversation around them at this point. Following the pause, I again take the

initiative and introduce a
new topic (29).

The next transcript is the beginning of the second conversation on
day one. This time the group consists of Terry, Suzie, Linda and Pat.
This particular transcript highlights the need the children had to know
whether these talks were to be defined as 'interview' or 'conversation'.
At the beginning the children tend to define the situation as interview
rather than conversation. This definition involves a heightening of
the formal rules of adult-child interaction* (e.g., they do not assume
reciprocal contingency in the interaction and they do not define their
day-to-day chatter as relevant). With some help from me this heightening of the rules breaks down fairly rapidly but it is not until the interview is defined as finished that they begin to initiate questions to me
about me. Up until that point they covered only topics which I defined
as relevant and relied on the information (about me and my interpretation of the situation) which they could gather without asking any
questions. While I felt free to ask them questions about themselves,
they deemed status and role-based information about me sufficient *for
the interview itself*, but sought further information of a personal nature
outside the interview as part of the process for moving on to more
intimate, less role-based terms. When they perceived this first interview
as finished they made a clear switch from interview to conversation. As
time progressed, however, the two forms of talk tended to merge. It
is not possible in later transcripts to make a distinction between interview and conversation as it is in this transcript. The taping begins, once
again, after I have discovered their names, and established that the tape
recorder does not bother them. When I turn the tape recorder on, Terry
picks up the microphone and begins talking:

Transcript 3.5: Terry, Suzie and Linda

| 1 | *Terry:* | 'I'm Gough Whitlam, as you know, your Prime Minister, I'm here tonight to talk about a very serious thing, it's about the um, um, um, the Darwin Appeal so please give generously, and you never know, it never might come to you, so it's just bye for now from Gough | 1 | The children have come in for an 'interview' with me. They have been practising inter- viewing on tape, and this speech of Terry's is his take- off of Gough Whitlam being interviewed by Norman Gunston. Thus his opening gambit in the 'interview' is to show how well he can 'play |

---

* These rules are discussed in further detail in Chapter 5.

Whitlam.'
(*Much clapping and giggling
from Suzie in the background*)
That's what we did on our
Norman Gunston show.

2   *B.D.:*   Is it?
3   *Terry:*   In fact, um, we had
an interview with Gough/
(*unclear*)
4   *Suzie:*   Are you going to have
that on while we are talking?

5   *B.D.:*   Yes, if that's all right
with you?

6   *Suzie:*   (*giggles*) No, no, yes,

at' being interviewed. Suzie
indicates that she finds this
very acceptable. When Terry
switches, however, to 'non-
interview' talk (end 1 and 3)
Suzie is not so sure that they
are 'on the right track'.

4   This natural chatter and
'talking' is clearly not a
formal interview. Suzie has a
distinction in her mind
between 'proper' interview
material appropriate for
recording and inappropriate
material.

5,6   This statement of mine is
received with giggles of
embarrassment from Suzie.
At the time I imagine her
enquiry relates to anxiety or
embarrassment about the
tape recorder so my reply is
in terms of this. My behaviour then becomes, in her
eyes, overly polite and so she
withdraws hastily, with 'no,
no' etc. (6). The giggles relate
to the humour attached to
the awkwardness of finding
appropriate forms of interaction in the beginning.
Despite the awkwardness and
giggles she has discovered that
I am interested in a wider
range of talk than she had
anticipated, and that I am
capable of excessive politeness to children – and *may*
therefore require politeness
back again (displayed in 6).

6   Says 'no, no' to reassure me

I was just wondering.

7 *B.D.:* Linda, how old are you?
8 *Linda:* Pardon?

9 *B.D.:* How old are you?
10 *Suzie:* We are all ten.

11 *Linda:* Nine.
12 *Terry:* At the moment, at the moment/
13 *Linda:* Oh, I'm ten in May.
14 *Suzie:* We're all, oh, Linda's/
15 *Terry:* Oh I'm not, I'm eleven at the moment. (*looks of disbelief from Suzie*)
16 *Linda:* He is!
17 *Terry:* I am!
18 *Suzie:* There's only one/
19 *Terry:* Because I've repeated second and I came here.

20 *Linda:* Look, that's how old he is.
21 *Terry:* I did. I happened/

that she was not criticising. She was checking to see if I intended to have it on while they were not actually being interviewed in a formal way – i.e., that her enquiry was not rude but helpful. In response to her enquiry however I am prompted to move over to 'interview' rather than 'chat' (7).

8 The switch is not easily achieved however – the mental set for 'appropriate' questions is not yet established, so Linda does not actually *hear* what I say.

10 Suzie recognises that their ages are relevant to me, so tries to give all the information I need. As it turns out her information is inaccurate.

11-21 Typical wrangle after the facts: statement, challenge, counter-challenge (sometimes *ad infinitum*, but in this case followed by information, assertion and interruption). Suzie's disbelieving looks (15) illustrate this common tendency of children to doubt each other's truthfulness. Terry recognises (19) that additional factual information is needed to sort out Suzie's doubt.

20 Linda adds the weight of her opinion to this reason.

21 Terry is about to add further information but I cease the argument by changing the subject.

22   *B.D.:*   OK, now tell me, first of all we start with Linda, what do you think of being in Mr Bell's class?

22   As adult I assume the right here first to interrupt and second to control who will answer first. They accept both these rights without demur.

23   *Linda:*   I reckon it's all right but I don't like the teacher we've got at the moment.

23   Linda zeroes straight in on the perceived problem in their classroom as she sees it. This had been hinted at by Garry and Warwick in the previous transcript (Transcript 3.4) and now, on second telling, I take it up as a topic of conversation.

24   *B.D.:*   What, that's the one doing prac. teaching?
25   *Suzie:*   Mm.
26   *Linda:*   Yeah.

24-26 In fact he is a relief as it turns out later. No one seems to have explained to them why he is there or for how long. There is a prac. teacher there at the same time.

27   *Suzie:*   Mr Cooley's all right.

27   Attempt to elaborate by saying that it is not all bad, the other teacher (who is temporary) is ok.

28   *B.D.:*   Why don't you like him?
29   *Linda:*   Ah, Ah,/
30   *B.D.:*   Just do that on the paper so you don't/

30   This is in reference to the plasticine I have given them to play with. Note the adult right to order their behaviour without excusing the interruption. This is accepted, not as rude, but as requiring an apology.

31   *Suzie:*   Sorry.
32   *B.D.:*   Put that mucky stuff on the table, that's the girl.

32   My formal role as adult is indexed by the use of these 'paternalistic' phrases in the early interviews.

33   *Terry:*   I do like him but sometimes he can be, a/
34   *Linda:*   I don't know whether I don't like him.

34   Very hesitant to commit herself at this point. This may be

35 *B.D.:*   Can you explain to me
what makes Mr Bell a good
teacher and what it is that/

36 *Linda:*   Well, he's a good
sort, and he takes jokes, and
you can sort of muck up a bit.

37 *Suzie:*   That's what she likes!
(*giggles*)

35 because she actually has not
made up her mind or because
she has not defined com-
plaints about the teacher as
appropriate at this stage.
I accept this situation as
normal and suggest a dif-
ferent way of coming at the
problem, i.e., by contrasting
the positive qualities of a
good teacher with the
negative ones of this teacher.

36 'Good sort' is an Australian
colloquialism for good-
looking or attractive.

37 Linda's straightforwardness
concerning Mr Bell's attract-
iveness and about mucking up
seems to be revealing too
much too quickly to Suzie
who tries to modify the claim
by suggesting this as peculiar
to Linda. Again it is
humorous to tell an adult you
like mucking up and hence
the giggles.

This and many of the topics raised in the ensuing conversation are
analysed in later chapters which deal with teachers and friendship. For
our present purposes it is more interesting to look at what happens
when one hour later the 'interview' comes to an end and 'conversation'
begins.

38 *B.D.:*   What about your first
day at the next school you
went to?

39 *Linda:*   Now that was some
school. I can't remember, oh
yes I can, I, oh yeah, we went
swimming and I nearly
drowned myself. The first day
we went swimming (*unclear*)

40 *Pat:*   Has anyone got a
watch?

41 *B.D.:*   No, I haven't.

42   *Terry:*   Mine says twenty-three minutes to one.

43   *Pat:*   Mr Droop took mine home.

44   *B.D.:*   Really! (*in response to 42*) Have we gone past the oh, it couldn't be that time! Do you want to go and find out what time it is? I don't want to keep you past your lunch hour.
(*Pat goes to find out*)

44   The children's lunch hour starts at 12.30.

45   *Linda:*   Oh no, we want to stay here! Please!

46   *B.D.:*   Mmm?

47   *Suzie:*   We want to stay here please!

45,47   These statements may indicate an actual pleasure in the conversation, or a wish to avoid some situation outside, or an attempt to establish a personal bond of liking, or all three.

48   *B.D.:*   Well I can come back another time. I have to um, I have to go at lunch time, but I'll be back tomorrow.

48   Defining the time boundaries of our talk is a task for the first day.

49   *Terry:*   Here well, we'll stay here a bit longer.

50   *B.D.:*   I can stay here till one o'clock.

51   *Terry:*   Yeah.

52   *B.D.:*   Or about ten to one actually.

53   *Terry:*   Goodie.

54   *Suzie:*   Are you married? I thought you were.

54   In contrast to my preliminary question (age) Suzie's first question relates to my marital status.

55   *B.D.:*   Ah, I was married but my husband died, so/

56   *Terry:*   Oh!

57   *Suzie:*   Just like my grandmother, a widow.

58   *B.D.:*   Yes.

59   *Suzie:*   Yes.

60   *Linda:*   Like my nanny, and my mother.

61   *Terry:*   (*unclear*) was killed in

57,61   The information I give them calls forth the tales of widows or deserted wives in their own families which they use to demonstrate that they understand my position.

a trucking accident, we don't
know what happened.
(*unclear*)

62 *Linda:* Yeah, in my next
school that was Hill school —
I can't remember.

62 Linda decides to continue the
answer to an earlier question
(38).

63 *Pat:* (*comes in door*)
It's a couple of minutes past
lunch.

64 *B.D.:* Really? Then your
watch is right?

65 *Terry:* Yeah, well, we'll just
stay here!

66 *B.D.:* I tell you what, If you
want me to come back this
afternoon I will.

67 *All:* Yeah!!!

68 *Terry:* Yeah, can we finish
this off we'll leave this until
you come back.

68 A fourth reason for wishing
to stay emerges. They feel the
interview is unfinished.

69 *Linda:* And we'll listen to
ourselves this afternoon.

70 *Terry:*)
) Can we listen to
Suzie:) this?

71 *B.D.:* OK

69,71 Part of 'finishing' recorded
work is to listen to it and see
how it sounds. Whilst Linda is
prepared to take such initiatives at this point, Terry and
Suzie (70) are still using the
rules more commonly apply-
ing to adult-child interaction,
i.e., to gain permission to do
what they want to do.

By the second day of interviewing the children had gathered something about what my interests were, something of my personal life, how
to address me, and how to balance the degree of informality I seem to
like with the standard rules of adult—child interaction. What I perceived
my purpose to be in talking to them was also something they needed to
establish, since the talk did not follow traditional interview lines. Their
interest in what I was doing is illustrated in the following transcript:

Transcript 3.6: Suzie and Pat

1 *Suzie:* What are you going to
call this book you're going to
write?

2   *B.D.:*   Don't know yet.
3   *Suzie:*   Oh! (*giggles*)
4   *B.D.:*   It's about children and   4   Repetition of earlier infor-
what they think.   mation, a substitute for lack
of information on title.

5   *Suzie:*   At school?
6   *B.D.:*   Mm.
7   *Suzie:*   And what you have
taped on the recorder, you
are going to write that in your
book?
8   *B.D.:*   Well, not all of it. If
there are any little bits that I
think are especially good or
interesting, I'll write them in
your words.
9   *Suzie:*   Oh!   9-15 Suzie and Pat seem im-
10 *B.D.:*   But other things will   pressed with the idea that
probably be in my words.   what they say is important
11 *Pat:*   Ooh!   to me.
12 *B.D.:*   But if anybody has
just said something that/
13 *Suzie:*   Hope it gets
published.
14 *B.D.:*   (*laughs*) really just
makes a good point/
15 *Suzie:*   When it comes out, I
will be the first to read it. No
second.
(*Conversation is interrupted
and not returned to*)

But who I am in relation to them is still something of a problem. Am
I simply a somewhat oddball (though likeable) teacher who sits in the
library and tapes everything that is said? Several days later, following
their observation of me talking to the school secretary about how long
we were using the library for and whether or not a group of parents
could use the library, Linda and Roddie pursue the following line of
conversation:

Transcript 3.7: Linda and Roddie

1   *Linda:*   I don't want to finish   1-4 Roddie and Linda are loath
off.   to return to the classroom.

2   *B.D.:*   Why?

3   *Roddie:*   I'd rather have you for a teacher than Mr Droop.

4   *Linda:*   So would I.

5   *B.D.:*   Why, would I be any different?

6   *Roddie:*   I dunno, you are much nicer.

7   *B.D.:*   In what way?

8   *Linda:*   Aw Roddie! Now we know Roddie.

They prefer to be with me.

5-7 I use this opportunity to explore their perceptions of me.

8   Linda can't resist the opportunity to tease Roddie. As a result, Roddie refuses to engage in further conversation about his relationship with me, though his smile and his facial expression remains friendly.

9   *Roddie:*   Mr Droop, he's always trying to argue with you.

10   *B.D.:*   Mmm.

11   *Linda:*   Yeah! God!

12   *B.D.:*   What do you think I would do if you started being a show-off in class?

13   *Roddie:*   I dunno.

14   *Linda:*   Probably ignore him.

15   *Roddie:*   Dunno, dunno.

16   *Linda:*   Probably tell you to stop showing off.

17   *B.D.:*   Would you bother showing off in class if I was teaching you? (*shakes head*)

18   *B.D.:*   Why not?

19   *Roddie:*   I dunno.

20   *B.D.:*   You think about it. Don't say dunno, that's too easy.

21   *Linda:*   No it's not. (*laughs*)

22   *Roddie:*   Got nothing else to say! (*smiles*)

23   *B.D.:*   Linda, what difference would there be?

24   *Linda:*   Every difference, 'cos

13-22 My question relates to the management of an *adult* role. Roddie shows no interest in the question and absolutely no concern about not being able (or willing) to answer the question.

23,24 When I pursue the topic with Linda she is more obliging and produces a

you're a woman, women are
more understanding than men,
I think.

25 *Roddie:*   Yeh, especially Mr
Droop.

generalisation which would
seem to suit the occasion.

25 Though Roddie gets on well
with Mr Bell whom he deems
'understanding' and does not
get on particularly well with
his mother, he concurs
with Linda's generalisation
because it helps in the negative definition of Mr Droop.

As time goes by many of the children develop an easy conversational style which ranges over a variety of topics. They talk, for instance, about their problems with their various teachers, their parents, and with each other, but there is a momentary hitch when what they have to say is something they would prefer to keep from the teachers. The following transcript reveals that my *team* membership in the school in relation to them and in relation to the teachers is not clear. As *adult*, my membership of the adult team may lead me to betray confidences given me by the children in the interview (team) situation.* The problem here seems to be not that I will tell directly but that I might allow the teachers to listen to the tapes.

Transcript 3.8: Roy, Roddie and Patrick

1 *Roy:*   Mr Bell upstairs, say,
you know, when, when the/

2 *Roddie:*   Yeah.

3 *Patrick:*   vroom vroom (*with
plasticine car*)

4 *B.D.:*   What was that?

5 *Roy:*   Mr Bell say/

6 *Roddie:*   Better not do it
on tape.

7 *B.D.:*   Better not do what on
tape?

8 *Roy:*   Oh — secret.

8 Roy rapidly picks up the cue
from Roddie that they must
be cautious.

9 *Roddie:*   Mr Bell. He

---

* See Goffman (1971, pp.83-108) for an analysis of the concept of teams.

mightn't like it.

10 *B.D.:* But Mr Bell doesn't hear the tapes!	10 Until this point it has not been necessary for me to define this particular boundary.
11 *Roddie:* Oh well! Don't worry about it then.	
12 *B.D.:* Only I do.	12 This statement was made and taken seriously – hence the pseudonyms.
13 *Roddie:* That's good.	
14 *B.D.:* So what was it you couldn't say on tape?	
15 *Roy:* Umm.	15,16 Since Roddie alerted Roy to the problem it is up to Roddie to say it is no longer a problem.
16 *Roddie:* Don't worry about it! It's OK now if he don't hear it.	
17 *Roy:* It was, you know, as I said about Mr Droop, he given – oh, what was that? (*etc*).	17 The children have been in serious trouble with Mr Droop. If Mr Bell hears about it, it may damage relations with him, or lead to further punishment.

A similar although more dramatic discovery of this same boundary occurred when Henry, recently returned to the school after a long period of absence, was boasting about what he was going to do to Mrs Hawkins, a new teacher in the school. He was outraged at her insistence that he use her name whenever he addressed her, and was saying what he was going to do to her, not realising that the tape recorder was on:

Transcript 3.9: Roy, Sally and Henry

1 *Roy:* Henry, he say to Mr Bell, 'You know that lady up there, she get wild!'	1 'That lady' is Mrs Hawkins.
2 *Sally:* Henry says he won't say her name.	2 Sally explains the problem.
3 *Roy:* When Henry's about 24, he'll get/	
4 *Henry:* Yeah when I get older mate, I'm gunna, I'm gunna shoot 'er. (*laughter from others*)	4 Henry's utterance, whilst leading to laughter, is said in a low gloomy voice.

5   *Sally:*   You need a licence
before you have a gun.

6   *Henry:*   Not all the time.

7   *Sally:*   Yes, you do.

8   *Roy:*   Not crooks.

9   *Sally:*   O-oh. (*Roy laughs*)

10   *B.D.:*   Are you going to be a
crook, Henry?

11   *Henry:*   Yeah, I'm going to
kill 'er.
(*Roy laughs again. Tape
unclear*)

12   *B.D.:*   What will happen
when you kill her?

13   *Henry:*   No one will know.

14   *Roy:*   Yeah, Henry will dis-
guise himself but they'll find
out like Kojak. 'E's always
findin' out things, Kojak.
(*Roy tells about Kojak and
a vampire.*)

15   *Henry:*   (*noticing tape
recorder*) Are you going to
take that to that (*points
in direction of Mrs Hawkins's
room*) up there?
(*Henry's expression is one of
total horror*)

16   *B.D.:*   No, I wouldn't do
that, that would be a silly
thing to do.

17   *Sally:*   She's going to take it
to the teacher's college and, ah
tape it.

18   *Roy and Henry:*   It's already
taped!

5-13 The conversation hinges on
the difficulty of carrying out
the task, not whether or not
the task is worth doing.

14 Television is an important
source of information on
such matters.

15 Request for reassurance on
Henry's part that his plans
for the future be protected.

17 Sally means the 'university'
and 'transcribe' — two
unfamiliar words.

18 Monitoring each other's
mistakes.

I reassure Henry. All the others were used to the tape recorder and I
had neglected to explain it to Henry as a newcomer. The others also
reassure him. They decide, however, to do some drawings, rather than
continue the fantasy.

Clearly my interactions with the children did not only occur when
the tape recorder was on. Much of their information was gathered outside of the 'interview' situation. Conversations took place outside the
school, in the corridors and before and after I had turned the tape

recorder on. As well, children staying overnight had become a feature of our lives over the period of interviewing. In this way their knowledge of me extended beyond what they could gather in the school setting, to what they could gather in the more informal setting of home.

A rather different glimpse of how one child perceived me occurred when I was unexpectedly called out of the room and the children went on recording in my absence. James, a sweet, baby-faced boy with glasses, after singing 'Boney Maroney', during one such absence, began breathing heavily into the microphone and whispered, 'Bronwyn, Bronwyn, Bronwyn, I want it now, tomorrow when you come to school. Head, give it to me. . . (etc.).' Such lustful declarations were rare, however, and gestures of liking were more commonly in the forms of cards or drawings, or simply an unwaning enthusiasm for talk.

Whatever other boundaries were established outside the recorded talk or which operated though never needed stating is impossible to say. Doubtless there were boundaries. What is clear from the information that is available through the recorded talk is that most of the children entered the situation easily through a previously developed knowledge of how to conduct themselves in similar situations with other adults. They extended and modified their talk as time went by and they developed a personal style with me which did not rely so heavily on the formal rules that were adhered to in the first days. The rules changed and became more complex as the We-relationship developed, and as we learned to take each other (idiosyncrasies and all) into account.

The Children's Accounts

A study of the children's accounts of their experiences reveals a power (made available through the use of language) to define and redefine these experiences. In the preceding section, the children's capacity to cue into what was wanted of them was examined. Though language and social structures are in an important demonstrable sense external and coercive, they are also the tools necessary for the creative exploration of oneself and one's relation to others.

When the children make an account of problems they are having with their friends and their teachers they are so engrossed in examination of the problem at hand that the researcher's consciousness (and what she wants) are a taken-for-granted background to the conversation. In other words, they are attending to the analysis of the events described, and the We-relationship, which makes possible the analysis of *other* relationships (outside the We-relationship), need not be attended to consciously (its workability can be assumed). This frees the minds of the children to analyse that which has become problematic and needs conscious attention. The conversation is used as a tool for working through the problem. As noted earlier, analysis of the classroom is difficult because of the extent to which our knowledge is taken for granted. The same is true of friendships. In this study the taken-for-granted became accessible for study due to the fact that when things go wrong in the playground or the classroom then the children do turn their conscious attention to what they normally take for granted if only to check whether they have misread it. They learn the rules of how to get on with their friends and their teachers and then they forget them. If suddenly they find themselves *not* getting on with these others, then they must examine what is going on carefully in order to see who is in the wrong. 'Is the other being stupid or am I?' Because I came regularly to the school specifically to listen to the children, I created a context in which this kind of talk could readily proceed.

It is possible, by examining their conversations in detail, to see the tension between a need for certainty, facts and knowledge of how the world works and a readiness to revise the knowledge they have in the light of ongoing experience. In their conversations the children are actively using language to make sense of complex situations (see Appendix 2: Analysis of the interaction between language and experience in the making of accounts).

In making their accounts the children tap into the apparent requirements of the situation, but are operating within a set of agreed-on rules for interaction which they and I know, and which do not involve them in misrepresenting their perceptions of events in order to please me. It is not part of the rules of communication that we should lose our own knowledge in order to discover the other's wishes. Certainly we *bend* to the other's wishes but *within limits*. Where these limits are broken people become disoriented and outraged, as the work of Garfinkel demonstrates only too well.

Reciprocity is an essential part of the person's social world – his world is built up out of the actions of others towards himself and his understanding of those actions. Reciprocity with the researcher is part of a pattern *already learned* by the child.

What the children say to the researcher (in relation to open questions) is within the range of acceptable statements for those people according to their perceptions of events. It may not be precisely what they would say to someone else but neither would it totally contradict what they would say to someone else (discounting occasional deliberate lies). They can make a variety of accounts explaining why they behaved in a particular way at a particular time. These form a mosaic of explanations and reasons rather than mutually exclusive accounts.

The understandings the children have of their relationships with each other and with the teachers is analysed in the next two chapters. Through the discussions which stemmed from breakdown in relationships the children examine their world taken-for-granted, and thus make it available to me, in the process of reaffirming it for themselves.

4
Friends and Fights

Children's Culture

As I pointed out in Chapter 3, in discussing the social location of children, there are critical ways in which adults do not want children to share their world. Parents and teachers encourage children to play with each other in order to have time to get on with their adult pursuits. Children's culture can be seen partially as a response to this separateness. When children first arrive at school they may be traumatised at the situation they find themselves in if they have no contacts amongst their peers. Until they make friends they cannot participate in children's culture (though some children in nursery school may regard the toys themselves as having social meaning, cf. Mead, 1934 and Silvers, 1977b). Once they have made friends, and gained access to childhood culture, they must be careful not to annoy or offend their friends, or they may find themselves alone again. The fearfulness of this aloneness, the possibility of being outside children's culture, should not be underestimated when seeking to comprehend the children's understanding of the world of friendship.

One of the questions I asked the children related to their memories of first days at school. My interest in Aboriginal children had prompted me to ask about these first experiences since I believed that their first experience of school would be more traumatic than that of white children, since Aboriginal culture is markedly different from white culture (McKeich, 1974). But white children also found their first day at school memorable and traumatic not only at their very first school but each time they went to a new school. The trauma does not relate to the subcultural differences in adult cultures (as I had anticipated) but to the empty moment of transition between home (with its attendant family relationships) and entrance into the culture of childhood.

The following transcript is Warwick's account of his first day in nursery (pre-) school, where he tells of the trauma involved in letting go of existing relationships:

Transcript 4.1: Warwick

1   *B.D.:*   Oh that's right, Warwick, we were up to your first day at school, weren't we? What was it like?

2   *Warwick:*   My first day at school?

3   *B.D.:*   At the very first you went to.

2-3 Warwick clarifies for himself precisely what it is I am asking. This kind of ground-work indicates an interest in the conversation and its success.

4   *Warwick:*   Pre-school. As soon as I got there I was cryin' 'cos I, you know, didn't want Mum to go. They had to close the gate on me and I ran out and I was kicking the gate and yellin' out to Mum. An' she said, 'No you had better go to school today.' After that I tried to get out and I couldn't, then I went inside and laid down and went to sleep. . . .

4   The teachers are perceived as 'they' who shut the gate on him. There is nothing familiar to comfort him in this new situation and so he resorts to sleep as an escape.

Anyone entering a new situation is bound to feel some uncertainty, fear and vulnerability if they do not know how to conduct themselves as a competent person within the terms of that particular situation. Friends can change the situation from one of uncertainty to one which is tolerable and even enjoyable. Roy, another Aboriginal child, describes his first school as a good one because all his cousins and friends were there. In contrast, his first day at the school he is at now was bad until he caught a glimpse of his friend, Henry, who lives next door:

Transcript 4.2: Roy

1   *B.D.:*   So you can remember your first day Roy?

2   *Roy:*   Um, yeah.

2   The question is answered

3   *B.D.:*   What can you remember about it?

4   *Roy:*   Um, when I first came here, I was a bit shy, then when you know the teacher, Mr Bell or someone took me upstairs and um, and then I saw Henry, 'cos he lived next door, and/

5   *B.D.:*   What did you feel when you saw, what was his name, Henry?

6   *Roy:*   Yeah.

7   *B.D.:*   Yeah, what did you feel when you saw him?

8   *Roy:*   (*pause*) Well, (*pause*) um, ah, you know, I wasn't scared when I seen Henry you know? 'Cos this was when I first came to this school. That's all.

9   *B.D.:*   What about the first day of school at M town, what was that like?

10   *Roy:*   That was better than every school I went to, 'cos all my friends were, all my cousins were mostly there.

11   *B.D.:*   Yeah, and so what, was this school mainly just for Aboriginal children?

12   *Roy:*   Yeah, mostly, and my cousin, Sam, he used, we used, to fight all the time. . . .

literally.

3   I produce a new question. As Malcolm (1977) has noted, hesitance in Aboriginal children's replies leads teachers (or in this case the researcher) to multiply their questions, a tactic he claims they do not like, at least in the classroom situation, since it focuses too much attention on them. Roy did not elaborate until another question was asked. He did resist my further questions, which suggest that the brief literal answer was not hesitance or resistance but an answer which he considered appropriate.

8   His 'that's all' tells me that he has had enough of that question.

9   So I change the tack.

10   Roy's voice has much more enthusiasm when he talks about a situation where he had nothing but pleasure.

11   A well informed guess.

12   Said with obvious delight at the pleasurable memory. Fighting is a complex activity actively enjoyed for the sheer physical (or verbal) skill involved, feared for the pain and isolation it may bring if things go wrong. Clearly Roy was confident with Sam that they could take on anybody

and come out well.

The trauma experienced quite recently by Jane when she first arrived at the New School indicates that the anxiety attached to uncertainty does not reduce as the children get older. The uncertainty she experienced is again alleviated by finding a friend.

Transcript 4.3: Jane

1   *B.D.:*   Tell me about your first day at school.

2   *Jane:*   Ah, I came at half past eight, 'n' nobody was in the office there, and um, I was sittin' there 'n' I was real shaky and started to cry a bit, and some of the teachers said 'ullo' then Mr, um, Mr Bell got me enrolment form and took me around there and I got in friends with Betty and then Vanessa came along, so I left Betty and went on with Vanessa.

2   This story is told in a small quavering voice. The trembling and tears that she experienced at the time are not far away when she recalls the experience. The fact that some teachers made some opening gestures is noted but the story of panic ends when she finds a suitable friend. Throughout, Betty is noted as an unsuitable friend, though she is attractive and popular with the teachers. She was rapidly rejected here in favour of Vanessa for reasons not stated.

To be alone in a new place without friends is potentially devastating. To find a friend is to partially alleviate the problem. By building with that friend a system of shared meanings and understanding, such that the world is a predictable place, children take the first step towards being competent people within the social setting of the school. Much of this building of shared meanings takes place through play. The intensity with which children play stems from aspects of the play whose meaning for outsiders is not readily discernible. The game* of 'sucked in' is an ideal example, since it encapsulates those aspects of children's play which are exploratory and yet which serve to confirm and reinforce their known, shared world.

---

* Denzin (1977) notes that 'play' becomes a 'game' if the same sequence is repeated often enough. That is, the play loses its enigmatic quality and takes on a known, formal structure.

The aim of the game is to lead someone on in such a way that they are sucked in to thinking they can come out on top of the situation (they are drawn into a pose), even though the pose is ill-founded.

A child who attempts to kick a goal whilst practising football, for instance, might find a jeering group of children yelling 'sucked in' when he misses the goal. In setting himself up as a goal kicker he is attempting an ill-founded pose. A more elaborate form of sucked in was described earlier in Chapter 2 (p. 18). The interaction went as follows:

Roddie (to Suzie):   You've been messing with my toy cars!
Suzie: I was not!
Roddie: You were!
Suzie: When?
Roddie: At break.
Suzie: How do you know?
Roddie: Garry said he saw you.
Suzie: I was with Mrs Thompson all of break!
Roddie: Why would he tell me he saw you if he didn't?
Suzie: Sucked in!
Roddie: Well you should get some new undies, Mond'y.
    (unrecorded, reconstructed from notes)

In this interaction, Roddie breaks two basic rules of childhood culture. He misrepresents the facts (his friends hadn't seen her), and he presents himself as better than he really is (poses) by acting out wounded innocence when he is in fact lying and trying to blame someone for something they didn't do. By drawing him into this pose, and then revealing it as such, Suzie is able to punish Roddie rather soundly by telling him he is sucked in. For to be sucked in is a fairly mortifying experience.

The game follows a pattern of challenge, counter-challenge (which is baited), a pose which is aimed at defeating the counter-challenge, and the cry of 'sucked in'. The poser is wounded and retaliates, but knows he has lost (see Figure 4.1).

Three basic concepts in children's culture are illustrated in this game: reciprocity, the facticity of events and the plastic quality of people. These will be elaborated later in this chapter (pp. 76–7).

Through such games, known patterns are used to make life more predictable and to introduce a greater degree of control over their own lives. Occasional incorrect playings of the game where the pattern is broken, require censure. These censurings reaffirm the rules of the game, and at the same time allow the children to discover or rediscover what the limits of the game are. The need for security and the need to explore are for ever in a delicate balance. What is known and secure will be guarded carefully and strict censures used to control people who

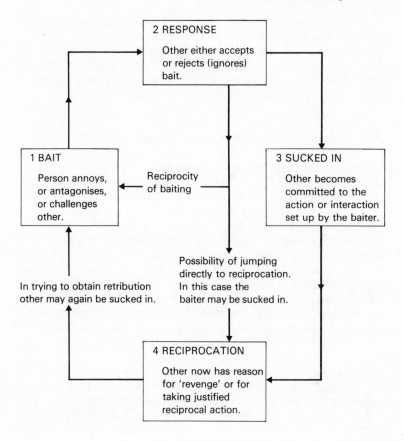

Figure 4.1 Sucked in

move outside the known. At the same time there is a constant challenge to move outside the known, to discover its limits and to explore possibilities as yet not grasped. The game of sucked in is fun for the victor. It often results in anger and tears. It encapsulates the secure and predictable by reinforcing the taboo nature of activities such as lying, posing, or misrepresenting oneself as better than one is, and it also provides the possibilities for exploration in an exhilarating fashion, since the aim is to come out on top. An almost identical game is called 'chopped'. This game, similar to the American game of 'sounding' (Kochman, 1972), involves an exchange of insults, the aim of each insulter being to come out on top by delivering the wittiest insult, whereupon the observers shout 'yah chopped' and the game is finished, the challenge withdrawn. The game breaks down when the insult is unacceptably close to a sensitive truth. The person insulted takes genuine offence, and the game gives way to violence.

I have analysed sucked in as an ideal-typical example of the children's play, in order to illustrate that what may appear to the adult outsider as futile, random and slightly unpleasant activity can in fact have a high degree of structure and a complex purpose.

Adults' Views Contrasted with Children's Views on Friendship

Adults and children, each from the perspective of their own culture, can be seen to have very different views on what friendship is. Beliefs about friendship from the perspective of adult culture are linked with notions of liking (or love), affection and loyalty. Children appear to have a rather fickle attitude towards friendship, and to engage in an unnecessary amount of fighting and bickering. In fact it would seem to adults that children do not 'really understand' what friendship is.* Certainly, during the earlier part of the year of the study, I had a great deal of difficulty understanding the ups and downs of the children's relationships with each other. The following field notes were made after several days taken out from interviewing to observe friendship patterns. I was able to describe what I saw and what I had heard and

---

* Speier claims that adults have difficulty in seeing children's culture. Along with Speier, I would see children's culture as existing in its own right, though intimately related to and developing partly in response to adult culture:

If there is any scepticism about the existence of children's culture, it is a reflection of our own adult ideological commitment which has all but obscured the fact of its existence. The work of parenthood consists mainly of the practical 'science' of child management in the family household. Likewise the work of a teacher is devoted largely to the practical 'science' of child management in the classroom and around the school establishment. Yet the Opies, for example, have documented the existence of children's culture among schoolchildren in Great Britain by accumulating a vast amount of data on children's traditional lore and games which do not originate out of the practical activity of child management. Likewise my own research on children's play activity at home, and my filming of children's interactions associated with school activity outside the classroom, indicates the existence of children's culture. It would appear to essentially be neither a miniaturized or a half-baked adult culture, nor an imitated version of it — but a culture in its own right. (1976, p.99)

yet was unable to find a satisfactory interpretation of what was going on. Despite the fact that the children seemed to know quite clearly what they were doing, I felt (quite incorrectly) that because I could not understand *why* they were doing what they were doing that *they* did not really understand what friendship was:

> Some insight perhaps into the extent and intensity of girls' fights. They seem to be experimenting with interactions to see how much power they have over each other and the boys, e.g., I witnessed Mandy ask Roddie for her pen back. Roddie had lost it. Mandy told him he would have to buy her a new one, Roddie then found that Warwick had it and called out to Mandy several times but was ignored and told again that he would have to buy a new one. She was deliberately being difficult and perhaps even stirring trouble. Later on she was playing with Roddie and Warwick and was turfed out by the other girls. She was deeply hurt and tearful because she felt no one liked her. Her power games had backfired, and she was a lost and unhappy little girl. Suzie and Linda were busy comforting her in the library at lunch time. She stopped crying when I suggested that she didn't really have a problem as long as Suzie remained her friend, which she very obviously was. The need to know that you are a likeable person is evident in this sort of situation. Two troublesome problems for children of this age:
> how to be likeable
> how to show others your liking.
> Roddie's solution is to hate everyone else but his friend so that the contrast can be seen. Warwick and Jane have been described as nice because they 'give things'. Mandy and Suzie have developed little rituals of hand hitting and twisting which are symbolic or affirmative of friendship. But since, in general, they have difficulty in defining what a friend is, they also have difficulty in *being* a friend because they are not quite sure what it is to be one. Thus they are offensive and hurtful without intending it, and so the conflicts flare up all the time, i.e., in this case it seems that lack of theory really does screw up the action. To further complicate the picture, the behaviour which they display in the library which appears to *me* to be friendly (supportive comments during traumatic personal discussion) are not counted as signs of friendship amongst the children.

The Opies, too, find childhood friendships chaotic and unpredictable, and acknowledge that it is from the adult perspective that they seem so:

> Children's friendships are far from placid. Perhaps because of the

gregariousness of school life they make and break friends with a rapidity disconcerting to the adult spectator. Two girls will swear eternal friendship, arrange signs and passwords, exchange necklaces, walk home together from school, invite each other to tea, and have just settled down together, so it would seem, when suddenly they are very 'black' with one another and do not speak any more. They seek a new friend, and have no sooner found one than they are with their old pal again. (1959, p.324)

The central argument put forward in this chapter is that, from the perspective of the children's culture, these makings and breakings serve two important functions, first in terms of the *maintenance of the orderliness* of the children's world and, second, in terms of satisfying their need for exploration and discovery of the dynamics of inter-personal relationships. Adults assume that the reason friendships develop is that people like one another. They construe their own friendships as developing from reciprocated feelings of attraction. Children, in contrast, whilst they do not negate liking as having some considerable importance, see proximity, or being with someone, as the first and basic element of friendships. Homans, in contrast with many social psychologists, would tend to agree with the children, that the nature of the other is no more (and perhaps less) important than the fact of being with the other. He says, 'an increase of interaction between persons is accompanied by an increase of sentiments of friendliness between them.' In other words, we come to like the people we associate with because we associate with them, rather than because they are intrinsically likeable. He goes on to say, 'You can get to like some pretty queer customers if you go around with them long enough. Their queerness becomes irrelevant.' (Homans, 1951, p.115).* An apparently simple proposition and yet one which seems contrary to what friendship should be. From our adult perspective, liking should come first. Children often mention liking as part of friendship. However, they are clearer about the pragmatic nature of the liking than most adults. One of the children of my study wrote, in an essay on friendship:

Why have I got a friend. Because if I dident have a friend, I would have nobody to play with. I think it is good to have a friend don't you. If I had a soccer ball I would give him a game of soccer.

Another wrote:

---

* See also Newcombe, Turner and Converse, 1965, p.316; Jackson, 1968, footnote pp. 22,23.

My friend is my friend because she looks after me and plays with
me and its good to have a friend. A friend is a girl or boy that plays
with you.

The children of my study, along with Homans, are not alone in their
observations. Other children, whose opinions on friendship have been
sought have placed being with your friend high on the list of the
defining features of friendship:

My best friend is John Corbett and the reason why I like him is that
he is so nice to me and we both draw space ships, and what's more
he plays with me nearly every time in the playground. (Opies, 1959,
p.323)

And the following conversation with 11-year-old Paul is reported by
Damon (who however maintains his own adult views on friendship):

Who's your best friend? *Don.* Why? *We hang around together.* How
did you meet him? *At school, he's the first one I met.* Is that why
he's your best friend? *Yeah, he showed me around the school.* Why
do you like Don? *'Cause we play football together and we like to
bike ride around.* Do best friends have to like the same things?
Not always. (Damon, 1977, p.159)

Damon claims that friendship as we have thus far described it based
on proximity, characterises *low level* friendship. Children who, in
contrast, have achieved a higher level, he says,

realise that friendship is subjective, in the sense that one person may
like or dislike another because of certain dispositions and traits of
the other. In other words, the bestowal of affection (and consequent
establishment of friendship) no longer is automatically associated
with frequent play contact but, rather, hinges upon subjectively
determined personal characteristics of the other ('niceness',
kindness, trustworthiness, and so on). (pp. 157-158)

Damon's analysis of 'higher level' friendship perfectly typifies the
adult position in which the liking is perceived as causal. He assumes a
higher quality inheres in the adult model, i.e., the model with which
children gradually learn to construe their friendships. Damon's model
implies that children have achieved a 'higher order' of friendship when
they cease seeing what is actually occurring within their friendships,
and see rather what they have learned from adults about what 'ought'
to be the case in friendship.

Certainly, when pushed, Paul went on to talk about these characteristics of his friend Don. He none the less mentioned being with Don and his happenchance meeting with Don as the first part of the equation. Along with Damon and the adult population in general, Paul will eventually learn to perceive the second half of the equation, the intrinsic likeableness of the other, as the essence of friendship. He will learn as well to feel some revulsion for the 'lower level' notion, that proximity leads to friendship. And thus the children's theories about friendship are difficult to understand because our own assumptions about what friendship is or should be cloud our vision. We apply the wrong mental set or template and do not understand what we see.

When children first arrive at school they are thrown on their own resources to a considerable extent. Making sense of this strange new world is a task they engage in with each other. The teachers may spell out the rules for classroom behaviour, but the sense to be made of it all is something adults cannot really provide. Friends are the source of meaning-making in this new situation. They are the source of meaning and therefore the source of identity. They can, by their presence and shared meaning world, render the world a sensible and manageable place. Their particular mode of viewing the world with its accompanying language, taboos, rituals and sanctions which function to maintain this meaning world, are developed in interaction with each other.

In Brunerian terms (e.g., 1974), the children develop their own templates for viewing the world. If Homans's propositions on friendship hold, the children's template may actually be closer to what happens in friendship both for adults and for children than the adult template. Be that as it may, the playing, the fighting, the making and breaking of friendships are necessary ingredients for the development and maintenance of the children's shared world.

Contingency Friends

Friends not only alleviate the uncertainty which stems from being alone, but via companionship and co-operativeness go on providing the means for warding off the vulnerability which attends being alone. *Being with* your friend, then, is important. Moreover, the more advantaged children have *contingency friends* ready for emergency situations where their friend is absent or where their friend offends them in some way. If they withdraw to their contingency friends their bargaining power over their 'best friend' is quite high.

In the following transcript Vanessa relates a tale of misery. Inadvertently, she failed to be with her friend Pat when Pat thought she should be. Unfortunately for Vanessa, Pat had contingency friends to turn to and she is now left alone in turn. The conversation takes place amidst, and parallel with, a noisy conversation with some of the boys, but with minimal prompting from me Vanessa tells her tale:

Transcript 4.4: Vanessa, Sally and Betty

1	*B.D.:* OK, I want to ask Vanessa how it turned into a horrible day.	1	Vanessa had earlier claimed that the day had started out well but it was now horrible.
2	*Vanessa:* Oh we were playing up in the bike shed I came down because, um, I wanted to come down just to sit on the bike (*unclear*) and when I came down and the bell rang while I was putting my bike away and I was saying, and I was talking to Pat, I was saying something to Pat and she went (*makes a rude sign with her thumb*) and ever since then, ever since the bell she won't talk to me.	2	Vanessa left Pat simply to do something she wanted to do and Pat took offence.
3	*B.D.:* And you don't know why she did that Vanessa?	3	I ask Vanessa for a causal explanation of the event.
4	*Vanessa:* I haven't had an answer.	4	Her reply is in the terms that matter to her. She has sent a message to Pat, and not had a reply.
5	*Vanessa:* If I go away and do something and I don't stay up with her she gets the cranks.	5	She then replies to my earlier question.
6	*Vanessa:* And she goes off to Linda or Mandy and then we're not friends.	6	She explains the contingency friendship plan.
7	*Vanessa:* I do everything she wants and I can't do anything I want, has to be all her way. (*20 minutes of other conversation*)	7	There is an imbalance in the relationship as to who calls the tune.
8	*Sally:* Pat is your friend.	8	Sympathetic reassurance

9   *Vanessa:*   No she's not.

10   *B.D.:*   You mean she's
cranky with you? And who
have you got for your friend
if Pat is not your friend?

11   *Vanessa:*   Nobody.
12   *B.D.:*   Betty. Betty just said
she's your friend.

13   *Vanessa:*   Yeah I know but I
got no one to talk, no one,
'cos Betty's with Mandy
mostly or/

14   *Betty:*   You gotta be kiddin'!
15   *Vanessa:*   But I'm with no/
I just gotta sit around and
do things myself.

. . . .

from Sally.
9   Clearly, Pat's actions are
strategic moves within the
friendship. Until she reaffirms
the friendship (which she
probably will do when full
reciprocation for offence is
carried through) Vanessa
will be alone and uncertain.

10   This indicates I have just
cottoned on to the fact that
Vanessa and Pat have fallen
out. The surrounding con-
versation had been distracting
me from paying attention to
Vanessa. I now ask who her
contingency friends are.

12   Betty is 'friends' with whoever happens to be around.
She explained in a separate
conversation with me that her
friend is whoever is doing
anything interesting. She had
noted Vanessa as her friend at
the beginning of the conversation simply because
Vanessa was there and doing
something interesting (talking
to me).

13   Vanessa knows Betty will not
do as a best friend because
Betty is a drifter, not having
the same wish or ability to
establish bonds as the others
do and thus forever breaking
friendships by simply not
being there with her friend,
when they expect she should
be.

16 *Vanessa:* Pat was good you know, good, and I, I've got really nobody in, ah, this school because the teachers are all against me. Mr Hunt especially.	16 In the event of no friends, the adult world is still obviously a possibility for contact. For Vanessa this possibility does not seem to be available.

Note here that an offer of friendship from Betty does not solve the problem. Betty is notorious for not allying herself with anyone for long, the others constantly criticise her for her behaviour and according to her account she hates sitting around talking anyway. (Her learning of the teachers' ideas of acceptable behaviour has apparently been more successful since she is well liked by the teachers.) Certainly she is no substitute for Pat, and Vanessa's misery at losing her friend makes life look very bleak indeed. Physical removal of one-self from one friend to another is one way of letting your friend know that her behaviour was inappropriate. For this technique to work, however, one must know who one's contingency friends are. The distress that Vanessa experienced when Pat left her need not have been so acute if she had had a contingency friend ready for the emergency. (The arrival of Jane at school provided Vanessa with a friend. In this unforeseen way, Pat's withdrawal backfired, since Vanessa was only too glad to start afresh with Jane.)

In the following transcript, Roddie and Garry are quite happily together on the contingency plan. They demonstrate, partly by explaining, partly by displaying, that one-time best friends can be an important source of contingency friends:

Transcript 4.5: Garry and Roddie

1 *B.D.:* You two are good friends at the moment are you?	1 I assume this because they have come in together and seem to be getting on well.
2 *Garry and Roddie:* Yeah.	
3 *Roddie:* Oh no, we don't hardly get around together but we are friends, good friends.	3 Roddie is not happy with straightforward agreement. They are friends with a difference.
4 *Garry:* Ah, before we used to but now we don't.	4 They were best friends once. A best friend can become a contingency friend.
5 *Roddie:* We are good friends but.	5-7 Note the continual reiteration of the fact of their friendship which is necessary to counter-
6 *B.D.:* You've always been	

good friends?

7 *Garry and Roddie:* Yeah.

balance the qualification of contingency which is being described. ('But' on the end of the sentence in 5 means 'though'.)

8 *B.D.:* But you don't hang around together all that much?

9 *Garry and Roddie:* No.

10 *Roddie:* Oh, but you know when I have a row with Warwick or somebody, you know, I'll go to Garry and Garry'll come to me and I'll go to Patrick or some of them.

10 They still are good friends but the friendship is only mobilised when things go wrong between Roddie and Warwick. Roddie has several contingency friends he can call on, unlike Vanessa who could think of no one.

Withdrawal to contingency friends need not spell the end of friendships. Negotiations such as that engaged in by Vanessa where messages are sent via others to find out whether the friendship is still on, take place fairly soon after the withdrawal, usually initiated by the least powerful of the duo. In the following conversations Suzie is quite upset because her best friend Mandy has withdrawn from her. Mandy will not open negotiations – she has the snobs – yet Suzie feels relatively certain that Mandy is still her best friend.

Transcript 4.6: Terry and Suzie

1 *Terry:* At the moment Mandy has got the snobs/

1 Terry and Suzie have become friends recently. Boy-girl relationships are potentially disruptive of same sex friendships. Another boy is involved in the disruption, but his role is not made clear.

2 *Suzie:* with me/

3 *Terry:* because, we don't know what happened/

4 *Suzie:* aw, something about Graham Hurley or something/

5 *Terry:* Hurley, yeah and at the moment she's a real you know, snob.

6   *Suzie:*   Yeah, because see Terry wrote on a piece of paper, 'What's the matter with Mandy', because he didn't want to say it in front of her, and Mandy, I think she still is my best friend, but she, see, she thinks I hate her now because Terry wrote this and she thought it was something else and she hates me now, and so does Betty Eggart. I never really did like Betty and that, because she's sort of spoiled.

6   Mandy has withdrawn and allied herself with Betty on the contingency friendship plan after sensing potential rejection from her best friend.

7   *Terry:*   She's a spoiled brat!

8   *Suzie:*   No. She's a show-off. She doesn't leave you alone, she came up to me the other day, I asked Mandy if she liked a drink of my drink and anyway, Betty, thinkin' she was smart, she was eating this apricot or somethin' and put the seed in it, just because I took it out and put it on the seat she comes up and punches me.

7-8   Betty is again noted as unacceptable though how to characterise her unacceptableness is difficult. It is easier to illustrate it with an example of her behaviour which speaks for itself.

The centrality of *being with your friend* for friendship, then, is illustrated through the effects that leaving your friend can have. Children do not like to be left alone but will leave their friend alone if it seems appropriate to do so. The contingency friendship plan is vital for the success of this strategy. Moreover, contingency friends increase the bargaining power of those children who know they will not be left alone if their friend chooses to leave them in the event of a disagreement or fight.

Finally, those children like Adrienne and Mandy, who consider they have quite high bargaining power, will play out the contingency friendship plan until all suitable apologies and appeals have been made. Adrienne, for example, in discussing a bout of fisticuffs she had just had indicates that however fearful she may feel, she expects the other to take the first initiative in restoring the friendship:

Because if you punch up your friends you feel, you feel that they

won't ever like you again. But they do make up with me. I'm not
the one that turns back and says 'will you be my friend?' They come
back and say 'will you be friends with me?'

The Rules of Childhood Culture

The advantage of the squabbles the children had among themselves
was that they created in natural form the sort of situation Garfinkel
(1967) was after when he had his students disrupt the order of things
to find out what was being taken for granted about the social order
before the disruption occurred. The disruptions described by the
children of my study were different in a significant way from
Garfinkel's, however, in that they were considered to be part of the
normal order of things, rather than as abnormal events. The transcripts
I have chosen generally deal with the disruptions. In case this is taken
to indicate an unusual lack of stability amongst the group studied, I
should remind the reader that there were several steady friendships and
friendship groups (see p. 13).

Even though these disruptions are considered normal by the children
('It's always normal, every year we have about three or four fights
through the year, but we always come back together'), they nevertheless prompt an examination or restatement of the taken-for-granted
rules attending friendship. Vanessa, for example, in wondering why Pat
has deserted her (Transcript 4.4), with little or no prompting, works
through the conditions of friendship as they operate amongst the
children. The ideas she produces were possibly not ideas she could
have produced before the incident. Only when she reflects on what has
gone wrong does she begin to make clear some of the basic rules of
friendship, i.e., that you should be with your friend, and that isolation
or reciprocation rapidly follows the breaching of this rule.

I have isolated three critical constructs within children's culture
which related to acceptable and unacceptable ways of behaving within
that culture. These are:

1 Reciprocity
I am a mirror to you which provides you with my perception of your
behaviour towards me.

This is a different proposition from the looking-glass self put
forward by Cooley: 'In imagination we perceive in another's mind some
thought of our appearance, manners, aims, deeds, character, friends and
so on, and are variously affected by it' (1972, p.231). Cooley proposed
the *imaginative* construction of self whereas the children's proposition
involves *active reflecting back* to the other of the other's self.

Related rule: I should behave to you as you behave to me. I should reciprocate any wrongdoing which you do towards me, and, less importantly, I should reciprocate correct behaviour as well. Behaviours which were defined as wrong from one's friends (though not necessarily wrong from others) were: getting the snobs, getting the cranks, teasing, lying, showing off, getting too full of yourself, posing, bashing people up, being piss weak, wanting everything your way, being spoilt, being stupid, dobbing (i.e., telling tales). On the other hand, you should be with your friend, play properly, share, be tough, stick up for your friends, and know each other's feelings.

(Dobbing was the only behaviour on the list which took cognisance of the adult world. In so far as it involved calling in extra and unhandleable adult forces it was regarded as totally unacceptable behaviour. For children who were unable to reciprocate bad behaviour, dobbing was a surrogate form of reciprocity.)

2 Events have a discoverable facticity
Children's constant quarrels about 'what happened' illustrate their belief in a single truth. Relativist philosophies were not relevant in their dealings with each other. Though over *time* what was true changed as a result of new perceptions and insights, and though they recognised a multiplicity of ways of explaining any event, they adhered steadfastly to the ideal of the facticity of events at any single point in time.

Related rule: The facticity of the phenomenal world should be maintained by challenges to inadequate approximations in others' talk. The behaviours which were unacceptable in relation to this rule were lying, posing, showing off, and getting too big for yourself (i.e., making yourself out to be better than you really are).

3 People have an existential or plastic quality
What is so about people today may be demonstrably untrue tomorrow. One's *character* is not assumed to have absolute continuity through time or across situations.

Related rule: One's actions towards others should be appropriate to the present.* Thus, behaviours which are unacceptable towards one's friend (such as leaving them) can become appropriate in the present if one's friend is behaving badly. Similarly with bashing up, getting the snobs and teasing.

---

* This proposition gives extreme cogency to Schutz's statements concerning the attentional modifications of meaning which are time related: '. . . the *meaning* of a lived experience undergoes modifications depending on the particular kind of attention the Ego gives to that lived experience. This also implies that the meaning of a lived experience is different depending on *the moment from which the* Ego is observing it.' (1972, p.73, emphasis in original)

These three constructs emerged in the children's talk, not directly, but indirectly. For instance, in the following transcript Jane expresses puzzlement at Mandy's failure to reciprocate apparently aggressive behaviour from Betty:

Transcript 4.7: Jane

1 *Jane:* It's funny, I'm not saying anything against anyone. We were having a game with Betty's ball, Mandy got bashed in the eye by Betty and then she's back sitting next to her. It's a wonder that she didn't get the huffs!	1 Jane is being very cautious here. She doesn't want the word around that she is criticising anyone. Nevertheless, reciprocity of action is both natural and important, even where the original offence was not intended.

It might be worth noting here that Mandy can't afford to get the 'huffs' since she and Suzie are still estranged and Betty is her contingency friend. To get the huffs with Betty would be to force the reconciliation with Suzie. Mandy's failure to get the huffs with Betty indicates that the groundwork for reconciliation with Suzie is not yet complete.

Except where such limiting conditions exist, reciprocation follows fairly rapidly. The following transcripts illustrate in a variety of ways trangressions against the rules, and the attitudes and responses brought to these transgressions. The importance of these transgressions, it must be remembered, is that it is through the breaking of rules that people discover or rediscover precisely what the rules are. That is, they discover the dimensions and limits of their taken-for-granted world.

Transcript 4.8: Anne and Adrienne

1 *B.D.:* Tell me about the fight you two had.	1 Referring to an earlier point in the conversation.
2 *Anne:* When?	2-4 Fights are sufficiently fre-
3 *B.D.:* Didn't you say earlier that you two had had a fight?	quent to need clarification as to which fight I am talking about, though the children
4 *Adrienne:* Oh yeah, that one. (*Anne giggles*)	may not find them memorable, nor regard them as frequent.
5 *B.D.:* Tell me about it.	
6 *Adrienne:* Anne said come	6 Anne suggested the two of

and do something and I had to do my number facts.

7 *Anne:* Yeah, Adrienne said 'I ca--ant, I have to do me wo--ork.'

7 Adrienne replied in a wingeing voice that she couldn't come (i.e., she was piss weak).

8 *Adrienne:* And Anne said 'all right then!' (*Anne giggles*) and then she walked out of the classroom.

8 Anne in response speaks huffily to her and then *walks away from her*.

9 *B.D.:* So you felt Anne should have come with you instead of doing her work?

10 *Anne:* I didn't know she had to do her number facts again! Just the way she said it!

11 *B.D.:* So it was just the tone of her voice she had that put you off. (*Anne nods agreement*)

9-11 It was not the fact that Anne refused to come with her that constituted a breach of rules. It was the *manner* of her refusal. By walking away Anne signals that she is temporarily withdrawing her friendship and spending her time with someone else.

Tone of voice has been noted as important to children. In some cases more important than actual words. They know if offence is intended through the manner of the delivery rather than the insult itself. In this case no offence was intended, but Adrienne discovered that her tone of voice had unwittingly delivered an unacceptable message.

The delicate balance between fun and serious fighting is illustrated in the following conversation with Vanessa and Jane. Mostly for these two it is fun but there is an air of exploration and challenge, of trying each other out, which leads on occasion to behaviour which causes genuine offence.

This friendship is a new one as mentioned earlier. Negotiations are still in progress as to how they will ultimately relate to each other, so the emphasis is on exploration, or trying out. Yet this exploration follows an orderly, rule-bound sequence of action and reciprocation. In what follows, the girls both talk about and display the reciprocity inherent in their relationship:

Transcript 4.9: Jane and Vanessa

1 *B.D.:* What sort of person are you at school?

2 *Jane:* (*laughs*) Aw, sometimes I get real low, and other

times I am real happy.

3   *B.D.:*   How would you describe her, Vanessa?

4   *Vanessa:*   (*laughs*) I dunno (*unclear*) squabbling.

5   *Jane:*   Yeah, Vanessa and me/

6   *Vanessa:*   She's a good friend when we are not squabbling, but when we are squabbling, ugh!

7   *B.D.:*   What sort of things do you squabble about?

8   *Vanessa:*   I dunno, just like/ (*giggles*)

9   *Jane:*   She might leave a letter out in a word and I'd say, 'Oh yeah, you've left out a letter in that,' and she says 'All right!' and I say 'OK I won't talk then!' Then she gets mad and then I get mad and we don't talk to each other.

9   Jane describes a pattern of criticism causing offence, then counter-offence, followed by withdrawal of friendship. This is told in a dramatic style which re-creates (displays) the incident for my benefit.

10   *B.D.:*   How long do you stay mad for?

11   *Jane:*   Aw, about ten minutes until we've said our pieces to each other and then we'll go back to good friends, won't we?

11   The pattern of mutual offence is typically followed by mutual reaffirmation of friendship after a period of no interaction. (Neither of them has 'contingency' friends to withdraw to at the time of this conversation.)

12   *Vanessa:*   Yeah, we are trying to stop our squabbling but we haven't succeeded.

12   The taken-for-granted rule of reciprocity is more powerful than the wish that either of them has to put an end to it.

13   *B.D.:*   Why are you trying to stop?

14   *Jane:*   Aw, we don't like it much.

15   *Vanessa:*   But we always do it.

16   *Jane:*   Every morning. (*both are giggling*)

17 *B.D.:* You're like an old married couple aren't you? Squabbling with each other. (*both giggle*)

17 In so far as they seem to have no clear alternative to their friendship with each other my joking analogy is quite apt.

18 *Jane:* I'll say, 'Are you buying your lunch?' and she will say 'No' and I say, 'Aw, well don't talk then, don't get the darkies with me.' And she goes, 'Aw god, I never even said nothing' and then we start squabbling, and then we make friends, 'n' I dunno.

18 The pattern repeated in another form. Jane's 'I dunno' indicates a feeling of helplessness or inevitability in regard to their bouts of offence and counter-offence.

19 *Vanessa:* She walks up to you and goes POW (*Vanessa punches Jane*) and nearly knocks you off your feet.

19 The children move from displaying through talk, to displaying through talk and action, how their 'squabbles' proceed.

20 *Jane:* No, I go like this. (*Jane punches Vanessa*)

21 *Vanessa:* Every day she has the habit of going (*punch*) and nearly knocking you off your chair.

22 *Jane:* And then Vanessa goes (*punch*) and then you get sore, and if you are trying to write she goes (*punch*).

23 *Vanessa:* You go like this to me (*punch*) and I've got a sore enough arm by now.

24 *Jane:* What do you think my shoulder is?

20-24 Several friendly (but painful) punches are thrown. They are challenging the other to take it in good spirits but risking genuine pain and consequent offence, exploring the limits of physical aggression within friendship, e.g., can Jane (22) get away with two punches and only receive one back? But two punches are returned by a punch and a complaint (23) and Jane hastily tries to defuse the complaint by pointing out that she has the same problem (24).

25 *B.D.:* Dear oh dear it sounds like you've got dreadful problems?

26 *Vanessa:* Yep.

27 *Jane:* Yes, we've got the same sort of personality I suppose (*pause*) we can be happy and mad at the same

27 In the process of interaction, or squabbling they discover who they are in relation to each other.

time, and we can change
our ways in just a second.

28 *Vanessa:*   We both seem to
change at the same time.

29 *Jane:*   We start squabbling
at the same time and we
always end at the same time.

28-29 As in 12, the pattern seems
inevitable, it can be described
but not controlled.

30 *B.D.:*   So when you get mad
at each other, do you not
really get mad? Is it all
part of a joke or are you
really mad?

31 *Vanessa:*   Yes, it's sorta, bit
of a joke, trying each other
out.

31 Vanessa recognises the
challenging and exploratory
nature of much of their
squabbling.

32 *Jane:*   Yeah.

33 *B.D.:*   What do you think,
Jane? Do you think it is really
a joke or is it serious?

34 *Jane:*   Oh, half and half.
Sometimes it's serious, sometimes it's a joke.

35 *Vanessa:*   Sometimes it's
serious, but it's really mainly
a joke, isn't it?

35-38 Vanessa seeks reassurance
that in fact their fighting is
acceptable within the friendship, i.e., joking not serious,
but repeats that their friendship would be better off with
less of it.

36 *B.D.:*   But you are able to
forget and forgive very
quickly?

37 *Jane:*   Yeah.

38 *Vanessa:*   Yeah, since the one
we had this morning, we
haven't done any more, and
we are not going to. We are
not going to continue it.

39 *Jane:*   Yesterday my foot
was aching (*Vanessa giggles*)
and um, Mr Droop went to
ring up me Mum — and
Vanessa goes, 'I'm doing the
experiment myself' and I go,
'Why?' and she goes, 'Aw, I
haven't got anybody to play
with at lunchtime. I don't
make friends easily,' and when

39 Even if your friend cannot
help going away (through
illness) offence can be taken
and retaliation in the form of
counter-withdrawal carried
out. Vanessa's relief that the
rift does not need to occur
warrants exclamations of
endearment ('Me old
buddy!').

I told her that Mum wasn't
home she said, 'Aw, that's good
me old buddy!' Changes like
that.
40 *Vanessa:*   Yeah, just change
with the weather, so me dad
says.

The unquestioning way in which reciprocal acts are engaged in clearly involves a controlling element, though the children do not necessarily accept 'control' as their motivation. Their actions, rather than having retribution as their major purpose, seem to relate more closely to equilibrating and maintaining the social world. This point was brought home to me in a discussion with Paul.

When Daniel (aged 8) was irritating Paul (aged 11) and Paul was handing out reciprocal irritation, I tried to persuade Paul that if he desisted, Daniel would grow to like him better and therefore spend less time finding ways to irritate him. Paul considered that a failure on his part to 'pay him back' would clearly mean that Daniel would repeat his irritating ways without cease. My response was, 'Well, if you want to control him to stop him from doing what he is doing, you are going to have to find more subtle ways of going about it. Simply paying him back each time isn't working.' With some anger and indignation Paul declared that he did *not* want to control him. Any approach I took to the argument, and I tried several, arrived at exactly the same point. If Paul didn't pay him back he would do it again and yet he definitely considered that he did not want to control him. Reciprocation is common sense, control is unacceptable. (Perhaps 'controlling' is what adults do.)

The rule of negative reciprocation seems to be a very basic law within childhood culture.

Interestingly, Gouldner in his 1960 review of the sociological literature on reciprocity, notes the frequency with which positive reciprocity is cited as a fundamental aspect, generally, of social stability. Homans's views on reciprocity (1951, p.290) once again coincide with the children's views. He claims that it is not individual acts of reciprocity which lead to social control, rather it is the interaction *itself*, the *process* of creating coherence, that leads to stability of action within a social group. Rosser and Harré (1976), further, analyse the equilibrating effect for the *individual* of reciprocated (negative) action.*

---

* The differences between adult and childhood cultures are subtle ones, and may often relate to what we *believe* we are doing rather than what we actually do. Thus, as adults in a modern Christian world we

The children of my study, and of Rosser and Harré's study, spoke most often of *negative* reciprocity. Perhaps this is because 'social rules seem to operate . . . more "in the breach than in the observance". We are not aware of breaking one until after the act' (Cook-Gumperz, 1975, p. 142). In other words, negative reciprocation will be more consciously engaged in, in the construction and maintenance of the world-taken-for-granted, i.e., in the creation and maintenance of a coherent world.

In the following description by Simon of the relationship between him and Roddie, the reciprocation takes a considerable amount of time, and offence (often apparently unintended) occurs regularly, so they are rarely in a state of friendship. They both want to be friends with Warwick, and they both wish that Warwick would cease being friends with the other:

Transcript 4.10: Simon

1	*B.D.:* You and Roddie don't get on do you?	1-6 Simon takes fighting as an indication of enmity (in partial contrast to Vanessa and Jane).
2	*Simon:* No, not much.	
3	*B.D.:* Why is that?	
4	*Simon:* 'Cos we keep on fighting.	Again, as with Vanessa and Jane, the fighting seems to be an unexplained fact.
5	*B.D.:* Why do you fight?	
6	*Simon:* Dunno.	
7	*B.D.:* Roddie said that when he first went to the last school that the teacher asked who wanted to look after him and you and Warwick said you would.	7 The friendship between Roddie, Warwick (and sometimes Simon) commenced on a happenchance proximity when Roddie first arrived at the previous school.
8	*Simon:* Yeah.	
9	*B.D.:* But then Warwick got on with Roddie and you didn't.	
10	*Simon:* Yeah.	
11	*B.D.:* What was it you didn't like about him?	
12	*Simon:* Oh, you know, he keeps on, you know, walkin' past goin' (*demonstrates*) hit	12 These punches, as with Jane's, are intended as a joking challenge and yet are

may adhere to certain beliefs about interaction (turning the other cheek), but in fact behave quite differently (eye for an eye).

me on the back of the head
for a joke, and I don't like
it, keeps on bumpin' me
when I'm workin'.

not acceptable to Simon.
After all, Roddie is not
Simon's only or even best
friend.

13 *B.D.:*   He just does little
things to irritate you does
he?

14 *Simon:*   Yeah.

15 *B.D.:*   Have you ever tried
to be his friend?

16 *Simon:*   Yeah.

17 *B.D.:*   When was that?

18 *Simon:*   Oh, when the show
was on and the times after
that.

19 *B.D.:*   And what happened?
What went wrong when you
tried to be friends with him?

20 *Simon:*   Oh, he done the
same thing.

21 *B.D.:*   Just sort of hitting you
and pushing you and that?
(*nods*)

22 *B.D.:*   How come he and
Warwick get on so well?

23 *Simon:*   'Cos, um, he isn't
game to hit Warwick.

24 *B.D.:*   Why isn't he game to
hit Warwick?

25 *Simon:*   'Cos Warwick can
beat him in a fight.

15-20 Despite the annoyance
Simon feels at Roddie's
challenge, Simon will be his
friend as long as he refrains
from challenging him. But
Roddie cannot resist
challenging him. (The 'show'
is the local fair.)

22-25 Simon reads Roddie's
challenges as deliberate
insults (though Roddie
may intend them as jokes)
since he does not behave in
the same way to a respected
person.

Roddie, in contrast, always sees Simon as the one who starts the
fights. (My attempts to unravel fights between my own children have,
similarly, always led back either to a point where one accidentally
offended the other, or else to a point where no one can remember
what happened before that.)

Transcript 4.11: Roddie

1 *B.D.:*   What's been going on
between you and the others
the last few days?

2 *Roddie:*   Oh, a big row up.

1 I have heard rumours of a
fight.

2 Enthusiastic tone of voice.

Pow, crash, bang!

3   *B.D.:*   What happened?

4   *Roddie:*   Oh, um, Simon?

5   *B.D.:*   Mm.

6   *Roddie:*   I think you had him in here before?

4-6   Roddie, aware that I am not as familiar with his world as he is, always checks whether new information is clear to me.

7   *B.D.:*   Yeah, oh wait a minute, have I talked to Simon? No.

7   This conversation took place before I had met Simon. He was later moved out of the teacher-directed class into the open-plan class and so came to talk to me.

8   *Roddie:*   Oh, no, he's in another class. Well, see he wants it all his own way and if I said that I'm goin' on his side, or goin' with Warwick and, um, he don't like me? So he just/

8   Roddie puts forward two basic propositions: first, Simon always wants his own way, and second, Simon doesn't like Roddie. In combination, this means Simon will insist on some things that Roddie doesn't like (e.g., not being in Warwick's team). It further means that Roddie's interpretation of Simon's action is not simply in terms of Simon's selfishness, but in terms of Simon's wish to offend Roddie.

9   *B.D.:*   So if you are friendly with Simon then Warwick doesn't like you? No?

9   I am obviously confused at this point.

10   *Roddie:*   See, Warwick always goes with Simon.

10   Roddie interrupts his story to provide the necessary information. It is interesting to note the use of the term to 'go with', which is a term more commonly applied to boy-girl romantic relationships. The exclusivity of the friendship that Roddie wishes for is emphasised here by the use of this term.

11   *B.D.:*   Oh, yeah, Simon.

11   I then remember Warwick mentioning Simon as a friend.

12   *Roddie:*   Yeah.

13 *B.D.:*   Yeah.

14 *Roddie:*   Well, um, see, we was playin' soccer there and I come on to Warwick's side, and Simon said, 'Go on the other side,' and I said, 'I want to be on Warwick's side the same as you do.'

14 Simon attempts to exclude Roddie from Warwick's team. Roddie becomes angry at a perceived offence and Simon walks away. Walking away is a fairly powerful device since it means Roddie is deprived of a game, deprived of Warwick's company, and left alone. Roddie had no alternative then but to reciprocate these multiple offences.

15 *B.D.:*   Mm.

16 *Roddie:*   An' then he just walked off and he expected us to follow him. Warwick followed him but I didn't. That's how it all started.

Roddie needs to find some way of getting back at Simon since he resents the power Simon has over Warwick and the use he makes of it to put Roddie down. After getting sidetracked into telling me about a fight between Roddie and Warwick, where Warwick had punched Roddie for supposedly saying something bad to Roy, another Aboriginal boy, Roddie explains that fights don't mean the *end* of a friendship; they are, like the contingency friendship plan, strategic moves inside the friendship.

17 *B.D.:*   So what did you think of that?

17 i.e., of the fight with Warwick.

18 *Roddie:*   Nothin'. It's always normal, every year we have about three or four fights through the year.

18-24 Roddie is not offended that Warwick hit him to the ground for something he actually had not done.

19 *B.D.:*   Do you? What you and Warwick?

20 *Roddie:*   Yeah, and Simon.

21 *B.D.:*   How long have you guys all been friends?

22 *Roddie:*   Since we come 'ere. Over at D School we was friends.

23 *B.D.:*   Were you?

24   *Roddie:*   We've been friends for a few years. You know we had arguments and fights in between and that, but we always come back together. (*Laughs a brief knowing laugh*)

24   Roddie's laugh is one which indicates that he has command of the situation with his friends; he knows how it all works so he doesn't need to worry unduly about the odd punch-up.

25   *B.D.:*   Are you friendly again yet?

26   *Roddie:*   Yeah. Not with Simon, I'm not with Simon. I wanted to fight Simon yes'd'y, but he wouldn't.

26   Reciprocation for the triple offence is yet to be achieved.

27   *B.D.:*   Why did you want to fight him?

28   *Roddie:*   Aw, 'cos 'e's the one that always starts it.

29   *B.D.:*   How does he start it?

30   *Roddie:*   'Cos see Simon's never liked me. And I sorta try to make friends wif 'im, and 'e just won't, and he just goes off and Warwick follus 'im. An' then Simon, you know, starts callin' me things, names and that, but when Warwick isn't around, but when Warwick's around he crawls to us, because he knows Warwick'll back up for him.

30   Roddie describes how Simon capitalises on Warwick following him. The gratuitous insults, i.e., calling Simon a crawler are an expression of the need for reciprocation and in fact a partial reciprocation, since Simon would not want me to think of him as a crawler.

31   *B.D.:*   Mm.

32   *Roddie:*   But when Warwick's around he always wants to be friends with me.

33   *B.D.:*   Mm hm. But sometimes like when you play soccer he doesn't try and be friends with you?

33   I immediately pick out the 'weak link' in the story.

34   *Roddie:*   Mm. Warwick made a promise 'e's not goin' with none of us.

34-36 Warwick will not be exclusively friends with one or the other. He is obviously fed up with the conflict so Roddie and Simon must sort out their differences without

35   *B.D.:*   Mm hm.

36   *Roddie:*   And 'e said that's how it's gunna stop. So me

and Simon's gotta fight it out ourselves.

using him. The manner of their sorting out involves a physical fight in which one is established as stronger than the other, that one presumably having the right from that point on to call the tune.

37   *B.D.:*   Mm hm.

38   *Roddie:*   But see I was round the side, waitin' for Simon to come round and fight me. Just around there.

39   *B.D.:*   Mm.

40   *Roddie:*   And next minute I looked down an' there was Simon ridin' home on his bike. And he wouldn't come back either.
(*I laugh and Roddie grins*)

40   I laugh at the image of Simon wisely and rapidly retreating from a bad situation.

41   *B.D.:*   Are you a better fighter than Simon?

41   If Simon was retreating it suggests he knew Roddie would win.

42   *Roddie:*   I've tried him once, we both/ no one won 'cos the bell rang. Oh, I'm urgin' to fight him again but. I just wanna see 'oo can win.

42   But Roddie admits he doesn't really know if he can beat him. He may not have been retreating at all – Roddie's description may just have been a pose which makes Simon look weak. On the other hand, Simon may well fear a denouement in which he is revealed as the weaker of the two, and therefore lower in the pecking order.

To sum up so far, the children have quite clear strategies for coping with unacceptable behaviour from each other. They can walk away from each other, either with the intention of being followed, or to seek out a contingency friend. Putting an end to reciprocal bouts of unacceptable behaviour is almost impossible if the freedom to walk away does not exist, as the case of Vanessa and Jane illustrates. An alternative to walking away, not used by Vanessa and Jane, is an all-out fight, though this is not always possible. These strategies do not spell the end of friendships: they are manoeuvres within friendships. A friend can walk away or fight with you and you can still count him as your best friend (after certain additional manoeuvres have been completed). To fight someone when it is not called for, however, is unthinkable, as Henry explains in the following transcript. This conversation takes place when Henry has just arrived back at school after some months of chronic illness. He explains that he will fight Roddie when the situation is right for it. At the moment they are friends, so fighting would be inappropriate. He is looking forward to the day when fighting Roddie will be appropriate.

Transcript 4.12: Henry, Roy and Sally

1   *Henry:*   I'm gonna drop Roddie.

2   *Roy:*   You gonna drop 'im? Pick 'im up and drop 'im?

2   Roy, fully understanding Henry, anticipates the lack of understanding I will have for the term, and plays on this.

3   *Henry:*   Sometimes you get me mad.

3   Henry does not like his claim to be treated in jest.

4   *Roy:*   Roddie's better'n me and he's eleven, twelve.

4   Roy acknowledges that Roddie can beat him in a fight.

5   *B.D.:*   So what are you going to do? Drop Roddie?

5   I am indeed baffled, and seek clarification.

6   *Henry:*   I'll drop 'im.

7   *B.D.:*   Why, Henry?

8   *Sally (Henry's sister):*   Last time he made me real wild when Henry was at the Far West. (*home for sick children*) Um, Jennie got 'it by Roddie. And she kept cryin' that 'e'd 'it 'er. And Roddie was sittin' down on the steps and I asked him, and I asked who hit her and I went over to Roddie and I said, 'Roddie why'd you hit Jennie for,' and he wouldn't tell me no reason so I 'it 'im. Then 'e 'it me back and then 'e ran.

8   Sally describes how, in the absence of her brother Henry, she had had to defend her younger sister. Amongst the Aboriginal children, reciprocation on the behalf of others was common. Amongst the white children it was rare. Sally is taking here an adult role of punishing elder rather than reciprocating peer. Her enquiry as to *reasons* for Roddie's action, rather than immediate reciprocation, is a further aspect of the adult role she describes herself as

9 *Henry:* 'e's scared.
10 *Roy:* 'e's scared, that's why.

11 *Sally:* I reckon Simon's the best.
12 *Henry:* I could drop Roddie.

13 *B.D.:* You're feeling mad at Roddie are you Henry?

14 *Henry:* No, I'm not mad at 'im *now* 'e's a friend now.
15 *B.D.:* But you could get mad at him now?
16 *Henry:* I *could*, I *could*, I can't get mad at 'im for no reason! You've got to 'ave a reason.

17 *Sally:* Say Warwick came up to my sister and she was only 5, and she had a bashed lip, and 'ed punched 'er well then what would you do?
18 *Henry:* Who? My sister?
19 *Sally:* Yeah, if it was your sister?
20 *Henry:* I'd punch 'im.
21 *Sally:* Yeah, right, so would I.

adopting.
9-10 An insult is offered when appropriate reciprocal action has been thwarted by withdrawal.

12 Henry points out that he is stronger than Roddie.
13 I am still not clear as to the precise nuance of meaning intended by Henry.
14-16 Henry finds my assumption rather silly and his tone of voice in 16 is indignant. Roddie's action towards Sally's and Henry's younger sister and towards Sally which occurred when Henry was absent does not constitute grounds for a fight, i.e., it is not Roddie's previous actions (or in some sense his character) which makes 'dropping' him appropriate. Dropping him will be in response to a particular action on Roddie's part. (See rule 3, p. 77, 'one's actions should be appropriate to the present'.) Henry will also, through such appropriate action, confirm that he is stronger than Roddie (12).
17 Sally points out that he would have punched him if he'd been in the situation she was in.

| 22 *Henry:* | I'd punch anybody. | 22 | Implied here is 'if it was appropriate'. |

This is a clear example of the children's concern to behave appropriately in the present. Friends do bad things and you react in the appropriate manner and fairly soon you are friends again, and the correct order of things has been maintained. Through appropriately reciprocated action a stable background of expectancies with which to interpret everyday action and interaction can be maintained. Though people will vary over time (one's friends can do apparently unacceptable things at times, and still be friends) reciprocal action can restore the balance and reaffirm the way things are, and ought to be.

Friends not only save you from being alone, they also help you to build up a working knowledge of who you are. This may be indirectly through facilitating certain ways of being or it may be directly through praise or censure. Friends are not enough, however, since non-friends seem necessary to provide the Garfinkelian element which clarifies or crystallises even more clearly who you are. One of the behaviours counted as inappropriate for friends was 'posing' or showing off, yet the children admitted that posing was something everyone did sometimes. Posing is seen as big-noting yourself or making out that you are better than you are. Even though everyone does it, posing is read by others as offensive, since it involves inaccurate presentation of self and also the possibility that by contrast to the posers one will be made to feel weak or inferior. There is a certain ambivalence, then, towards posing.

Transcript 4.13: Sally, Henry and Roy

1	*Sally:*	Everyone 'ates Mr Droop 'cos, you know, everyone talks behind his back. 'Specially Mandy.
2	*Henry:*	Yeah, she's a freckle face! I'm going to shoot her too.
3	*Sally:*	She sticks her thumb up at Mr Droop. She do's all that stuff. (*unclear*)
4	*B.D.:*	Why don't you like Mandy, Henry?
5	*Henry:*	She shows off.
6	*Roy:*	Yeah, she shows off.
7	*Sally:*	She follows Roddie

around.
8 *Roy:* And Warwick.
9 *Henry:* And Roddie don't
want 'er/
10 *Sally:* And Roddie likes, um,/
11 *Henry:* Anne.
12 *Sally:* Yeah, Anne.
13 *B.D.:* But Anne doesn't like
him.
14 *Sally:* Sometimes.
15 *B.D.:* But you don't like
Mandy because she shows off?
16 *Sally:* Yeah.
17 *Henry:* Yeah.
18 *Roy:* What's the use of saying
that because we show off too
sometimes.

Teasing is closely related to posing. It can be a pose if you tease
(i.e., making out that the other's style is inferior or wrong and therefore
to be teased) or teasing can be a response to posing (you are teased for
making out that you are superior). Teasing is generally taken to be
offensive, and not many children can receive teasing with cool. In fact
rarely is it seen as appropriate to receive it with cool, since such cool
may be interpreted as weakness, or inability to reciprocate the offence.
Friends generally place a taboo on teasing each other (except where it
is agreed to classify the teasing as a joke, and even then it might run the
risk of being taken as a serious challenge). They reserve most of their
teasing for others. Another way of looking at this would be to say
that friends have usually negotiated and agreed upon the details of
acceptable behaviour and therefore have no need to tease, though
teasing may well have played some part in the negotiations.

In the following transcript Linda explains that she has modified her
school behaviour as a result of teasing.

Transcript 4.14: Linda, Suzie and Terry

1 *B.D.:* You are more responsible at school?

1 Linda has claimed she is quite
different at home from at
school. She is having trouble
formulating the difference so
I make a suggestion.

2 *Linda:* Yes, at home I sort
of do everything, I sorta show

2 She agrees, but subsequent
conversation indicates I am

off a bit at home.

3   *Suzie:*   Yes!

4   *Linda:*   I don't show off at school 'cos, you get called/

5   *Terry:*   'Poser! Poser!'

6   *Linda:*   Yeah, 'Poser! Poser!' Or if you are a flirt they call you/

7   *Suzie:*   Yeah and they call ya, they say/

8   *Linda:*   'Flirt! Flirt! Flirt!', something like that.

9   *Suzie:*   And if you're goin' round with a boy or somethin', talkin' to him or somethin' like that and somebody says somethin' about you or somethin', and your family's going around with a boy and you also those people would say/

10   *Linda:*   'Oh now you've got a boyfriend.'

11   *Suzie:*   And the people who are going around with a boy will just say, 'You're jealous.'

12   *B.D.:*   So what the other kids say about you at school has a big effect on what you are at school?

13   *Suzie:*   Yes, see, whenever I'm being called a name or somethin' like that, I dunno what happens, but it feels horrible.

14   *Linda:*   I sorta really go, I sorta really get the snobs.

15   *Terry:*   Yeah, me too.

16   *Suzie:*   And Betty comes up and says, 'Don't get the snobs.'

off beam.

3   Suzie has witnessed this behaviour at home.

4   The reason she is different at school is that she would be teased if she didn't modify her behaviour.

5   Said in a sing-song teasing voice.

6-8   Chanted in a teasing voice. Being teased for flirting is a response to people who are thought to be setting themselves up as more attractive than anyone else.

9   Suzie explains you can even be teased however for aspects of your home life which are unavoidable, i.e., if your family goes out with another family who has a boy of your age.

10   Sing-song teasing voice.

11   But there are words you can use to defend yourself which deliver a reciprocal offence.

12-15   The recognition and acceptance of the power of social pressure is quite strong.

14   'Snobs' is a withdrawal into offended isolation.

16   So if you are teased and withdraw, that, too, is worthy of

more teasing.

So the teaser attacks the person he fears is setting himself up as a poser in the first place. Teasing is at once a fear of the possible superiority of the other and an attempt to place oneself (the teaser) in the superior position.

Transcript 4.15: Terry, Linda and Suzie

1 **B.D.:** So posing is being sort of smarter than everyone else?	1 Posing is a word which was quite new to me at the time.
2 **Terry:** Yeah, showing off.	
3 **Linda:** Yes, you just have to be the best.	
4 **Terry:** Sometimes Graham will say, 'Aw don't pose,' when he's posing, oh, sometimes, I'll pose on my bike and he'll pose chucking wheel stands on his sister's bike, and he'll go down skating and pose. I just say, 'Oh don't pose Graham,' anyway he just takes no notice of me.	4 Posing is something Terry admits to doing himself and admits to criticising others for. He further criticises Graham however for not being affected by the criticism.
5 **Suzie:** Well, that's what you should do, take no notice.	5-6 Suzie finds this commendable, however, and Terry agrees. The possibility of non-reciprocation (if done with cool) is acknowledged but rarely acted upon.
6 **Terry:** Yeah.	

Sometimes the physical violence itself is the pose. Fist fights were not uncommon among the boys and the girls.* If your friend is tough and bashes others up then you are all the safer since he will most likely defend you when necessary, so to be tough is admirable. On the other hand you may be on the receiving end of the toughness in which case it is no longer perceived as admirable. The tough guy from the point of view of the loser and perhaps of the loser's supporters is seen as a poser — someone who is fighting to big-note himself. To be

---

* Though I was surprised that the girls fought physically, other researchers (see for example Meyenn, 1980) have found fisticuffs amongst girls accepted as the norm.

seen as a poser does not feel very good — the word in itself can act as a form of social control to prevent someone from posing. Paradoxically then, the tough guy in a fight can find himself either admired or despised or even both.

Transcript 4.16: Garry, Vanessa and Suzie

1   *Garry:*   Ian Wilkins, he's a poser because he can beat me in a fight.

1   To win a fight is to be a poser (or to run the risk of being called one), i.e., Garry may mean that he poses because he wins or the very fact that he wins makes him a poser by definition.

2   *B.D.:*   Mm hm.

3   *Vanessa:*   So's Mandy because she beats me.

3   This applies to the girls as well.

4   *Garry:*   And Terry! God he's a pose. Ian Wilkins, when everybody's around he gets in and fights me and beats me just so everybody'll get around 'im and be his friend and that.

4   Winning fights and posing call for admiration and friend-ship — at least so it seems from the loser's point of view.

5   *Vanessa:*   'n, have a look.

5   Everyone will look at you being beaten.

6   *B.D.:*   So if you're tough, everybody likes you?

7   *Garry and Vanessa:*   Yeah.

8   *B.D.:*   What happens if you're not tough?

9   *Vanessa:*   Nobody likes you.

10   *Garry:*   Yeah, they call you chicken.

10   Moreover you will be teased about it.

11   *Vanessa:*   They call you words that wouldn't be very good to say on tape.

12   *Garry:*   They call you chicken. (*laughter*)

13   *B.D.:*   What do they call you?

14   *Garry:*   They call you chicken, they go pk, pk, pk.

15   *Suzie:*   No, they go like this,

aak! pk! pk! pk!

16 *Garry:*   They call you p.o.o.f.

17 *Vanessa:*   They do, that's what they call you.

18 *Garry:*   They hit you on the shoulder.

19 *B.D.:*   So it's the tough people who know that they are tough who go around bullying the people who aren't?

20 *Garry:* Yeah. Say I was Warwick and I was fightin' her, Warwick's come up and hit her there. Just there.	20 Garry explains that Warwick, a high status person, can get away with things that he, Garry, couldn't expect to get away with.
21 *B.D.:* For no reason?	21 Interpreting the indignation in Garry's voice.
22 *Vanessa:* The word they get around calling you is deadshit and that's not very nice really.	
23 *Garry:* I call people dead-head.	

So to be weak is potentially quite devastating. If you are beaten by someone and are weak about it you risk some fairly unpleasant teasing. Garry, in the following transcript, has just been bashed by Roddie. He does not blame Roddie for this since that would be being weak, instead he poses himself by telling a tale of his own prowess.

Transcript 4.17: Garry, Linda, James and Jane

1 *B.D.:* So sometimes you get on OK with Roddie?	1 Garry and Roddie were contingency friends in Transcript 4.5.
2 *Garry:* Yeah we get on a lot of the time.	
3 *B.D.:* Why is it so important to him to prove he's so strong?	3 Another tale of Roddie's prowess had just been told. This time of Roddie over Garry.
4 *Garry:* I don't know, everybody reckons they're strong	4 Garry recognises posing as something everyone must do

sometimes.

sometimes. (Compare this with Harré's notion that the 'pursuit of reputation in the eyes of others is the over-riding preoccupation of human life' (1979, p.3).)

5 *B.D.:*   Yeah.
6 *Linda:*   Strong in which way?
7 *B.D.:*   Everybody or just boys or/
8 *Linda:*   Betty, Mandy, Suzie.
9 *Garry:*   Girls, everybody. Everybody reckons they're tough some time in their life. Like my cousin, he's only as tall as me and he's 16 this year, he reckons he's great in soccer and everything, and the other day he scores a fight with me and he went home, he had a bleedin' nose, all blood was comin' out of his nose.
10 *James:*   You're just posin' 'cos you won!

9-10 For example, he is tough because he beat his 16-year-old cousin in a fight. Garry makes himself sound very tough in this story. The boys in Willis's study (1977) noted with some surprise how tough they sounded when they read the draft of Willis's book. These choices of stories to illustrate one's toughness are, as James points out (10) attempts to present oneself in as impressive a light as possible without straying too far from the facts, i.e., telling a tale (if colourfully) of your own prowess is in itself posing.

11 *Garry:*   He always starts fightin' me.
12 *B.D.:*   But why is it that everybody needs to prove or to show that they're smart or tough?
13 *Jane:*   I don't know, they just wanna pose.
14 *Garry:*   Yeah, that's all.
15 *B.D.:*   But why do they?
16 *Jane:*   They need attention.

11 Garry only has a lame defence prepared.

13,16 It is a basic need — it does not really require explan-ation. The children, in this discussion, confirm Harré's point that striving to be noticed and respected is a very basic human desire: 'We prefer to risk the contempt or pity consequent upon public failure for the chance of the respect and even admiration accorded to public success' (1979, p.22).

17 *Garry:* They'll get no friends – everybody won't like them.

17 But it won't always work. You may get attention but there are some who won't like you for it.

18 *B.D.:* How do you mean?

19 *Garry:* Oh well, say I went up to Warwick and I could beat Warwick in a fight and if I was Warwick and Warwick was me, and Warwick started fightin' with me and I hit him and no one else liked me because he was all their friends, then I'd have no friends.

19-22 If you know you are stronger (as Warwick does) there is no need to fight. If you don't know you are stronger you might feel the need to prove you are tough. In fact if you fight when you know you are tough people might think less of you.

20 *B.D.:* Yeah, but it's not a good idea to fight because you might lose friends.

21 *James:* Sometimes you fight 'cos you've got to prove you're tough.

21 There is a dynamic tension between how we take ourselves to be and how others take us to be. We may have, as James says, to do quite a bit of work to gain credence from others for the model we have of ourselves (cf. Harré, 1979, p.26).

22 *Garry:* Yeah sometimes.

So who can do what to whom depends on their popularity and status, and on the particular situation. Warwick is exceedingly popular with everyone. He is well liked by both the girls and the boys. He is never seen as a poser and when he fights, it is because he has to – at least that is how it is perceived by Roddie: 'He just stops out of it, we 'ardly have a fight me and Warwick, only unless it's called for,' i.e., he knows how to be appropriate, given his status.*

Fighting is a *natural* response to irritation and it protects you and your friends from outside attack. It is a useful skill to be developed and

---

* And he may well have this status because of his knowledge of appropriate and inappropriate behaviours.

therefore requires practice. Most importantly, it gives you a reputation as someone to be respected and taken into account. It is the most direct form of negotiation engaged in by the children in establishing *who* they are, but it takes place within carefully defined situations.

The complex strategies that the children develop to maintain the friendship are not necessarily for love of the particular friend, but because of the functions friendship fulfils. Children may 'make and break friends with a rapidity disconcerting to the adult spectator' (Opie and Opie, 1959, p. 324), but that is perhaps because the adult spectator does not actually understand what is going on. The friendships are in fact quite stable as I have indicated. What appear to be breakages are, rather, manoeuvres within the friendship. The children have developed words and related concepts which describe or explain what it is they are doing. These words and concepts are alien to adults. They belong to the social world of childhood.

Examination of the temporary breakdowns within this culture facilitates an examination of the interpretations the children make of their world, and how these interpretations are related to the functioning of the children's reality. Leaving one's friend for contingency friends, posing, teasing, fighting are all integral to the children's functioning within, and maintenance of, the world as they see it.

Romance

The children rarely talked about their romances and they especially carefully skated around the topic of sex when it was mentioned. They personally felt that there was nothing *wrong* with 'kissing and cuddling' but knew that adults could get quite heated about it. Many of them were well aware of adult sexual activities and felt adults were hypocritical in their outrage at the children when the children engaged in sexual activity. Though for the most part kissing and cuddling was all they did, some fellows claimed to have had a number of 'naughties'. The former they were sure was not 'wrong', though they knew that adults tended to assume it was. The latter they were not quite sure about, and kept the details carefully to themselves.

There was some kudos to be gained from being able to say that you had a boyfriend or girlfriend (though at the risk of some teasing). Most of the children on one occasion or another claimed that they had such an alliance, either with someone at school, someone at another school or someone they had met on holiday. Some few children resisted the idea totally, saying they had no interest in members of the other sex. Some found themselves caught up in romantic relationships even though they considered it all a bit foolish. Yet others threw themselves wholeheartedly into exploring the world of sexual activity.

As with friendships, romances did not necessarily blossom through love of the chosen. There were some children, usually in the high status groups, who were considered attractive by everyone and therefore well worth attempting to ensnare as a romantic partner. Suzie and Mandy for instance were both interested in Warwick and each on different occasions claimed him as their boyfriend. More usually the particular boy or girlfriend of the moment seemed to be based on happenchance: who the others had lined you up with for a party, who happened to sit near you in class, or who didn't currently have an alliance with somebody else. Generally romantic alliances lasted only a short time, and then ceased altogether. When an event like the local annual show (fair) was on, there was a rush of romantic partnering up so that couples could meet at the showground and go on the rides or into the sideshows together. Soon afterwards, for most of them it would be as if nothing had happened. They were, in a sense, relationships of convenience that ended when the need for them ceased. And there was in fact little *need* for them beyond exploration and kudos. They did not serve the powerful functions as same sex friendships and so could be taken up and let lapse with little emotional investment.

The reverse is more typically true amongst adults. It is within marriage, or marriage-type relationships, that reality is negotiated, and isolation and vulnerability kept at bay. Breakdown of marriages, and fights within marriages, have the same emotionally stressful effect as the fights amongst same sex children. It is perhaps partly in anticipation of the reversal that the children begin to explore heterosexual relationships.

The ambivalence towards romantic relationships is illustrated in the following transcript. Those who feel they are not ready for romance are good bait for teasing if they do get caught up in an apparently romantic relationship. Suzie has been friendly with Terry for the last few days. This conversation about their relationship develops from a conversation about name-calling, which Terry and Suzie have engaged in towards each other.

Transcript 4.18: Pat and Suzie

1	*Pat:*	Terry O'Dell calls her 'undies'!
2	*Suzie:*	Who?
3	*Pat:*	Terry O'Dell.
4	*Suzie:*	Oh yeah. He won't leave me alone. We call him Smelly sometimes.
5	*B.D.:*	What do you think of

1-4 It has long been noted that little boys show their interest in little girls by antagonising them.

4 Both nicknames are of simple rhyming origin (cf. Morgan, O'Neill and Harré, 1979).

5-7 My question stems from my

Terry? (*Pat giggles loudly*)

6   *Suzie:*   Aw, everybody is asking me this.

7   *B.D.:*   No, I mean the two of you, not you in particular, what do you think of him as a person?

8   *Pat:*   I hate him. (*whispered*)

9   *B.D.:*   You hate him, Pat, why? (*Suzie giggles*)

10   *Pat:*   I hope that didn't come out.

11   *B.D.:*   Mm?

12   *Pat:*   I hope that didn't come out. (*giggles*)

13   *B.D.:*   Well it doesn't matter 'cos he won't hear it.

14   *Pat:*   Oh, 'cos he's a boy.

15   *B.D.:*   (*laughs*) That's not a very good reason! Do you hate all boys?

16   *Pat:*   Yes.

17   *B.D.:*   And Terry more than others, or the same as others?

18   *Pat:*   The same as others.

19   *B.D.:*   What about you Suzie, do you/

20   *Suzie:*   Well, I don't hate anyone really, I don't hate, I don't hate Betty but I just don't like her that's all.

21   *B.D.:*   Well let's talk about Terry. (*Pat giggles knowingly*) Does everybody ask you because they think that you and he get on very well?

22   *Suzie:*   Oh, sort of, in a way anyway. I get teased because everybody thinks he's my *boy*friend!

interest in Terry rather than in the budding relationship.

8-18   Hate is one way of resisting the immanent and apparently inevitable heterosexuality.

14   In answer to my question (9).

20   Suzie has some strong moral imperatives which influence the way she interprets her feelings.

21   Pat's giggles are a form of teasing.

22   *Getting on very well* and *being a boyfriend* are only 'sort of' similar. Because it is generally the more attractive children who first engage in romantic alliances it is interpreted as a pose and therefore worthy of teasing. Further it is to break well

23 *B.D.:* Would it matter about having boyfriends? Are you kids still worried about that?

established patterns of distance between individual boys and girls and is therefore resisted through teasing.

23 Smaller children often make much ado about the horrors of contact with the other sex.

24 *Suzie:* I'm not worried, but it's silly the thought of it.

24-28 Suzie feels that romance is as yet inappropriate amongst them.

25 *B.D.:* Why?

26 *Suzie:* I dunno, little people about 10 or somethin' havin' a boyfriend! It's stupid.

27 *B.D.:* What age is the proper age to start having a boyfriend?

28 *Suzie:* About 15 or somethin'.

29 *B.D.:* So at this age, you are just all friends whether you are boys or girls.

30 *Suzie:* Yeah, I don't care if I have a friend as a boy or anything like that, they are still human beings like yourself.

30 She prefers to think of Terry as a friend rather than a boyfriend but will probably not gain any social recognition for her wish.

31 *B.D.:* And how is Terry different from other boys?

32 *Suzie:* He is not really, he's the same. I just like all the boys.

Suzie presents herself as a moral, concerned little girl, as someone who likes others regardless of sex and who enjoys being with others. She is both vivacious and pretty. That, and her enjoyment in being with the boys and playing sport with them led one of the male teachers to comment that she was a bit fast and bound to run into trouble. This stereotypical perception of Suzie would, I think, have shocked her and certainly it did not do her justice.

In fairly stark contrast to Suzie's attitude to romance, is the boys' attitude as illustrated in the following conversation. Their attitude towards romance comes over as a rather crude chauvinism where the girl is a possession to be fought over and boasted of, and who is hopefully instrumental in their sexual explorations. Their chauvinism is on occasion tempered by some ambivalence and embarrassment. The

conversation starts when I am talking to Vanessa about the girls who
are perceived as a group when it comes to talk of boys: Mandy, Suzie,
Betty, Adrienne and Anne.

Transcript 4.19: Vanessa, Ian, Roddie and Patrick

1   *B.D.:*   Would you like to be
like the girls that are in that
group?

2   *Vanessa:*   Oh yeah, I suppose
so, I dunno, but I wouldn't
like to have as many fights
as they do.

3   *B.D.:*   What do they fight
about?

4   *Vanessa:*   Oh, other girls/

5   *Ian:*   Who's prettiest!
(*giggles*)

    5   Ian jokingly projects the
kinds of discussion the boys
have onto the girls.

6   *Vanessa:*   They fight about
all the girls and that, and boys
and that, being bossy and
things.

7   *Roddie:*   Oh yes, us boys.

    7   Roddie enjoys the thought
that the girls are interested
enough to fight over the
boys.

8   *B.D.:*   The boys are popular
with that group of girls are
they?

9   *Ian:*   )
)
   Patrick:)
) Yeah!
   Roddie:)
)
   Vanessa:)

10   *Roddie:*   Very popular.

11   *Ian:*   I don't/

    11   Ian tries to declare non-
involvement.

12   *Roddie:*)
) Oh I-a-an!
   Vanessa:)

    12   Roddie and Vanessa tease
him as a result.

13   *B.D.:*   Do you see that group

of girls as being the most
attractive group in the class?

14 *Patrick:* No I don't.

15 *Vanessa:* No.

16 *Patrick:* One girl, Roddie
was fightin' over her, Kirsty?
No um/

16-20 Last year, an attractive girl
had been sought after by the
boys but rejected their atten-
tions. The assumption
among the boys seems to
have been that the strongest
boy wins the most attractive
girl. An archetypal image.

17 *Roddie:* Suzie?

18 *Patrick:* No! She's left, um,
Sandra.

19 *Roddie:* Sandra, yeah. None
of us got her.

20 *Patrick:* (*laughs*) She left.
She wouldn't take none of
them. They all kept fightin'
over her.

21 *B.D.:* I didn't know you
were old enough to have girlfriends. (*they all laugh*)

22 *Patrick:* What about my
brother, he's only 13 this year.

22 The idea that they are not old
enough is belied by the fact
that children just a little
older have clear romantic
associations.

23 *Roddie:* I had a girlfriend.
(*unclear*)

24 *Patrick:* He lost Kirsty.

25 *Roddie:* I've been all round
the school to tell you the
truth.

25-28 Roddie loves to boast
of his prowess.

26 *Patrick:* Yeah.

27 *B.D.:* Dear! you're a bit of a
playboy aren't you?

28 *Roddie:* Yeah. (*everyone
laughs*)

29 *Patrick:* He had, ah, first he
had what was her name?

29-35 Patrick plays up to
Roddie's pride in his activities
by providing details of past
relationships.

30 *Roddie:* Denise.

31 *Patrick:* Nah!

32 *Roddie:* Lynette.

33 *Patrick:* Lynette, when I
first came here, and then he
had Kirsty.

34 *Roddie:* Yeah! Yeah!

35 *Patrick:* And this is only

when *I* was here (*Roddie laughs*) I was only here about a year ago,

36   *Roddie:*   I got in front eh!

37   *Patrick:*   And now he's got two, he's got Anne, and he's goin' to get another one! (*giggles*)

38   *Roddie:*   How do you know Patrick?

39   *Patrick:*   Oh I know!

40   *B.D.:*   What does having a girlfriend mean at this age?

40-41   Roddie gives an air of mystery, excitement and knowingness to the having of girlfriends.

41   *Roddie:*   Ah, a lot of things!

42   *Patrick:*   He's got a girlfriend, Kirsty, she's twice as tall as him! (*Patrick laughs, they all laugh*)

42   Patrick can't resist a tease. Roddie, is after all, posing. But Roddie is in fact very small and Patrick is moving too close to a sensitive truth.

43   *Roddie:*   She's not.

44   *Patrick:*   She's a bit taller than you.

45   *Roddie:*   She's not.

43-45   Roddie's denial causes Patrick to back down. He doesn't want the challenge to be taken seriously and lead to fighting.

46   *B.D.:*   Listen, so what do you do, do you just talk to her, or do you go out together?

46-47   Talking is certainly not the picture Roddie wishes to create at this point. He later admits to talk as part of the relationship (71-2).

47   *Roddie:*   Nah, don't talk to her. Nah.

48   *Patrick:*   Kiss 'er (*giggles*) Cuddlin' up.

48   Patrick is more direct but in a teasing voice.

49   *Roddie:*   What about you and Mandy, Patrick?

49   Roddie counteracts Patrick's over-directness by turning the attention to Patrick's romances.

50   *Ian:*   Yes Patrick?

51   *Patrick:*   I hate her.

51   Just as Pat (Transcript 4.18, 8-16) hates all boys, Patrick now automatically hates the girl to whom he had once been attached.

52   *Roddie:*   Oh, don't gimme that, Patrick!

53 *Ian:* Oh yeah!
54 *Roddie:* We don't want him upset.
55 *B.D.:* So you just decide that they are your girlfriends, but you don't do anything about it?
56 *Roddie:* Nuh, unless you get into trouble with the teachers.

57 *B.D.:* What do you mean?
58 *Patrick:* Go tell his girlfriend his problem!
59 *Roddie:* I been in trouble a few times over Kirsty.
60 *Vanessa:* He quitted cricket just for her.
61 *Patrick:* Just for 'er!
62 *B.D.:* He what?
63 *Vanessa:* He quitted cricket just for 'er.
64 *B.D.:* Why would he do that?
65 *Vanessa:* He wanted to stay with her, so he quitted cricket.
66 *Patrick:* Yeah! (*laughs suggestively*)
67 *Ian:* He's pretty mad, eh?
68 *Vanessa:* He just quitted for his girlfriend.
69 *B.D.:* What, she didn't want you to play?
70 *Vanessa:* No, he just didn't want to go.
71 *B.D.:* You wanted to talk with her, to stay with her?
72 *Roddie:* Yeah.
73 *B.D.:* Do you see her at weekends or out of school?
74 *Patrick:* No.
75 *B.D.:* How come when you were listing your friends you didn't mention her? (*giggles*

54 Roddie suggests they should not push Patrick too far.
55 I am puzzled. Their romances seem to be a bit of a non-event.

56 You don't have sex because the teachers will get upset, and (by implication) there isn't anything else to be done about a romantic relationship.

58-72 Patrick suggests in fact that Roddie does talk to his girlfriend and this too is worthy of a tease. Roddie suggests (59) that he and Kirsty do not *just* talk. Whatever they do, male pursuits have been set aside in favour of her company. This is seen as a bit mad by the others.

75-76 None of the children mentioned other sex children as friends. In so far as the

from Patrick)

76 *Vanessa:*   You don't like her no more.

romances are so brief, they do not really qualify as friends. Also to list them would be to risk teasing from the others.

77 *Patrick:*   He don't like her no more. How about Anne? She's a little thing about this high! (*giggles*)

78 *Roddie:*   A bit small.

78 Bravado. Anne is the only girl in the class as short as, or shorter than, Roddie.

79 *B.D.:*   What's Anne like?
80 *Roddie:*   Good, to me! (*Patrick giggles*)
81 *Vanessa:*   Big jumper, you go like that and she jumps!
82 *B.D.:*   Is Anne part of that group of girls?
83 *Ian:*   Yeah.
84 *Vanessa:*   No.
85 *Patrick:*   Oh, yeah, sometimes she isn't, when she gets mad with 'em.

85 The boundaries of the larger girls' groups were fluid, in contrast to the dyadic friendships which were more stable.

86 *B.D.:*   What about you Ian, do you have a girl?
87 *Roddie:*   Yep.
88 *Ian:*   Yeah!
89 *B.D.:*   Who's your girl?
90 *Ian:*   She don't go to this school anyway.

90 Schegloff (1972) analyses this phenomenon where information which would have no meaning for the listeners is omitted from the conversation, i.e., we don't need to know the name because it wouldn't mean anything to us.

91 *Patrick:*   Oh god.
92 *B.D.:*   Does she live near you at your home?
93 *Ian:*   No, she lives up West Hill.
94 *B.D.:*   How did you get to

know her?

95 *Ian:*   Aw, Dad worked with her father. (*High-pitched giggle from Patrick, and Roddie bursts into fits of laughter*)

95 Patrick and Roddie find this amusing. The joke is beyond me.

96 *Patrick:*   Ian!

97 *B.D.:*   What about you, Patrick?

98 *Patrick:*   No, I haven't got one.

99 *Roddie and Ian:*   Aw Patrick!

100 *Patrick:*   No I haven't. (*laughing*)

101 *B.D.:*   Who did you used to have?

101 Interpreting the innuendo in Roddie's and Ian's voices (99).

102 *Patrick:*   I didn't used to have no one.

103 *Ian:*   Aw, don't gimme that, Patrick, 'cos you used to like Mandy. (*Patrick laughs*) No you did, Patrick, don't give me that.

103 Patrick's denials (reservation, caution?) are not allowed by the others, now that they have confessed as much as they have.

104 *Patrick:*   She's got freckles all over.

105 *Ian:*   Oh, you used to like her.

106 *Patrick:*   No, I didn't.

107 *Ian:*   You used to like Vanessa.

108 *Patrick:*   Erh!

108 Insult intended only as defence is often, as in this case, quite cruel.

109 *Vanessa:*   Aw shut up!

110 *Ian:*   He used to like Vanessa and he loves Lynette.

111 *Patrick:*   So does Ray, and um/

112 *Vanessa:*   Oh, who told you that?

113 *Patrick:*   He said, 'If you don't go with me, I'm tellin' on you!' and she didn't know

113-124 Patrick takes the heat off himself by telling this story about a boy in another class

what for!

114 *Ian:*   Yeah 'e says something to 'em that they never done.

115 *Patrick:*   He *makes* 'em. That's what he said to another girl.

116 *B.D.:*   Who is this strange person?

117 *All:*   Ray Elliott.

118 *Patrick:*   Strange all right.

119 *B.D.:*   So he makes the girls go with him?

120 *Patrick:*   Yeah, he forces them. He's a dirty worker.

121 *Ian:*   Yeah. (*all laugh*)

122 *Patrick:*   He says, 'I'm tellin' on you,' and they say, 'what for?' 'Aw I won't tell on you as long as you go with me,' that's what he does. If they say 'what for' and keep on saying 'what for' he just walks off and says, 'I'm telling on you' and the girl runs up and says, 'I'm going with you, don't worry.' Mad!

123 *B.D.:*   Goodness me! How peculiar!

124 *Patrick:*   Yes, he is.

who manipulated girls into being his girlfriend out of fear of what he might do to them. Machismo is alive and well, though regarded as 'mad' and 'dirty' by the others.

Much of this talk of boys and girls is accompanied by giggles. This is partly because of the awkwardness of the situation (one does not normally confess these things to adults and it is difficult to know how much to tell), and partly too because the relationships they describe are in large part not to be taken too seriously. Further, the anticipation of serious relationships between boys and girls in the near future makes them both nervous and excited because massive changes in their taken-for-granted patterns of interaction will sooner or later have to take place.

Race Relations

Amongst the particular group of children studied there were two Aboriginal girls, Sally and Teresa, and three Aboriginal boys, Henry,

Warwick and Roy. Adrienne and Simon were fair-skinned and did not identify as Aboriginal though their grandmother was Aboriginal. They were not antagonistic to Aboriginality however. Simon counted Warwick, Henry and Roy as his closest friends and Adrienne claimed that she often played sport and other games with Sally and Teresa and the Aboriginal girls in other classes.

The Aboriginal children did not like to be thought of as different from the other children. They would not consider aspects of their behaviour which did in fact set them apart as indicating difference. They accepted at one and the same time an incorrigible proposition that 'we' are the same as 'them' and yet quite often referred to themselves as a separate group. They perceived their own separateness but did not want others to perceive it or take it into account.* This wish was generally respected by the others. As Roddie said, 'There isn't (any difference) actually except their skin. And that don't make no difference.'

Henry and Warwick were highly respected and liked for their prowess in fighting and Roy was appreciated for his sense of humour. The girls fancied Warwick for his good looks and his quiet and generous manner and regarded him as the highest status catch. This was despite certain knowledge, in some cases, that parents would heavily censure playing with Aboriginal children even of the same sex:

Transcript 4.20: Patrick

Patrick: Yeah, my Nan, my first day at school, she asked me who I was playing with and that, and she told us not to play with Aboriginals, and I say, 'Henry and Roy and them', and she said, 'Don't play with them.'
B.D.: Did she give you a reason?
Patrick: No.
B.D.: Did it make any difference?
Patrick: I've been Henry's friend a long time. I was Henry's friend when we were up at D School.

Sally and Teresa were not considered high status and did not often play with the other girls but were not automatically excluded as possible friends by all of the girls.

Racial tension was not high amongst this group of children. That is, I think, in contrast to other schools and other groups of children. The

---

* I have observed the same apparent illogic in some 'women's libbers', which is, I think, related to the concept of *passing* (which includes passing to oneself). See Goffman (1968b) pp. 92-113.

Aboriginal children's capacity to fight and protect themselves from white prejudice was respected.

Transcript 4.21: Vanessa, Roddie and Patrick

1   *B.D.:*   How do you think that they feel when they come into this school, and they're one and you're a group and they are on the outside?

2   *Vanessa:*   They feel like us.

2   Vanessa reminds me that each person, regardless of race, can feel loneliness.

3   *Roddie:*   They don't worry. 'cos, you know, they can fight. See, if anyone picks on them, all they've got to do is tell them to leave them alone or they'll get into them and if they don't see, they can start it.

3   Though they may be picked on, they are safe because of their known fighting skills and can therefore establish that they are not to be messed with.

4   *Patrick:*   Yeah, they fight.

They fight to protect themselves, and generally they don't fight these boys (unless, of course, 'it's called for'.) As Ian says, 'Look. You know Henry and Roy. We're Henry and Roy's friends and they don't bash us up at all.' Further, they are reliable as contingency friends. Patrick says, 'One thing about Aboriginals, they, well, if you haven't got a friend or anybody you can always turn to an Aboriginal person.'

In general, the children claimed that race was not sufficient reason to assume that someone was different. They were aware of a different-ness about Aboriginal adults and were aware of racial tension and prejudice between Aboriginal and white adults but they did not feel that this signified anything for their relationships with each other.

Conclusion

The children indicate through their accounts that they recognise a wide range of appropriate and inappropriate behaviours for different situations. They are less concerned with consistency of action from individuals than they are with consistency within given situations. They are not bothered, for instance, if a friend's home behaviour is different from his school behaviour, or if friends display non-friendly behaviour when the situation requires it. (If the situation does not require such inconsistency in a person's behaviour then inconsistency is unthinkable.) In this sense they are like the Japanese mentioned by Harré and Secord (1972, p.93) who see behaviour as *role-* rather than *person*-dependent. Detailed rules relate to situations and people may be seen as not following the rules appropriate to one situation although they may behave entirely satisfactorily in another situation. Censure does not fall on them as a person, but it is recognised that they have not followed the rules of a particular situation and reciprocal action is usually called for. The variables which seem to be important in the definition of any given situation are status (who can call the tune), place (school, home, playground, classroom), who is friends with whom and whether anyone is trying to pose as better than he is. This detailed awareness of the definition of the situation and its power to dictate appropriate behaviour may well be associated with the fact that school children experience frequent and regular changes of situation over which they have little control. They must pay close attention to the requirements of any one situation such that within its own terms it becomes predictable. Once a situation is predictable, then competent, appropriate behaviour is possible. Censure must fall on those who threaten the reading of each situation. Friends behave in predictable ways towards each other, thereby providing a secure arena for competent behaviour. The children have developed a complex culture centred around these friendships, a culture they recognise as having little to do with the adult world, but which they recognise as having much to do with being a child.

Postscript to Chapter 4. When Paul was helping to correct the page proofs he pointed out to me that the saying 'sucked in' originates from a longer saying, 'sucked in, chewed up, spat out and trodden on'.

5
Pupils' Attitudes to Teacher Organisation and Discipline

boys peering at spunky teacher

children laughing at teachers uglyness

Adult-Child Interaction

Children, when they enter school, are asked to take part in a world where they are relatively powerless strangers (Schutz, 1971), where the new rules are strange, where there are often no previously established relationships, and where 'success' is based on a capacity to cue into what the teachers want of them. Yet it would seem that this strangeness need not really bother the children, since the world of play, and of other children, can function anywhere, and does so in the nursery school classroom as soon as the children make social contacts (either with each other, or with the toys). This play forms the basis of children's culture. The teachers can, and do, share in this world of children's play, but their specific task is to introduce children to the adult world through adult structures. The introduction of adult structures need not be at the expense of children's culture, however. Mehan (1979a, 1979b) and Griffin and Mehan (forthcoming) have observed (in infants' classrooms) children's culture existing in parallel with, and even complementing, adult culture. They observe children successfully attending to both the 'pupils' agenda' and the 'teacher's agenda', at many points during the day, each agenda designed to fulfil the purposes of the cultural group in question. Cusick (1973) has observed the same parallel management of agendas amongst adolescents in high school.

From the pupils' point of view, there are two cultures with their related agendas, each running parallel with the other, sometimes each of mutual benefit to the other, occasionally each conflicting with the other. One potential source of conflict between these two cultures may come from the teachers' attitudes to pupil culture, which they may construe as an illegitimate 'underlife' in the classroom and which may, if they are not careful, take over the classroom. In other words, that which is not part of the official world of school is a potential threat, and should not be allowed.

The official line on schooling is that teachers are responsible for the *socialisation* of their pupils; socialisation, that is, into the adult world. Socialisation has been distinguished from *education*, however, as less liberating for the individual though more useful for the society. Mehan cites Parsons, for instance, as having claimed that we cannot really afford to 'educate', since education is subversive to the *status quo*. Each community, he says really wants its youth socialised.

Mehan (1979b) introduces a different perspective on socialisation. Through detailed analysis of classroom interaction he shows that children need to be 'socialised' into the rules of classroom behaviour in order to participate in the 'educational' aspect of schooling (cf. also Sharp and Green, 1975; Edwards and Furlong, 1978). He indicates that socialisation is a necessary rather than an anti-educational process, and that socialisation and education, rather than being alternatives, are part of the same process. Children and teachers collaboratively assemble the interactional form appropriate to their classroom through selecting appropriate behaviours from the children's repertoire of behaviours already learned through their various interactions with adults. Through learning the appropriate form, the children can participate in the educational enterprise. The children of my study actively sought to discover the interactional rules relevant to each of their teachers. They recognised that the successful carrying out of the *teacher's agenda*, whether that be to 'socialise' or to 'educate' them (or both), involved following the teacher's rules. *Alongside* the teacher's agenda, they quite busily pursued their own agendas which related to matters specific to the culture of childhood (cf. Mehan, 1979b; Cusick, 1973), and which involved the conceptual framework and related interactional rules outlined in the previous chapter. Mucking around, and having fun and interacting with each other were as much, if not more, part of the school day as learning lessons. The pupil agenda need not disrupt the teacher's agenda, however. Mehan (1979b) shows how teacher and pupil agendas can run parallel and even complement each other during the school day. For the children, freedom to pursue their own agendas was essential for the continued maintenance and construction of their shared world. As well, they recognised the importance of learning about the adult world. Their involvement with adults in adult-oriented activity gives them partial membership of the adult world. Neither adults nor children expect this to be full membership (cf. Aries, 1962). Both, however, assume that the adult world with its peculiar order be attended to with some seriousness. As far as the children were concerned they wanted teachers to allow them sufficient freedom in the classroom to pursue their own agendas – that is, to have fun and to muck around and, as well, they wished to get on with the business of learning, recognising that to do this they needed to learn the rules appropriate to each teacher. This recognition was not simple and straightforward however. The children built up background expectancies for teacher behaviour which they used in their interactions with teachers. When their interactions failed they became annoyed with the particular teacher. Much of their talk involves discussion of such instances. Through these (and presumably other) conversations they came to recognise and accept the *particular* characteristics of the teacher, thereby rendering that teacher unproblematic, and thereby, also, creating a modified set of background expectancies.

The children recognised that even the most open of teachers had rules, limits and expectations however complex and however difficult these might be to discover (cf. Sharp and Green, 1975). Ideally, from the children's point of view, each teacher's rules should be presented straightforwardly and made sufficiently clear that they can be learned quickly and effectively such that teacher and pupil agendas can proceed smoothly and harmoniously.

Some teachers make this process problematic by handing over to the children partial responsibility for the teacher's agenda. Those aspects handed over may be curriculum planning, or they may be formulation and control of interaction patterns in the classroom. Yet in handing either or both of these over to the children, it is still in an important sense part of the teacher's agenda since it is still the teacher's responsibility. Schools are, after all, adult institutions. Adults choose to have children attend school, adults choose to make this compulsory and adults dream up the various educational philosophies which affect how they choose to teach. It is not surprising, then, that despite liberal reforms in education towards pupil initiatives and independence, the children believe that their learning is the teacher's responsibility, especially when, as Gracey (1975) notes, the teachers teach children very early in their schooling to take it on *trust* that the teachers know what they are doing. Where teachers appear not to know what they are doing, children feel a certain indignation and betrayal of trust combined with an anxiety for their future in an uncertain world of work.

Further, inviting children to participate with adults as equals gives rise to complex interactional problems. In traditional classrooms the primary initiative for action and interaction comes from the teacher. Children are generally powerless to initiate action; their choices are more in terms of how to react to the teacher's initiatives (see, for example, Malcolm, 1978; Mehan, 1979a). An open teacher may introduce a different perspective to the classroom on the origin of initiatives and on the value of the children's own thoughts. Where the open model is a novelty for the children, they may have to discover, through trial and error, how such initiatives can and should be used. The majority of open teachers will opt for initiatives from children that relate to interest or project-centred learning. They will not necessarily extend these pupil initiatives into the personal sphere of teacher-pupil relationships. Where these initiatives are extended into the social interaction sphere, however, a fairly radical departure from traditional teacher-pupil or adult-child interactions may be called for.

Researchers such as Leiter (1976), Speier (1976) and Mackay (1974) have illustrated that adult-child interactions are usually asymmetrically contingent, i.e., 'the behaviour of one participant is highly contingent on the other, but the behaviour of the second participant is only partially contingent on the other', whilst reciprocal contingency, more usual in adult-adult or child-child communication, involves 'reciprocal influence and mutual dependence' between the participants (Hargreaves, 1975, p.70).* Despite this traditional asymmetry between adults and children, the rule of reciprocity is none the less frequently brought to bear by children and by adults on their dealings with each other (see for example Werthman, 1971, and Rosser and Harré, 1976). Moreover, it can be seen by children as basic to their interactions with adults. For example, in a recent discussion conducted by a colleague with my own children and one of their friends, the children proffered the following advice to prac. teachers:

G. M: What's the most important advice you'd give to a prac. teacher?

Paul: Don't treat kids badly, or else they'll treat you worse than you treat them. If you treat them badly on the first day, they'll absolutely murder you. (unequal, negative reciprocity)†

Friend: Oh well, if they be nice to us, we'll probably be nice to them, you know, we wouldn't be naughty or anything. Any teachers that can take a joke we really like and we treat them really well. (equal, positive reciprocity)

Also, respect, usually anticipated from children to adults, was seen as an important element of a 'good' teacher's treatment of children:

Jacob: I reckon ones that, you know, treat you with a bit of respect. Like, you know, they just don't tell you to get over there, they tell

---

* Gouldner (1960) distinguishes between reciprocity and complementarity. Complementarity exists in asymmetrical relationships where the rule is 'what is your right is my duty' or *vice versa*. Reciprocity exists, he says, where there is equality of obligation, and each party has rights and duties. Complementarity is therefore appropriate in traditional adult-child relationships and reciprocity in relationships where there is assumed equality.

† Gouldner (1960) and Homans (1951) state that acts of reciprocity are usually roughly equal. Unequal reciprocity can tentatively be explained in this case by the unevenness in power between children and adults. To regain a sense of equality or equilibrium, children may have to return more than they get.

you why, and they don't order you, they just ask you to. And if you tell them to go away, or something like that, they can take it as a bit of a joke.

When an open teacher endeavours to move from the traditional asymmetrical contingency existing between adults and children to symmetrical contingency, very complex interactional problems can ensue. Given the greater power, accorded by the school to the teacher, and by the society to adults in general, the teacher can in *fact* only move to the outward form of adult-adult interactions with children, i.e., he may treat them with *respect*, but he cannot in the final event *be* equal with them. Adult-adult interactions are characterised by equality (symmetry) and by the rules of politeness which accord automatic respect to the other, at least ideally (the emphasis being on positive reciprocity). Child-child interactions are also characterised by equality, but reciprocity is *more* important than respect. Traditional adult-child interactions are asymmetrically contingent: there is no equality, and respect is expected from children to adults but not necessarily from adults to children. Further, adults assume the right to *control* what children do. If open teachers wish to introduce equality (symmetry) into their interactions with children via the rule of polite adult-adult interaction they may encounter some difficulties.

Children do not and cannot know all the subtleties and complexities of adult rules, nor can they always bring them into play. As Cook-Gumperz (1975) points out, there is a foreground and a background to social rules. The foreground rules are the explicit, stateable rules of social interaction (e.g., mutual respect). The background rules (the tacit knowledge) are difficult to state and are only learned through prolonged interaction within the culture. Children, as partial members of adult culture, have not had sufficient experience to be able to use them competently with any consistency. Their ability to engage in the adult-adult forms of interaction may well be limited to stateable rules. Further, children may be *allowed* symmetrical interactions but the asymmetrical contingency of traditional adult-child interactions will none the less remain latent and emerge whenever it suits the adults to call on their greater power in order to control children. This use of asymmetrical power where adult-adult forms of interaction are being used may not be obvious to the adults using it, i.e., it remains tacit. Berlak and Berlak (1975, p.6), for example, quote a teacher whose *expectations* are that children will do as she bids them, even though she *asks* them in such a way that an outsider might well assume that they had choice, i.e., the outward form is symmetrical, but it is tacitly recognised by children and teacher that the symmetry ends there. When adults engage in symmetrically contingent interactions with children, breakdown can occur if the child inadvertently breaks the background rules of adult-adult behaviour, e.g., by reverting to child-child behaviour. Or, alternatively, they may break down if the adult inadvertently reverts to the foreground or form of asymmetrically contingent interactions. Where this latter breakdown occurs, children can become quite indignant and revert to child-child interactions (where reciprocity for rule-breaking is foremost) in order to express their annoyance.

To illustrate this point, I will take an actual conversation used by Speier to illustrate traditional adult-child (asymmetrically contingent) interactions. I will then contrast these with hypothetical adult-child conversations where adult-adult rules are followed, and where these break down. In this conversation, the two children's (Cs) attempts to present their point of view are defined as 'back talk', and are terminated by the two adults (As):

C   Oh, oh. Here comes Dad.
C   Yeah. Mine always watches hockey and we never/
A   O.K., kids.
C   Yeah. See?
C   Aw, gee.
A   See what, T?
C   Aw, it's just like always, Mr B. Why can't/
A   Come on kids. 'It's hockey night in Canada.'
A   Heh, heh.
C   Aw, Dad. This *our* show!
A   R., why don't you go and see what mommy's doing?
A   Yeah, S. Go ask mother for some ginger ale. Would you like some pop, R?
A   Sure you would. Wouldn't you/ Tiger?
C   Gee, and we got here *first too*!
A   That's enough.
C   Aw, gee. (Speier, 1976, p.102)

If the interaction were influenced by a wish on the part of the adults to treat the children with respect and as equals the scenario could have been very different. Imagine, for example, the following:

C   Here comes Dad.
C   He may want to watch the hockey.
A   Hi, kids. What are you watching?
C   *In The Wild*. It's a really good show.
C   Do you want to watch the hockey?
A   Yes we do actually. How long before this show finishes?
C   About fifteen minutes.
A   O.K. fair enough, can you let us know when it's finished?
C   Sure.

If, however, the children had been led to expect equality and respect but the adult inadvertently slipped into a traditional mode the following scene might have developed.

C   Here comes Dad.
C   He may want to watch the hockey.
A   O.K. kids.
C   What do you want? (*with a tinge of hostility*)
A   Come on kids. 'It's hockey night in Canada.'
C   But we were watching a really good show! (*Angrily*)
A   Don't talk to me like that!
C   (*flounces out of room in a huff, leaving both adults feeling annoyed.*)

Here the adult begins with a traditional adult-child interaction. The children try to turn it into an adult-adult interaction but are slightly annoyed and so do not present themselves in an adult manner. The adult is confirmed in his adult-to-child mode. The child becomes outraged at the disrespect and moves into the reciprocal contingency of child-child interactions, handing out rudeness in return for perceived rudeness. In reverting to child-child behaviour, the child is responding to 'rudeness' from the adult with the only tools he has available (having been cast in the *child* role he cannot play *adult* and explain to the actual adult that he has behaved unacceptably, nor can he reverse roles and reprimand the adult as if the adult were a child). Huffy withdrawal at least lets the adult know that the interaction was unacceptable.

These imaginary scenes are based on experiences with my own children and breakdowns, such as those in the last imagined scene, have served to socialise me into a more careful awareness of the rules of interaction, such that I am now less likely to engage in unintended or inadvertent role switching in my interactions with children.

The children of my study find themselves involved in similar scenes with their teachers, where, for example, they assume equality only to find that the teacher is offended by their assumptions, interpreting their behaviour as inappropriate and rude. As Suzie says, 'The teachers reckon they're just *it* sometimes.' Pat told of a particular instance of different readings of the situation which occurred when a teacher took offence at a child initiating conversation with him in relation to words he had just spoken to another teacher. His reported response, 'You wait 'till you are addressed to before you speak to me and call me 'sir' thank you,' was told by Pat with both amusement and horror.

Interactions with each of the different teachers that the children of my study encountered followed different patterns based on differing understandings of the rules of adult-child interactions. This is not to suggest that the children were helpless victims of circumstance. They were in fact aware of complex sets of reasons for their failures to interact positively with any one teacher. They were aware of administrative/organisational problems as well as of personal interaction problems. Their task was to discover how to act as competent people when the basic ground rules for interaction shifted from teacher to teacher and on occasion from one day to another with the same teacher. In the discussion I had with them after the ground rule shift on Mr Bell's part (Transcript 3.1), the children talked at considerable length about what they considered the nature of proper teacher behaviour to be.

It was apparent from the children's perspective that knowledge of how to behave in a variety of situations is necessary for successful functioning in a world run by adults (see rule 3, p. 77). Where punishment follows rule-breaking, it is indeed critical for children to know precisely what each adult defines as right and wrong, and thus what they can expect will follow from 'wrong' behaviour. They felt angry if they made predictions concerning the normative pattern and these turned out to be wrong. If their predictions succeeded for some length of time and then failed, as in the incident under the blankets, they felt the adult had betrayed their trust and was unworthy as a teacher: a highly favoured teacher could temporarily become, in these circumstances, an object of derision. Their anger in this particular discussion related not to the fact that the teacher had punished them (they could handle that if they considered it was justified) but to the fact that he had become unpredictable, reducing the control they had over their lives.

In the following sections of this chapter, I will show that the children wish to be *socialised* into whichever mode of interaction is compatible with the teacher's agenda, whatever that agenda might be. This socialisation is a prerequisite for competent action within the social setting of each teacher's classroom, competent action, that is, in relation to the teacher's agenda. (Action in relation to the pupils' agenda will be occurring in parallel with the teacher's agenda.) Once the teacher has thus 'framed' (Goffman, 1975) his teaching he can be as *educational* as he likes and he can produce whatever liberating thoughts he likes. He can make the children more aware of their cultural heritage through time-honoured materials or he can introduce them to new perspectives and ideas linked to materials they themselves produce. As long as the frame is clear, education or socialisation, whichever the teacher prefers, can proceed.

The Teachers

The children had three different teachers during the year of the study.

Mr Bell, the headmaster, was their teacher intermittently and at the beginning. He regarded the class as his. When Mr Bell found he could not carry out all his duties satisfactorily, Mr Droop, a relief teacher, was brought in to teach the class and thus take some of the pressure off Mr Bell. The possibility also existed, as mentioned in the introduction, that the pupil numbers would reach the point where Mr Bell was no longer required to teach. But it was expected that the pressure would ease as the year progressed, and that Mr Bell would be able to return to full teaching duties. Mr Droop and Mr Bell were both committed to 'open-plan' teaching, but had serious clashes about how this should be carried out. Mr Bell believed that learning related to the curriculum was less important than learning related to the development of self and of social relationships. He felt that when the children had all learned to relate to each other, enthusiasm for work would come naturally. Mr Droop was appalled at the children's 'backwardness' and felt they needed some solid work to catch up on what they had clearly missed. The children's anger at the changes he brought was perceived by Mr Droop as the kind of disruptive behaviour one would expect from a classroom of 'disturbed' and 'backward' children who had been taught in the way Mr Bell was teaching them. He found the kinds of interactions Mr Bell had encouraged to be quite unacceptable. His previous class had been one in which there were many resources and the children had busily got on with learning through independent use of these resources. Mr Droop had simply been the resource advisor, waiting for the children to come to him whenever they needed help. Unfortunately, the New School had few resources, since their money had not 'come through' and so Mr Droop's model left the children quite often with nothing to do. Occasionally Mr Bell would come back into the class and make suggestions as to what they could do, or fill the blackboards with colourful, highly skilled drawings accompanied by suggested tasks for the children. Mr Droop, meanwhile, explained to me that even though the class was OP (open-plan) and not TD (teacher-directed) the teacher should adapt his teaching style according to the subject matter — sometimes he should do directed work with the whole group, sometimes open work with small groups and sometimes remedial work with individuals. With the continued presence of the charismatic Mr Bell and his wish that the class should run his way, Mr Droop's switches from one teaching style to another were perceived as irritating and confusing:

Transcript 5.1: Vanessa, Patrick, Roddie and Terry

1   *B.D.:*   Now let me/
2   *Vanessa:*   Get something

straight.

3 *B.D.:*   Yeah, get this straight. You don't like OP at the moment but reckon you will when Mr Bell gets back?

4 *All:*   Yeah. (*enthusiastic*)

4 'Yeah' has many meanings, all the way from very doubtful to total support. This yeah is telling me I've got the story exactly right.

5 *Vanessa:*   Yeah, well see Mr Bell, Mr Droop is giving us half OP and TD, and he reckons that it's just OP. Mr Bell's opinion of OP which I've told you is that you do whatever you like and tell the teacher, as long as it's good work; and that is Mr Bell's idea of OP.

5 Mr Bell has taught them, first, that in OP you plan your own work routine; second, that you get your work done; and third that, it should be good work (the meaning of 'good' being tacitly understood).

6 *Patrick:*   I done a story and he blows me up.

6 Indignant tone of voice.

7 *Terry:*   He blows *me* up.

7 Terry feels he is the one who gets all the trouble.

8 *Vanessa:*   He blows you up for nothing!

8 Moreover, Vanessa explains, there is neither rhyme nor reason for his anger.

9 *Patrick:*   You do a page and he blows you up and says 'go and do another half page' and you might be lucky.

9 i.e., it might be what he wants and it might not. It is pure luck if it is what he wants. Their previous knowledge of what constituted 'good work' for Mr Bell no longer holds with Mr Droop.

10 *B.D.:*   But now you reckon you prefer TD so why don't you like it when Mr Droop does TD?

10 I understand their complaint to refer to the change in rules from OP to half TD, rather than the introduction of unpredictability into the situation.

11 *Vanessa:*   Aw, I dunno, he's just a bit too fussy.

11 Maybe it is Droop himself who is the problem, since he fusses over unexpected

12 *Roddie:*   Mr Bell is a better man.

12 Roddie concurs with this judgment.

13 *Vanessa:*   He gives you more chances.

14 *Patrick:*   Yeah, Mr Droop he/

15 *Terry:*   Mr Bell he/

16 *B.D.:*   Hang on, don't all talk at once, I can't listen to everybody at once.

16 Adult right to insist on 'orderly' conversation.

17 *Patrick:*   He gave Garry the cane yesterday, caned 'im.

17 Patrick apparently decides that a specific example of his horribleness might help.

18 *B.D.:*   But Mr Bell gives people the cane and nobody minds?

18 The rational adult/researcher, always looking for the flaw in the story.

19 *All at once:*   He gives ya a chance. Yeah, but he gives us a chance first. Yeah but not/

19 Mr Bell's caning is different because he defines right and wrong before he gets out the cane.

20 *Patrick:*   Mr Droop says 'Right, git out there and stand in the corner,' and when it's home time all he does is wack! and Garry came out bawling 'is 'ead off.

20-22 This is an interesting type of conflict which occurs several times during my conversation with the children. They dramatise a story to make it more interesting and convincing, but whichever children are listening pick them up very quickly if they stray from the facts as they perceive them. Tiresome quarrels eventuate if each has a different version of the 'facts', since neither will give way. In this case, Patrick gives way immediately since he happens to agree with Roddie's version of the 'facts' (cf. p. 77, 'Events have a discoverable facticity').

21 *Roddie:*   Did not.

22 *Patrick:*   I know but 'e was nearly crying. He got the cane.

23 *Vanessa:*   You miss Mr Bell.

23 Vanessa becomes nostalgic for the good old days.

24 *B.D.:*   No hang on. Vanessa was explaining why Mr Bell was a good teacher, why you

24-26 Note the adults' right to declare what it is that children are saying.

would like to be with him
in OP.

25 *Vanessa:* Was I?

26 *B.D.:* Yes. ·

27 *Vanessa:* Well I dunno, he
just gives you more chances
and that, if you wanna say,
he might give you say one
little thing in OP to do and
say, 'I'll give you a little bit
of TD to do,' say, 'you have
to write something out of
this book,' well all right, if
you didn't want to do that
straight away you didn't
have to, you wanted to
finish your project or somethin' that was all right. If you
want a project on something
well you can have that project
to do. It's just that he's (*Mr
Droop*) I dunno, it's hard to
explain, he's a nice teacher
and that when he wants to be.

27 Vanessa goes along with my
version. She elaborates her
earlier statement (5) by
giving a more concrete example. Mr Bell might direct
them sometimes, but he
would say that that was what
he was doing and he would
not fuss about when things
were done, i.e., he leaves
some freedom to the children
to make decisions.

28 *B.D.:* But somehow he
hasn't managed to work out
how to get on with you kids?

28 An intuitive leap.

29 *All:* No, nah, nh, nh.

29 Very emphatic (in agreement).

30 *Vanessa:* Mr Droop, well we
were having this council
meetin' one day and he said
somethin' to Mandy and
Mandy told him what she
thought of him.

30 Mr Bell has encouraged the
children to have opinions of
their own. This has led them
to believe that it is acceptable
to state what they think of
their teacher if he is being
unacceptable (i.e., to adopt
child-child rather than
adult-adult reciprocity).

31 *Roddie:* Yeah, told 'im off.

32 *Vanessa:* He gets all wrinkled
up here, and goes real funny
when somebody says some-
thing to him like that. You
walk up to him and say something and he gets all these

32 Vanessa sounds worried and
puzzled by Mr Droop's
visible upset.

wrinkles up here and that.
He goes real queer! As if he's
startin' to bawl.

33 *B.D.:* He really *wants* to get
on with you but he doesn't
know how?

33 Again an intuitive leap,
influenced probably by the
end of 27, and by the concern in their voices.

34 *All:* Yeah.

34 Emphatic. They like this
version, perhaps because it
accounts for quite a lot of
what they have said, i.e.,
that he is a nice enough
person and yet they don't
know how to get on with
him.

35 *Roddie:* Aw, you know, in
a way I feel sorry for him.

35 This change in tune from
Roddie may well be partly
in response to my words
which render Mr Droop in a
more sympathetic light (28,
33).

36 *Vanessa:* Yes.
37 *Roddie:* 'Cos I suppose I
haven't been very nice to him,
you know.

37 Musing tone of voice.

38 *Vanessa:* Yeah.

38 Vanessa agrees. Roddie has
been mucking around a lot
in class.

39 *Roddie:* I've been, you
know/
40 *Vanessa:* A bit/
41 *Roddie:* I reckon 'e was in
the right to tell me about the
tape recorder, but see I didn't
know what tape recorder to
use. I don't reckon 'e's got
the right to blow me up about
that.

41 Roddie may feel sorry for
him but it's hard to get away
from the fact that Mr Droop
has acted in an unacceptable
fashion.

The conflict between Mr Droop and Mr Bell was not only stressful
for the children, but for both of the teachers as well. Mr Bell eventually
moved Mr Droop to another class when a relief teacher was needed
there, and attempted to take over the class on his own again. Again his
duties as headmaster intervened and this time he managed to acquire a

permanent teacher to take over the class and Mr Droop was moved to another school.

Miss Love was a down-to-earth, no-nonsense kind of person. Though Mr Bell was unhappy about her teaching style as well, he did not intervene to the extent he had with Mr Droop because the class now officially belonged to Miss Love. Miss Love had to work hard to gain the children's acceptance. As Mr Bell's class they had fought and won the battle to rid themselves of Mr Droop only to find another teacher coming to take over their class. Moreover, her ideas on how classrooms should be run were a far cry from Mr Bell's. She too found the focus on interpersonal relations, at the expense of getting on with lessons, quite unacceptable. She believed in very clear teacher framing of the teacher agenda, though she was sensitive to the children's construction of reality. After an initial battle, the children capitulated and accepted Miss Love as their teacher. Their talk about classroom changed from talk about interpersonal problems to enthusiastic discussions about the work they were doing.

These three teachers, each with their different expectations of the children, created problems for the children in terms of learning how to get on with them. Because Mr Bell had introduced ideals of equality to them, their negotiations with subsequent teachers were made quite difficult. At the beginning of each school year, children are generally aware that they will have a new teacher and therefore a new set of ground rules to learn. This they seem to accept willingly. Where the new teacher is temporary (such as practising teachers and relief teachers) the children may resist the new ground rules introduced by the teacher. Considerable research has indicated, however, that children are prepared to co-operate with teachers if they perceive it to be in their best interest to do so. Where they feel the teacher is going to teach them something, they co-operate (Werthman, 1971; Furlong, 1976), or where they avoid fear and humiliation and gain teacher approval they go along with the teacher (Holt, 1969), or where they feel the teacher is prepared to move some way to meet them (in cases where the pupils' and teacher's cultural background are radically different), they are prepared to co-operate (Dumont and Wax, 1971). Where they feel that the teacher is not teaching them or that they have nothing to gain from co-operating with the teacher, or that the teacher is, in some important sense, oblivious to their perspective they will defend the ground rules that they already understand. Mr Droop was unable to accept the children's attempts at the reciprocally contingent interactions encouraged by Mr Bell. He was not interested in their attempts to explain their perspective, and he was temporary anyway. There was, apparently, little to be gained, as far as some of the pupils were concerned, in accepting the ground rule shift required to interact with this teacher. These pupils exerted group pressure on wavering and pro-teacher peers to go along with their opposition. They reiterated the ground rules as established by Mr Bell, and became heated and angry about their uncertainty in the face of new rules which to them did not seem workable. Once they had decided Mr Droop was bad they looked for and played on any evidence that this was so. This process seemed to be an attempt to make their opposition seem more rational, i.e., if you can find specific examples of unfair behaviour on the part of the teacher your general antagonism is justified. Another slightly different way to put this point is that they 'knew' they did not get on with the teacher. They did not, on occasion, know why. Instances of classroom friction, or descriptive examples of failed interactions may not explain but rather help to illustrate failure: over-dramatisation and a degree of misrepresentation of these instances may better serve this illustrative purpose; sense-making will go on, even in the face of the apparently senseless; explanations which are not entirely satisfactory will do in the absence of better explanations, and perhaps the most straight-forward sense to be made of failed interactions is that the teacher is a bad one. Confirmation of this will therefore be actively sought in the interpretations brought to bear on the teacher's actions (cf. McHugh, 1968).

During periods of opposition to their teachers, the children appeared to be under considerable stress. They talked a lot about their failure to learn anything, and about the fact that there was no room for fun in the classroom. Neither their agenda nor the teacher's was being carried out satisfactorily. They were especially concerned about the failure in the teacher's agenda.

Under pressure, ironically, they themselves readily reverted to the assumption mentioned earlier of a traditional model of teacher-pupil relationships, namely, that it is entirely the teacher's responsibility if no learning is taking place. This type of interaction was, after all, one in which they had had much practice throughout their schooling. The assumption made their anger and opposition to the teacher quite rational, since, if teaching and learning is the teacher's responsibility, then the teacher is at fault in so far as they are clearly not learning. They became justifiably angry that their teacher was not fulfilling his part of the teacher contract. They were not prepared to co-operate with teachers who could demonstrably not teach. As Adrienne commented, 'He wants to teach doesn't he? That's what he's trained for. If we don't learn he might stop and take a look at what he's doing.'

What the children were saying, in essence, could almost be cast as a Laingian-type knot:

You don't listen to us so we won't listen to you. We're not learning anything so you must be a bad teacher. We will not co-operate with

you because you are a bad teacher. Because we do not co-operate
you will not listen to us . . .

This 'knot' with Mr Droop was never in fact unravelled. Miss Love
grappled with the children's hostile attitude and did seem to untie the
'knot'. Not without initial pain, as the children had become disruptive
and militant with their previous teacher. She had some advantages. She
was not temporary, she took clear responsibility for framing and
carrying out the teacher's agenda, and while she was not prepared to
engage in reciprocally contingent interactions, she did seem to have an
intuitive grasp of and appreciation for their perspective and could thus
allow for the presence of the pupils' agenda in the classroom. After
violent antagonism, the children capitulated and accepted her as their
teacher and therefore as someone they would co-operate with. Once
having made such a capitulation they went out of their way to find
illustrative evidence of her goodness and to excuse aspects of her
behaviour that could previously have been construed negatively. They
seemed to forget their earlier commitment to the interaction patterns
established by Mr Bell, and buried themselves in the work they had
missed while the protests were on. The *adult* world did not make
sense – could not be made to make sense. In the end the children
simply went along with the system their current teacher favoured. They
may have thought nostalgically of past teachers, or they may, as some
children did, recall the *problems* involved in past models, thereby
rejecting them in favour of the present model. And the present model
is all important if one is bent on survival. It may not be entirely sensible
but if one understands it sufficiently to function within its terms, it
may well have to suffice.*

Discovering How to Get On in a New Classroom

The children of my study were in the OP classroom. Their parents had
chosen this rather than the TD classroom, even though there had been
a great deal of unrest amongst the parents in response to open-plan
education in the previous year. The reason for their choice did not lie
so much in a commitment to a set of educational beliefs and values but
simply on the pragmatic assumption that if the children were happy
they would be more likely to work.

---

* There is a parallel here with the attitudes of the patients described
in Kesey's *One Flew Over the Cuckoo's Nest*. Such parallels point to
the importance of the *situation* the children are in. Though substan-
tively childhood culture is clearly different from adult culture, there
may well be much to be learned from these children about strategies
adults develop in parallel situations.

Suzie and Linda, in the following conversation, explain how they came to be in the OP class and express some of the puzzlement they were experiencing in finding out how OP works. At the time of this conversation their new teacher, Mr Droop, had taken over the class from their original teacher Mr Bell:

Transcript 5.2: Linda and Suzie

1   *B.D.:*   Now let me just ask you some more questions.

2   *Suzie:*   Uh huh.

3   *B.D.:*   Well, so, in this class that you are in, ah, first of all Linda, did you choose that or did your parents?

4   *Linda:*   No, my mother brought me in and that.

5   *Suzie:*   Just like me.

6   *Linda:*   And um, Mr Bell said, 'Right now, Mrs C. would you like your child to go in open plan or TD, teacher directed?' and Mum said, 'Well she had a couple of weeks last year and she said she liked it and I can't really make up my mind if she goes into teacher directed or an open plan, and if she's not happy she probably won't work,' and that and I'll get lazy and that, 'cos I'll just do nothing and get into trouble all the time, and that. And Mum said, 'Well I'll leave it up to Linda to decide'.

7   *Suzie:*   Yeah.

8   *Linda:*   And I decided to go into open plan as a trial and Mr Bell said, 'If Linda,' he said this to Mum, 'if Linda complains about an open-plan class, I'll put her in the TD

8   Mr Bell's ideal was that each person should make their choice and go on having a choice if they found themselves unhappy in the choice they had made.

class if you want me to.'

9   *B.D.:*   Mmhm.

10   *Linda:*   TD is all right because, I mean, open plan is all right because I do work. I like working, we have ERA cards, books, and things like that, that sort of interests me, and we've got a maths book and I like maths and that, and yeah, I like open plan.

10   Linda states that open plan is satisfactory because she likes the resources they use. She has accepted Mr Droop's resource-based model. Her criterion of success is that she does work.

11   *Suzie:*   Yeah, but see, um, Linda and I aren't used to it, because we did teacher directed last year/

12   *Linda:*   All our lives/

13   *Suzie:*   and that, and we have both been in the same class anyway, I don't think I really know it yet. I know how to do it but see, the more I try to understand it, you know, kids take you off it and that.

11-13 But Suzie is not so sure. She explains that her knowledge of classrooms is based on teacher-directed classes. She knows how to use the resources, but there is a problem relating to the other children, or some element of the working of open plan which she has not managed to sort out.

14   *B.D.:*   Mmhm.

15   *Linda:*   Yeah, 'cos they say, like in the council meeting when you bring it up they say, 'Oh you should know,' and they go on to something else.

15 Council meetings were instituted by Mr Bell as the primary arena for the thrashing out of the values, principles, understandings and forms of interaction which he saw as constituting openness. However, discussions about open plan itself have not really got under way in council meetings. Apparently the other children do not see open plan itself as their problem, since they had experienced and liked open plan the previous year.

16   *Suzie:*   See, 'cos, at D school they got an open-plan class,

16-17 At her previous school Suzie had experienced an

Mr Fairway's, and I understand their class and that. See, Mr Fairway was our singing teacher last year, and I really got on well.

17 *Linda:*   We could go down to his class, and that, whenever we wanted to, sort of.

18 *Suzie:*   It was really nice, but here at the New school, now/

19 *Linda:*   It's sort of different.

20 *Suzie:*   Kids don't get on and that, I don't get it.

21 *B.D.:*   So you feel that, um/

22 *Linda:*   Oh, that's not really the same with me.

23 *B.D.:*   But we'll try just with Suzie now, you feel that you, ah, haven't quite worked out what you should be doing?

24 *Suzie:*   Yeah.

25 *B.D.:*   And when you do settle down the others tend to disturb you a bit?

26 *Suzie:*   Yeah, sorta, see 'cos I'm used to gettin' on to work, and not chattin' and all that with teacher directed.

27 *Linda:*   We had a good teacher last year, and she was strict, but not too

open-plan class which she could understand. This was the class run by Mr Fairway. Mr Fairway allowed the children from other classes to drop in on his class whenever they wished, even though, officially, he was only responsible for teaching them singing.

20   Suzie returns to the problem with other kids. Her model of open plan is akin to Mr Bell's in so far as problems are connected to interpersonal relations. Confusion in the functioning of the pupil agenda is related, in Suzie's view, to a confusion in the teacher's agenda.

22   Linda repeats that she does not have the same views as Suzie.

23-25 I asked whether the problem is simply one of children not letting her get on with her work.

26   Suzie agrees that there is a sense in which my formulation is accurate, but it would be more accurate to focus on the fact that she is used to another system.

27   Linda explains that a good teacher is one who acknowledges the pupil

strict, she was good. She had a few jokes and then, 'Right, shut up and get on with your work.'

28 *Suzie:* Yeah and anyway when I came here, Linda was here too.

29 *Linda:* We were at D School/

30 *Suzie:* 'Cos we were good friends and that, and anyway because Linda went into it, I thought if I went into any other class I wouldn't have any friends, so that's why I went into OP sort of.

31 *Linda:* Yeah, and anyway, I had friends here, but I thought, well, if they give up with me like that, well, I've still got Suzie.

32 *Suzie:* Yeah.

33 *Linda:* 'Cos that's sort of the same with me, I said to Mum, it just depends sort of what Suzie might be going in. If Suzie is going into open plan then I would like to go into open plan, if Suzie is going into TD I might go into TD with Suzie.

34 *Suzie:* Yeah, the class doesn't get what an open plan is, they think it is to muck around and that/

35 *Linda:* Yeah, and do nothin'.

agenda and even contributes to it with jokes, but sets a clear boundary for the commencement of the teacher's agenda.

28-33 Suzie and Linda acknowledge the importance of ready access to the pupil culture in the classroom. The continual modifier 'sort of' is probably due to the fact that Linda and Suzie are contingency rather than best friends. Linda points this out in 31.

34-5 The others think open plan means that the pupil agenda can dominate classroom activity. Total time spent on the pupil agenda is, in the classroom context, to do 'nothing'. As far as Linda and Suzie are concerned the major emphasis should be on the teacher's agenda, even though the choices to be in OP were made on the basis of friends, rather than a commitment to the teacher's agenda.

36 *Suzie:*   It's exactly the same
as teacher directed in some
ways, but it's just that/
37 *Linda:*   You've got more
responsibility.
38 *Suzie:*   Yeah.

36-38 Linda and Suzie see the
teacher's and pupils' agendas
as separate and with different
functions. To be in an open
classroom entails carrying on
with the teacher's agenda
through a personal choice to
do so, i.e., the children take
responsibility for the carrying
out of the teacher's agenda,
though it is still the teacher's
agenda.

Though Suzie and Linda see the rest of the class as not understanding what OP is, because they think it means you muck around all
the time, it would seem that the whole class in a council meeting had
decided that getting on with your work is very important. Garry
explains that the council has made it a rule that people who fight and
thus prevent others from getting on with their work should get the
cane. He goes on to say:

Transcript 5.3: Garry

1 *Garry:*   Oh, it's good really
for the school, because if you
can stop the fighting then you
can get your work done and
everything.
2 *B.D.:*   You all agree that's a
good rule then?
3 *Garry:*   Yeah.

But counterbalanced with the concern for work is the love of fun.
Mucking around (or pursuing the pupil agenda) is essential. One needs
to work and to muck about. As Garry indicated, however, in Transcript
5.3, if the mucking about turns into fighting the children agree that it
should be stopped. In the following transcript, Warwick, Garry and
Roy further demonstrate that they are prepared to accept certain
rulings or constraints on their mucking around, if these constraints are
enforced in acceptable ways.

Transcript 5.4: Warwick, Garry and Roy

1   *B.D.:*   You said Warwick that you go into the music room to muck up. Does that mean that when you feel like being noisy you sort of get away to the music room rather than be noisy in the classroom?

1   An attempt to get at the function/ meaning of 'mucking up'.

2   *Garry:*   Oh, not really, sometimes we're not allowed in the music room, we muck 'round with the band there.

2   The music room is not always available. One is supposed to make music in there. By mucking around with the band they combine their own agenda with the teacher's.

3   *Warwick:*   You're allowed there without a teacher there.

4   *Roy:*   You can play a cassette or records.

5   *Warwick:*   Now and then we check to see how far away the teachers are.

3-5   Because the teacher is not there, the pupil agenda sometimes dominates in a manner which is against the teacher's rules. When this happens they keep a weather eye out for the teacher.

6   *Roy:*   Everybody gets out the things, like a bass/

7   *Warwick:*   Yeah, Barry Wilkins was muckin' up in there, and Mr Bell, we were muckin' 'round, you know, he went in, we all stopped, you know, 'cos we knew someone was comin' in the door and we all stopped, and then Mr Bell went away, and then he come back and he opened the door real quick and looked in (*mimics Mr Bell looking in very quick, which makes me laugh*) and Barry Wilkins was there with the drumsticks in his hand banging them into a box.

7   Warwick's mimicking of Mr Bell catching them out is extremely funny. The grin on his face indicates that everyone considered the catching of Barry Wilkins to be entirely fair, given that the teacher's rules are explicit and yet not being followed.

8   *Roy:*   Yeah.

9   *B.D.:*   Yes. (*still laughing*) So I guess he was in trouble was he?

10 *Garry:*   Yeah.
11 *Roy:*   Yeah.
12 *Warwick:*   He was banned from the music room.
13 *Roy:*   He was banned for a week.
14 *B.D.:*   So it's not really supposed to be the place where you go away to muck up in?
15 *Roy:*   Nooo, we like playing cassettes in there/

15 Long drawn out no. Not sure what my 'supposed' in 14 means — supposed according to whom?

16 *Warwick:*   Cassettes and a record the most.
17 *B.D.:*   How do you think it would be if you didn't have the music room?
18 *Warwick:*   Terrible.
19 *All:*   'Cos you don't/ the music room/ you would have to work all the time.

19 To have a separate room generally unsupervised by teachers creates a clear physical boundary with which to demarcate the carrying out of teacher's and pupils' agendas.

Thus there are elements of the children's behaviour, mucking about and fighting, that can interfere with work, though the children would prefer that this didn't happen. Their wish is that work and fun can co-exist harmoniously, and they will accept restraints or rulings which allow for this co-existence. This harmonious co-existence Mehan refers to as 'mutually constitutive socialisation'.

Mehan further points out that where teachers are unaware of the pupils' agenda, they may perceive children as being at fault within the terms of the teacher's agenda, not realising that the act constitutes correct behaviour in terms of the pupils' agenda:

When the fact that students have agendas they want to accomplish is incorporated into the analysis, it casts 'students' errors' in a new light. Before accepting the conclusion that 'students' errors' stem from a lack of competence, it is necessary to determine the part that the behaviour in question plays in the students' scheme of things. Not all wrong answers stem from a lack of academic knowledge, not all disruptions stem from a lack of interactional competence. Borrowing a metaphor from Wittgenstein, students may make mistakes as a move in a different game. Instead of being an incompetent move in a teacher's game, the behaviour in question may be a very sophisticated move in a student's game, a move calculated to manipulate the teacher's normative arrangements in order to accomplish items on the student's agenda. (1979b, p.34)

Where the teacher's agenda is problematic or faulty it *becomes* part of the pupils' agenda to respond to that faultiness. Though the children do not see it as their role to take control of the teacher's agenda, they may see it as appropriate to respond, or reciprocate wrong action:

Transcript 5.5: Pat, Terry, Suzie and Linda

1 *B.D.:* Do you do homework at home too?
2 *Pat:* Yes, sometimes.
3 *B.D.:* What about you, Terry?
4 *Terry:* Umm, at home doing homework? I hardly do any.
5 *Suzie:* Yes, Terry! He wagged school yesterday.
6 *Terry:* I'm sort of one of those lazy waggers. You're lucky to get, say, two words out of me.

6 Terry identifies himself as the type of person who does not work at school.

7 *B.D.:* At home and at school?

7 Apparently this is in contrast to his home identity, though this contradicts 4.

8 *Terry:* No, I do a fair bit at home, but at school you'll only get about two words out of me.
9 *Linda:* Yeah.
10 *B.D.:* Why's that?
11 *Terry:* Because I'm not, I don't know! I just don't like working.

11 The answer is difficult to formulate. 'I don't know' in this context indicates that there is no single clear answer to why he is as he is. What he does know for sure is that he

does not like working in his present school situation.

12 *Suzie:*   Why do you come to school then?

12 Even though Terry has no real choice in the matter of school attendance, Suzie feels some indignation at the foolishness of coming to school and not working.

13 *Linda:*   Yeah, well my mother won't/

14 *B.D.:*   Shh. Can you just let Terry talk for a while?

15 *Terry:*   And um, well, Mum prefers me to go into a TD class, 'cos Mum and Dad did put me in the TD class, but only that Mr Bell put me into an OP class.

15 Terry's antagonism to school directly relates to adminis-trative decisions which ignored his and his parents' point of view.

16 *B.D.:*   Why did he do that?

17 *Terry:*   Because there are too many in TD and not enough in OP. He went through the things and they picked out ten I think it was, and then they called the names out and people who didn't want to go, well they could, had to sorta stay there, but Mr Bell said 'I think you would be better in the OP class', anyway he stuck me in OP.

17 Despite Mr Bell's ideal that pupils should have their choice, he was forced to deny some that choice and move them into the class they had not chosen. Clearly he had explained to the children the necessity for the move, and yet Terry feels pushed around. Some had choice and and he didn't. He was 'stuck', object-like, where he did not choose to be. Wagging school and not working are two ways of getting even.

18 *B.D.:*   But did you used to work in TD?

19 *Terry:*   Yeah, I used to work with Mrs Wright upstairs, we used to move around the room and we'd have our, oh we sorta had a contract and, we would have to have about seven things done in a day, like maths, reading and science and all that, when you finished,

19 Terry clearly enjoyed the routine of work in Mrs Wright's class. He was not a 'lazy wagger' then. It was probably on the basis of his 'good pupil' behaviour in Mrs Wright's class that Mr Bell chose him for the OP class. But for children

like, you went to maths first, and then you went to reading and you stayed there for a fair while and you had lessons with the teacher in the morning and in the afternoon and that.

20 *B.D.:* You said you don't work at all now, is that because you are in OP?

21 *Terry:* Yeah, cause open's just like, um, just like staying home, you just muck around there, you don't, at the moment we are doing, some of the kids are doing TD because we are not doing enough work. Mr Droop got them out this morning, he's wroten them down a contract and they have to do that contract and I thought to myself, well, here I'm one of them, and um, I never, I wasn't put down as one.

22 *B.D.:* Would you be pleased if you were?

23 *Terry:* Yes, because, you'd get more work out of me.

24 *B.D.:* Why don't you suggest it to him?

25 *Terry:* I don't know. (*laughs a slightly embarrassed laugh*) I might try that. (*uncertain*) In some ways I don't like Mr Droop, and some ways not, and you just, say, he's like, some days you can really get on well with him, but sometimes like when I'm playing in the room and you say, um, jump on the cushions and that, he'll just tell you off and that and um, one time Patrick flew a plane at me so I just

identity is not a fixed quality and the new situation required a new set of responses, a new role, a new identity (see rule 3, p.77).

21 Terry does not like the dominance of the pupil agenda which he experiences in OP. He was disappointed at missing out on a contract which would spell out more clearly for him the teacher's agenda in this classroom.

25 This idea of asking for the sort of order he wants seems odd to him because it is the teacher's responsibility, not his. Sometimes Terry and Mr Droop get on. Basically they want the same thing, i.e., for Terry to get on with some work. But when Terry acts in ways which he assumes are acceptable and Mr Droop does not, there is conflict. When Mr Droop sends Terry to Mr Bell, Mr Bell does not

flicked it back so anyway, I had to sit in the corner, anyway he reckons that I swore at him, anyway I never swore at anybody, anyway so he sent me to Mr Bell, anyway Mr Bell just told him that I was just paying back at him.

seem to have supported Mr Droop's perspective. He simply tells Mr Droop that Terry's response made sense under the circumstances. While this may be so, it does little for Mr Droop's credibility with the children.

26 *B.D.:*   If you just had Mr Bell in your open classroom would you do work then?

27 *Suzie:*   Yes, I *think* so.

27 Suzie is careful when she says this, she is obviously not 100 per cent certain. The working of an open-plan class is a dubious thing.

28 *Terry:*   'Cos Mr Bell he did quite well, he'll start you off on a lot of things, like, whereas Mr Droop, he'll start you off on a couple, and you have to stay with those until Mr Bell will come in, because we haven't got all our supplies yet, and um, and we have to sorta just do those things for, say, a couple of weeks.

28 Terry provides a further explanation for the failure of the current classroom. The resources so necessary for Mr Droop's teaching have not yet arrived. He did not mind OP while Mr Bell was in charge of it, since Mr Bell created his own resources.

Terry was happy with teacher control of the teacher's agenda upstairs. Downstairs in OP where responsibility is left to him to proceed with the teacher agenda, he ceases working. He wants to work and he wants the teacher to provide a situation in which he can work but he has been offended and appropriate response as he sees it is in fact to walk away from the situation by wagging and by not working, by, in fact, becoming the sort of person appropriate to this new situation.

The constant concern of these children is that work should be done. The harrassed Mr Droop would probably have been astonished if he had realised how anxious they were to be getting on with their work. Vanessa, another victim of administrative decisions, announced gloomily that teacher-directed classes were better for you because you get more work done: 'The teacher forces you, which is a, and my mother reckons that is good for you, especially if you don't know nothin' much and that.'

Vanessa and Jane have, in contrast to Terry, made an effort to follow their own initiatives and work. Unfortunately, through a fairly gross misreading of the situation, they have got it all wrong because the initiatives they took were not acceptable. There is a danger that they too, with parental support, will cease their current efforts:

Transcript 5.6: Vanessa and Jane

1   *B.D.:*   So you have both got contracts?
2   *Vanessa:*   Yeah, we have a joint contract together.
3   *B.D.:*   What do you think of that?
4   *Vanessa:*   We haven't started yet. I was doing one by myself and we decided to do one together. We have always done everything together.
5   *Jane:*   Yeah, we started a project on mice.
6   *Vanessa:*   We did a project on cities together.
7   *Jane:*   Which we haven't started yet.
8   *Vanessa:*   Oh that's complicated, we didn't like it, we should have done the other one. I wasn't going to do it, but she come up to me and said, 'Why don't we do cities?' So I said 'OK' not knowing anything about cities/
9   *Jane:*   Yeah, I thought it was going to be easy/
10   *Vanessa:*   And so we tried cities and it turned out to be very hard.
11   *B.D.:*   Why's that?
12   *Jane:*   Oh, we done about three pages on countries and it turned out to be about cities.
13   *Vanessa:*   We had to tear it out.
14   *Jane:*   And we had to tear it

1-12 Mr Droop has written out individualised contracts for some of the children (as noted by Terry in the previous transcript). Vanessa and Jane have been allowed to do theirs together, but they have spent days of hard work doing it wrong.

13-16 They had enjoyed the hard work sufficiently to press on with it instead of having fun.

out and everything. We spent
a lot of time in the library,
about four days we spent in
the library, getting, missing
out on a lot of things.

15 *Vanessa:*   Missing out on the
fun we normally have.

16 *Jane:*   Just working as hard
as we could on our project.
It took a long while to look
up the information and now
it's just ruined.

17 *B.D.:*   Why couldn't you just
change the name of the
project to countries?

18 *Vanessa:*   He wouldn't let us.

19 *Jane:*   There is a theme, there
is theme 1 and theme 2, we
should have done resources,

20 *Vanessa:*   which we tried to
change, but we couldn't get
to it, like you find out things
about/

21 *B.D.:*   So what are you
supposed to find out about
cities?

22 *Jane:*   How trains go.

23 *Vanessa:*   What are their
problems.

24 *Jane:*   Resources, how does
one kind of resource, get to
another place, and/

25 *Vanessa:*   It's all very
complicating.

26 *Jane:*   I said to Mum, 'Do we
have to do it?' and she goes,
'Find out a bit more about it.
If it is too hard you don't have
to do it.' Mum don't like open
planning.

27 *Vanessa:*   Neither does my
mother.

28 *Jane:*   I was supposed to be
put in TD but I changed to OP
and I don't like it meself.

When it turned out to be
wrong they felt very badly
about having to tear it out
and start again.

17-25 The work has a specific
structure which the girls
understand now, but which
they did not understand
previously, because they were
used to Mr Bell's less
structured projects. The kinds
of projects they had done
with Mr Bell had not been of
the pre-structured variety. He
had, rather, encouraged them
to do research in an open-
ended way, pursuing what-
ever seemed of interest. The
girls realised too late that Mr
Bell's idea of research was not
what was being called for
here.

26-34 The children's anxiety and
frustration is shared by their
parents. The children
recognise that Mr Bell was
forced to move some chil-
dren, but they do not see
why they were chosen.
Perhaps Mrs Wright didn't
like them. They have
struggled in good faith with
the work in OP but it is not

29 *Vanessa:*   It was all Mrs
Wright's fault really, because
she had thirty-six children, she
had a lot of children, carrying
all us in Mr Bell's class. And
she wouldn't take them to
herself, she wouldn't take it
and that. So she's got thirty-
six in her class now, and she
was the one. And she picked
out all us kids, 'cos she doesn't
like us probably.

30 *B.D.:*   She picked out the ones
that should go into OP?

31 *Vanessa:*   Yeah, I don't think
I should, because I'm not
really good at anything, and
Mum agrees that I'm not. Dad
doesn't want me in OP. He
reckons I should be in TD.
And I wanna be in TD too,
but Mr Bell just put me in OP
'cos Mrs Wright wouldn't have
any more.

32 *Jane:*   I didn't think it would
be like this. Mum goes to me,
'What have you learned today?'
she goes, 'What have you
learned today?'

33 *Vanessa:*   Aw, that's what I
always get. Then if you say
something, she'll say, 'Oh,
surely you learnt somethink!'

34 *Jane:*   I show her me work
and she goes, 'Only a page!'
Stupid, I only do a page of
work nearly all day. It's
stupid open planning 'cos
you get lazy.

working out for them.

34 In the final event, the
appropriate response seems to
be to get lazy, like Terry. Yet
this is a source of anxiety
both to the girls and to their
parents.

It is not only the children who can't get by in Mr Droop's classroom who would like a clearer structure. Linda, who has settled down reasonably well and found a way of getting enough work done, would prefer a system where the teacher's agenda was more clearly structured.

Transcript 5.7: Linda and Suzie

1   *Linda:*   I sorta work, sorta more solidly at home when I do my homework.

2   *Suzie:*   Yeah.

3   *Linda:*   Because the kids don't um, disturb you and Mum says, we've got a study, a sort of study, TV room, except there's a desk in the corner and when someone has homework the TV isn't allowed to be turned on. I mean we do our homework and when we are finished it, we can turn on the TV, and Mum sort of says, 'Right, I'm not going to disturb you.' We have to do our chores first though, and then she says, 'Right, is everything done? Get on with your homework now.' So we do our homework and, in complete silence, oh, except for Mum, she's making tea or something and I get on, I work more solidly, because say I come out to get a drink or something, and then I try to sorta get off homework, Mum says, 'I know you are only trying to get off homework, go and do your homework.'

3   Linda describes the rules surrounding homework in loving detail: the physical setting; the rules her mother has made; and the way her mother responds to attempts to 'get off' homework with predictable, though accepting, authority.

4   *Suzie:*   Yeah.

4   Suzie also apparently experiences such 'relief' at home.

5   *Linda:*   And the teachers don't say that, I wish they did in some ways.

5   Note that Linda only wishes this in 'some ways'. Mucking around, is after all, fun.

Each teacher will strive to structure the classroom in his or her own way. It is clear that the children want this structure made clear and are concerned if it is difficult to follow.

If it becomes problematic, the children's agendas may also become problematic. Some of the children were prepared to keep on trying to find out how to work in Mr Droop's classroom. They felt in time they were bound to figure it out. Other children, in contrast, were simply engaging in reciprocal activity – for every perceived wrongdoing on Mr Droop's part, wrongdoing was delivered back. Reciprocation in the child-child mode was a straightforward way of responding to an unclear situation.

Roddie was often named as the leader of the anti-Droop contingent. In the following conversation where the children discuss their problems with Mr Droop they can be seen, metaphorically, to be orchestrating the theme that the teacher is no good. They allow, briefly, distortion of facts against the teacher to assist in this orchestration. This would appear to be a result of the fact that they do not get on with him and yet have difficulty in formulating precisely what the problem is. Dramatising the facts in description of his horribleness helps to illustrate their feeling that the situation with him is not a good one.

Transcript 5.8: Roddie, Terry, Roy and Vanessa

1	*B.D.:* So you think that when Mr Bell comes back to take over your classroom you'll like OP?		
2	*All:* Yeah, Mr Bell is nice.	2	Open plan will work with a nice teacher.
3	*Roddie:* Mr Droop is a bit daggy.	3	Spontaneous reference to their dislike of Mr Droop. 'Daggy' is derived from the Australian slang 'dag' meaning dried excreta on a sheep's tail.
4	*Terry:* He puts Roddie on teacher directed!	4-5	This complaint is lodged against Mr Droop in tones of righteous indignation.
5	*Roy:* Yeah, for nothin'!		
6	*Terry:* We was taping/	6-7	The second complaint is lodged with the same measure of indignation.
7	*Roddie:* We was taping songs and that, and he came out and blew us up for no reason whatsoever!		
8	*Vanessa:* Oh be like me and/		
9	*Roy:* Those tapes are not for recording though.	9	One of the first complainants points out that the second complaint might have a shaky

basis.

10 *Roddie:*   Well we didn't know!

11 *B.D.:*   But Roddie said that he wasn't getting any work done anyway, and it would be quite a good idea to have a contract?

11 I then point out that the first complaint also has a shaky basis.

12 *Roddie:*   Mmhm! (*laughs*)

13 *Roy:*   Yeah, it's good with a contract.

13 They then quite happily undo the basis of the first complaint saying they prefer direction. Interestingly enough this does not reduce the outrage they feel towards the unhappy Mr Droop. They *know* they do not get on with him. They do not, at this point, know why. The complaints made can be seen as attempts to illustrate their failed interactions in the absence of a more satisfying explanation, i.e., they adhere to the facticity of events, even though it suits them to do otherwise in the construction of a coherent world.

14 *Vanessa:*   Especially TD. I reckon TD is better than OP.

15 *B.D.:*   Why's that, Vanessa?

16 *Vanessa:*   You get more work done, the teacher forces you, which is a, and my mother reckons that is good for you, especially if you don't know nothin' much and that.

This conversation illustrates a search for a satisfactory explanation, though in this instance it takes the form of description rather than analysis. Generally they know things are bad and they react to that knowledge, i.e., any action on the part of Mr Droop can be construed as confirmation of his badness. The two contrasting points of view in the classroom, one, that they will get to understand Mr Droop's style, given time, and two, that he should receive measure for measure are illustrated in the following transcript:

Transcript 5.9: Terry, Linda, Suzie

1   *B.D.:*   O.K. Now tell me, first of all we start with Linda, what do you think of being in Mr Bell's class?

1   As adult I assume the right here to initiate a new topic and to indicate who should answer first.

2   *Linda:*   I reckon it's all right but I don't like the teacher we've got at the moment.

2   My question is answered but their dislike of Mr Droop is mentioned immediately.

. . . .

3   *B.D.:*   Why don't you like him?

. . . .

4   *Terry:*   I do like him but sometimes he can be a/

5   *Linda:*   I don't know whether I don't like him.

4-5   The children are hesitant to state categorically that they do not like him, once asked.

6   *B.D.:*   Can you explain to me what makes Mr Bell a good teacher and what it is that/

6   Since they are hesitant over going into details as to why they don't like Mr Droop I guess that it might be easier to contrast him with Mr Bell whom they do like.

7   *Linda:*   Well, he's a good sort and he takes jokes, and you can sort of muck up a bit.

7   A good teacher is good-looking ('good sort' in Australian slang means good looking or attractive), humorous and gives you some leeway in the class-room.

8   *Suzie:*   (*giggling*) That's what she likes!

8   Suzie teases Linda for making such an admission.

9   *B.D.:*   And so how is the other teacher that you don't like different from that?

10   *Suzie:*   He is strict, very strict I reckon.

10   In an earlier transcript (5.2 27), Linda had described a good teacher as 'strict, but not too strict'. Goodness and

badness in teachers is related
to something more complex
than strictness.

11 *Linda:*   Quite strict.
12 *Suzie:*   Sometimes you
    know/
13 *Linda:*   Sometimes he's quite
    a good teacher, but sometimes/
14 *B.D.:*   Describe him being a
    good teacher. (*pause for 6
    sec.*)

14 Attempts to get them to
    place their descriptions of his
    goodness in a context lead to
    silence, followed by an
    analysis of the problem from
    a different angle.

15 *Suzie:*   Um, well, um (*giggles*)
    it's just that all the other
    kids don't like him and that's
    why.

15 While they could readily
    describe Mr Bell, they cannot
    do the same for Mr Droop.
    They can, however, pinpoint
    the problem in so far as the
    children as a group have
    decided they don't like him.

16 *Linda:*   It's sorta hard to like
    him. Or maybe it is that
    we don't know him/
17 *Suzie:*   Very well and/
18 *Terry:*   Yeah!
19 *Linda:*   When we've had him
    a bit more/
20 *Suzie:*   When we get to know
    him.
21 *Terry:*   When we get to know
    him more.

16-21 A second aspect of the
    problem with Mr Droop is
    that they do not yet know
    him well. They agree that
    knowing him better could
    resolve their current prob-
    lems. They indicate here a
    willingness to like him and to
    get to know his particular
    ways, i.e., they acknowledge
    that people are plastic. He
    who is bad today may be
    good tomorrow (see rule 2
    p. 77).

22 *B.D.:*   What you were saying
    Suzie about the other kids
    not liking him means that
    you feel unsettled in the
    classroom when he's there?
23 *Linda:*   Yeah.
24 *Suzie:*   Yeah, you sorta feel
    um/
25 *Terry:*   Out of the classroom.
26 *Suzie:*   Yeah.

22 Again I use adult 'rights' to
    ignore 16-21 and ask them
    to elaborate on 15.

24-31 The children describe the
    feeling of being isolated if
    they do not go along with the
    majority opinion against Mr

27 *Terry:* If I don't, just say, if I don't agree well I'm out of the class.	Droop, i.e., this is a third aspect of the problem: social pressure not to like him. Note that they ignore my formu- lation of 'unsettled' and elaborate in their own terms.
28 *Linda:* Yes, we sorta all/	
29 *Terry:* We sorta all/	
30 *Suzie:* We pick on Terry.	
31 *Terry:* Yeah, pick on/	
32 *Suzie:* Like see, well I dunno, but it's Roddie and all the others pick on every- body.	32 Suzie introduces a new aspect of the problem which is that they do not now get on with each other. This develops into a long description of their last council meeting. This is the fourth dimension to the problem: their own relation- ships with each other are now unsatisfactory.
(*The children go on to describe how their council meetings have become ridiculous, the classroom is chaotic, some kids are too bossy and some are too rude. The council has made ridiculous rules which make for more disorder. Suzie then returns the conversation to Mr Droop.*)	
33 *Suzie:* In a sort of way he tries his best, in a *sort* of way.	33 As in 4, 5, 13 and 16, there is an indication that Mr Droop is all right, though there are some misgivings.

Mr Droop is strict and yet this strictness has not led to a workable structure. Some children have decided to actively resist his control and to try to ensure that the whole class goes along with this resistance. Suzie, Terry and Linda feel that the problem may relate simply to the fact that they have not yet figured out Mr Droop's style and that time, therefore, may solve the problem. They are concerned, however, about the increased conflict amongst themselves. They have learned from Mr Bell to engage in reciprocally contingent interactions and so feel justified in saying what they think in response to teacher initiatives. But in attempting to confront Mr Droop with the problems they perceive in his classroom, they find that he does not perceive the same links between pupil and teacher agendas as they do.

Transcript 5.10: Betty and Linda

1 *Betty:* Mr Droop gets too cranky when you tell him your

problems.

2 *Linda:* He just says 'nothin' to do with me, it's your problem not mine.'

3 *Betty:* Mr Bell doesn't, he helps you sort it out.

4 *B.D.:* How does he help you sort it out?

5 *Betty:* Well he'll talk to you about it and all that, but Mr Droop won't. Mr Droop gets real cranky if you tell him about him and all, hey? If you told Mr Droop he'd get real cranky.

5 Mr Bell will negotiate but Mr Droop simply gets angry.

6 *Linda:* Like we had a bit of a talk all about, er, hours and that and I sorta wrote him (*Mr Bell*) a little letter saying, 'Your talk was boring but I s'pose it was interesting.' He said he'd reply but he hasn't yet.

6 Linda wrote to Mr Bell telling him he was boring, and he wasn't angry – he simply promised to write back.

Mr Droop is confronted with children wanting to behave in ways he doesn't accept or apparently understand. He perceives them as not willing or not able to work, and unsettled due to the unreasonable 'freedom' allowed them by Mr Bell. In his attempts to sort the classroom out and establish his own ground rules, he seems to get further into the mire. Time does not seem to be sorting things out. The children continually find him unpredictable and incomprehensible and therefore unacceptable.

They try to challenge him in council meetings but he simply becomes upset. While they can see that they have given him a bad time they also consider that he has broken the rules of acceptable teacher behaviour as they see them, for example, he has been overly angry for a misdeed which was only an error (see Transcript 5.1). The children tried to understand Mr Droop's model of open plan but they continually alienated him with their attempts to negotiate over what it was that constituted acceptable behaviour in his classroom. He grew angry at what he deemed unacceptable in them and they, in turn, resorted to more closed forms of negotiation: quitting work, wagging school, refusing to learn, talking in class, laziness and general 'mucking up' (cf. Woods, 1980). The children became more and more conscious of the fact that they wanted to learn as less and less learning took place.

The third teacher the children had during the year was Miss Love. Similarly to Mr Droop, she found reciprocally contingent interactions with children unacceptable. When she first arrived to take over the class, the children were not prepared to co-operate with her. Once again, Mr Bell had been removed from them and once again they had to figure out a new system of rules.

Miss Love entered into open battle with the children. She recognised the power that Warwick's, Henry's and Roddie's group had over the class and focused on Warwick as the person to be battled with and won over, following perhaps the same lines of thought as Mr Dadier in *The Blackboard Jungle* (Hunter) when he singled out Miller as the ringleader and sought to get him on his side. Warwick, who had not previously had trouble in the classroom, suddenly found himself singled out for attention.

Transcript 5.11: Roddie, Warwick and Roy

1   *B.D.:*   So how's the classroom these days, Warwick?
2   *Roddie:*   No good, Awful.
3   *Warwick:*   Awful and a bit good, a *bit* I said.

2-3 Roddie is keen to dramatise the situation with Miss Love. Warwick, who is becoming reconciled to her, must emphasise how small the 'goodness is in order not to spoil Roddie's production.

4   *Roddie:*   A bit!
5   *Roy:*   Warwick mostly gets in trouble, eh?
6   *Roddie:*   Yeah! (*indignant*)

5-6 Roddie and Roy are concerned and sympathetic.

7   *B.D.:*   You didn't used to get in trouble all the time did you?

7   Until this point I had not heard any tales at all of misbehaviour on Warwick's part.

8   *Warwick:*   Nuh.
9   *B.D.:*   What do you get in trouble for?
10   *Warwick:*   Well see, there was this, there was a little toy truck here on this table, a little toy truck over here/
11   *Roy:*   Yeah and Patrick/
12   *Warwick:*   And Patrick was sittin' here and he owned this

10-14 The details are important, because Warwick wants to make it clear that he was not the only one involved. The fact that Miss Love chooses him alone to pick on places him in a quandary. As the

little truck, and Roddie got
that little truck and he was
pushing it on the table, and
Patrick got this truck and
pushed it and it made a noise
and um/

13 *Roy:*   It went brrrrrrrrrrrrr!/
(*high pitched noise*)

14 *Warwick:*   And Miss Love
said, 'Warwick, get out of
the classroom.' When I was
going out I said, 'Why me,
why not Roddie?' and she
just said 'get out.'

15 *Roy:*   Yeah and then/

16 *B.D.:*   Shh, let Warwick tell
it.

17 *Warwick:*   And then, ah, I
went around and ah she told
me to get away from the door
'cos I was blocking up the
door and then, um, she said,
'As a matter of fact,' she said,
'You can go to one of the
other classes,' so I went, I
said, 'Can I go and get my
pencil and my book then?'
and she said, 'No I don't want
to see you in this classroom
while I'm in, I don't want you
in this classroom while I'm in
here.'

18 *Roddie:*   Yeah, yeah/

19 *Warwick:*   I went in to get
it and she said, 'Who told you
you could come in here?' I'd
asked Patrick and Roddie could
they get 'em for me when Miss
Love wasn't around so, um/

20 *Roy:*   She said 'come in'.

21 *Warwick:*   And she said 'come
in' and I said, 'No, I thought
I wasn't allowed,' and then I
fought, 'OK, I might as well go
in,' and when I went in, she just

only Aboriginal boy in the
group, Miss Love may be
choosing him on the basis of
his Aboriginality rather than
on the basis of his actions.

14-21 Warwick tells a tale of
attack and counter-attack
between himself and Miss
Love. He gains some pleasure
out of sucking her in to
becoming angry at him for
'innocent' behaviour, thus
making her look foolish and
in the wrong.

told me, she grabbed me and
said, 'OK you're goin' up to
Mr Fife.'

22 *Roy:* And Mr Fife/

23 *Warwick:* And then um, I
was goin' up to Mr Fife and I
fought, 'why should I go up
to Mr. Fife I didn't do much
wrong' so I went 'ome.

24 *Roy:* And Mr Fife was good
to you eh?

25 *B.D.:* Why do you think that
she was doing all that,
Warwick?

26 *Warwick:* Because she was
blaming me for mucking up
there.

27 *B.D.:* For just that one
time?

28 *Warwick:* Yeah.

29 *B.D.:* Was she mad at you
for other times too?

30 *Warwick:* Not that day.

31 *B.D.:* But other days she got
mad at you too?

32 *Warwick:* Oh Friday she got
mad at me.

33 *Roddie:* Oh yeah but she
was up everyone Friday!

34 *Warwick:* Yeah.

35 *Roddie:* She wouldn't leave
no one.

. . . .

36 *B.D.:* So what's going to
happen now, is she all right
with you now?

37 *Warwick:* Yeah.

. . . .

38 *B.D.:* What did your Mum
do when she came?

22 The Deputy Head.

23 Aboriginal children seem to
find it easier to leave the
school situation (to think
outside the institutional
framework) when conflict
arises than do white children.

25-30 The pragmatic interpretation is that *this* trouble is
due to *this* action. Warwick
does not consider that Miss
Love's anger is part of a larger
scheme of things. He assumes
that behaviours are interpreted for their relevance to
the present situation.

36-37 (see also 49) The same
pragmatism which prevents
Warwick from seeing beyond
the reciprocated action and
reaction in the trouble he has
with Miss Love also allows
him to get on with her when
things are going well (see also
rule 3, p. 77).

39 *Warwick:*   Nothin'.
40 *Roddie:*   She just had a
little talk to her.
41 *Warwick:*   Mum didn't say
anything to 'er.
42 *Roy:*   She wouldn't even give
her a chance, Miss Love.
That's what Aunty Jean
(*Warwick's mum*) told me
last night, she couldn't get
a chance to talk. (*giggles*)
43 *B.D.:*   Why was Miss Love
talking to you this morning?
44 *Warwick:*   Because I went
'ome and got Mum . . . and
she kept on talking to me and
saying 'why did you go 'ome?'
and that, and I said 'because
why did I have to go to Mr
Fife and not Roddie?' and she
kept on saying 'oh 'cos there
was a reason' and I said 'why
didn't you send Roddie *and*
me?' and she said um, ''cos you
were doing other things' and
I said 'come on, what was I
doing?' and she just said 'you
know what you were doing'
and I wasn't doing anything
else, I was/
45 *Roy:*   She didn't even know,
she just said that. He got kept
in at recess.
46 *Roddie:*   Warwick didn't I
did.
47 *B.D.:*   You got kept in at
recess for what?
48 *Roddie:*   See um I was there
and I was doing me work and
Miss Love couldn't stop
looking at me, so I done a ugly
face at her, so she'd stop
lookin' (*giggles*) and then she
kept me in at recess for doing
ugly faces at her (*laughter*) it

44 Warwick's reasoning is that he
is justified in doing wrong
because Miss Love did wrong.
She picked on him unfairly,
so he went home to get his
mother. His constant
reference to Roddie is not
because he wanted Roddie
punished, but because it
seems that Miss Love is being
unfair (and perhaps even
racist).

47-48 Roddie also has moved over
to child-child interactions
with Miss Love. If she does
something wrong, then he
will reciprocate. Even though
adult power prevails and
Roddie is punished for his
reciprocation, there has been
a humorous pay-off.

was funny actually, I wasn't
worried but.

49 *B.D.:*   Hang on I want to ask
Warwick some more questions.
So do you think she'll be nice
to you now?

50 *Warwick:*   Yes she is.

51 *B.D.:*   She's been nice to
you this morning, why's that?

52 *Roy:*   'Cos/

53 *Roddie:*   Boyfriend's upset.   53 Roddie introduces a
                                                 humorous explanation for
                                                 the current problems.

54 *B.D.:*   (*laughing*) I beg your
pardon? (*laughter*)

55 *Warwick:*   Dad keeps on   55 The adult world as a resource
saying that to me. He said like   for humour is discussed in
if any of the teachers say to   chapter 6.
ya, like Miss Love said 'why
do youse always have to
follow Roddie?' and ah, dad
said to say to her 'didya have
a bad weekend with ya boyfriend?'

56 *B.D.:*   (*laughs*) Oh dear!

57 *Roddie:*   Yeah we're friends,   57-60 After the talk has ranged
we like going round together!   over the events in the class-
                                                 room and humorous explan-
58 *B.D.:*   She's bothered that   ations suggested, the root of
you kids hang round together?   the matter is brought up for
                                                 discussion. Miss Love is trying
59 *Roddie:*   Yeah, yeah, just   to break up the group which
because we're friends.   she sees as powerful.

60 *Roy:*   Just because we're
friends! When we wanted to
sit next to each other she
wouldn't let us.

In trying to separate these children, Miss Love was trying to break
down the strength of the children's agenda in the classroom, which she
perceived, quite rightly, as being opposed to her and her agenda. But by
entering into such an attack, perhaps especially with children who have
been encouraged to think for and express themselves, she ran the risk
of counter-attack. In this case the counter-attack took the shape of
a negation of Miss Love as a person. The children established just who
did or did not like her, and then told her who didn't like her. ('Don't
treat kids badly, or else they'll treat you worse than you treat them. If

you treat them badly . . . they'll absolutely murder you' (see p. 117).)
The announcement was too much for Miss Love, and she fled the
situation declaring she would never come back. Attack, counter-attack
and withdrawal. Children's culture dominated the scene, and they were
the victors. They went to fetch Mr Bell back to their classroom (after
all you can't *be* a class without a teacher!) but he refused to come.
They had created the problem he said, and they must sort it out. He
wanted no part of it. The children sent deputations up to the staff
room to speak to Miss Love, but she refused to talk to them. The
children were shocked to see that she *was* genuinely upset, and that this
was no adult play acting in an attempt to control them. Reciprocity
had been played out in full measure and it was time to make amends in
whatever way they could.

Mandy, Suzie and Linda told me the story when I returned from a
two-week absence from the school, and after reconciliation had been
made:

Transcript 5.12: Suzie, Mandy and Linda

1	*Suzie:* Are you writing that book?	
2	*B.D.:* I was actually teaching.	
3	*Mandy:* Did you write a book?	3 Mandy had missed this information because she and Suzie had been fighting at the time we talked about why I was there.
4	*B.D.:* I'm going to write a book.	
5	*Mandy:* What on?	
6	*Suzie:* Children. Us.	
7	*Linda:* Yeah, that's why she interviews all of us.	
8	*B.D.:* Would you like to do some drawing? (*discussion on their drawings*)	
9	*B.D.:* So tell me what you've been doing since I was here last.	
10	*Linda:* Work.	10-13 Work has become a central defining feature of classroom life.
11	*Suzie:* Very hard work too.	
12	*Mandy:* Oh, not all of it.	
13	*Linda:* Well, some of it, most	

of it. (*further discussion on their drawings*)

14 *B.D.:*   So since your new teacher came you've been doing lots of work.

15 *All:*   Yeah it's better than/ she's better than/

16 *Mandy:*   She's used to TD I think.

16 The children put forward explanations for some of the difficulties they have had. Miss Love is not used to OP.

17 *Linda:*   Yeah, she was a TD teacher.

18 *Suzie:*   But she likes us to get on with our work.

19 *Mandy:*   One good thing is she takes a joke.
(*The children then talk about Mr Droop, discussing why he left, putting forward a variety of hypotheses, including the idea that he had left because of them*)

18-19 Miss Love gets them to work and lets them have fun.

20 *Suzie:*   When Miss Love first came everybody hated her/

21 *Linda:*   Hated her. She got really upset and Henry, Warwick, Roddie and Roy, they're all mucking around, you know, and saying, 'Yeah, well why should I work?'

21 Why Indeed? This is a fundamental question which is probably only asked when taken-for-granted controls break down to the extent they had here. But the question negates the unwritten, even unspoken agreement that the teacher is there to teach them and the pupils to learn.

22 *Mandy:*   They were not.

23 *Linda:*   Yes they were.

24 *Mandy:*   They went around the class and asked who liked Miss Love and who didn't and then they told her, and she went up to the staff room crying.

25   *Linda:*   I don't blame her.

25   Crying *could* be interpreted as 'piss weak' so Linda supports Miss Love's action by saying it was under-standable.

26   *B.D.:*   So what happened then?

27   *Suzie:*   Oh well you know, Mr Bell came in/
Mandy: I hope you won't tell this tape to her because there are too many secrets. See we've got a piggy bank and we've been putting money into it up in the cupboard, and we're buying a necklace for her. It's either got 'Janet' on it or it's going to have a key on it, we don't know yet.

26-27 Suzie starts to tell about Mr Bell's part, but Mandy inter-rupts with the details of the recompense they intend to make.

28   *B.D.:*   So you like her now?

29   *Mandy:*   Mm, yeah, except for when she sends mine and Suzie's favourite boy out of the classroom. (*laughs*)
(*discussion about Warwick*)

30   *Linda:*   Sometimes we all have a blow up because some cranky/

31   *Suzie:*   Oh well you would too.

31   They have worked out how to accept and explain Miss Love's occasional angry outbursts: 'anybody would do the same.'

32   *Linda:*   Yeah, I'm not saying anything against it.

33   *B.D.:*   So that day that she, that you made her cry, what did that make you think?

34   *Linda:*   Really guilty you know.

35   *Mandy:*   But Roddie he was really upset.

36   *Suzie:*   He gave the class a talking to, and all this and we decided/

36-38 Laughter and tears – both shock responses to what they had done. This asking of the

37 *Linda:* Oh but James, he got really upset. He was saying/

38 *Mandy:* Everybody was laughing because Miss Love had been crying. And James, he came down from the staff room and said Miss Love was crying up there and she couldn't even talk 'cos she had a lump in her throat and he, um, everybody started laughin'.

39 *Suzie:* And Roy said um, 'and you're nearly crying,' and ah/

40 *Linda:* No that was Roddie.

41 *Suzie:* Was it? Oh well, all the, I said it too, and then he started crying because he was really upset Miss Love was going to leave and then he sorta blubbered out that she's the best teacher we've ever had.

42 *Linda:* Which she is.

43 *Mandy:* Which is true.

44 *Suzie:* Mr Droop, everybody hated Mr Droop.

45 *Linda:* Oh well I think/

46 *Suzie:* Mr Bell was always out of the room.

47 *Mandy:* But with Miss Love in the room it doesn't matter if he's out he's not here.

48 *Suzie:* She's our permanent teacher.

question (in 21) may be reasonable but it is not answerable within the framework of the school.

41-43 Miss Love changed then from the target of their anger to the object of their love. She threatened to leave the school and they found that they did not actually want her to go.

44-48 They contrast Miss Love with the other teachers they have had, and she comes up well. She is after all, their permanent teacher, and Mr Bell's continual absences need no longer matter.

When Miss Love returned to the classroom, redefined as a good teacher ('the best we've ever had') the children worked with her to make the classroom a coherent and predictable place. Though there were still problems, and occasional 'blow ups' the children generally worked hard to get their contracts finished (so they could have time to muck around) and she rewarded them for their hard work in a variety of ways, including taking the best workers to town each week and buying them a small gift. In a sense they each recognised the other's agenda and went out of their way to contribute to it. The children took to bringing their school work into the library and reading me their poems and stories and showing me how much work they had done on their contracts. They did not have much to say about Miss Love after this major blow up. Conversations turned more to each other and to their own agenda. Miss Love grew to appreciate these children and became very attached to them, and they to her. When administrative wheels turned and Miss Love was moved to another town, the children were shocked and traumatised to lose her. Their upset when they heard she was leaving was expressed most poignantly by Roddie who threw his arms around her and sobbed, 'What's the use, what's the use?'

Conclusion

The process the children describe whereby they so strongly oppose new teachers and then finally capitulate is a natural response to a situation where new adults impose systems of interaction so that the children's taken-for-granted world no longer 'works'. In this case, the taken-for-granted rules established with Mr Bell were continually being reinforced by his presence and by his status. Specific objections to Mr Droop and Miss Love were usually of a superficial and sometimes patently inaccurate kind. They looked for and played on any 'evidence' which supported the idea that the teacher was a bad one. They *experienced* failure in interaction which they found difficult to fully explain. The stories they told were attempts to make their experience sensible.

Their actions seemed to be an attack on the teacher's world view. They frequently talked about the teacher's 'rights' and expressed a sense of moral indignation when teachers were unpredictable. These 'attacks' were often simply 'paying the teacher back' for his apparently uncalled-for attacks on them. But the children were not wantonly destructive. In their defence of their own sense-making they inadvertently hurt others. This was a source of great concern to them when they realised that the adult in question was actually suffering. Their sense of guilt and horror is stronger than their earlier wish to have the world maintained on familiar and predictable lines.

In so far as the children's focus is in part on *discovery* of the world taken-for-granted, when they find that the rules they were working on no longer work, they discard them and become open to new sets of rules as imposed by the new situation they find themselves in. In a sense their conflicts with the teachers can be compared to elements of the game 'sucked in'. Sometimes they inadvertently go too far, move outside the acceptable rules of the game, thereby discovering or rediscovering just what those rules are. Since acceptable behaviour changes from teacher to teacher, then discovery and rediscovery of rules is a constant activity.

This openness makes them, on occasion, seem fickle or conversely, remarkably ready to forgive. A best friend one day may not even be mentioned as a friend the next day – a teacher they are angry with one moment may be declared a good teacher the next.

Much of what the children described about their understanding of classroom process became available for conscious inspection because their classroom was problematic, and their taken-for-granted rules no longer worked. In more 'normal' circumstances they may have taken for granted that the teacher was in control, that pupil and teacher agendas existed harmoniously side by side and that the twofold purpose of school is to learn and to have fun.

The process whereby children are socialised involves exposure to different adult worlds or different sets of taken-for-granted rules, which the children have to discover. As well, they learn to behave appropriately with each other according to the rules of their own childhood culture, and they learn how to interact across cultures according to varying sets of rules. Though they may sometimes be put out by the confusions involved in rule-switching (especially where adult anger or punishment follows) they seem to maintain a remarkable facility to switch from one rule set to another and to accept a variety of views on the correct modes of interaction between adult culture and childhood culture. This switching is similar to the code-switching observed in some adult cultures. (On code-switching, see for example Blom and Gumperz, 1972.) The children tend to accept that they do have to learn the rules imposed by adults, but will set limits where the adults move outside what the children consider to be their adult rights.

When introduced to Mr Bell's model of open teaching they embraced it willingly and tried to extend it into their interactions with all teachers. Those tensions inherent in their attitude to school between work and mucking around, between having teachers in control and not allowing them to control, between the teacher's agenda and the pupils' agenda, were in a state of balance with some teachers. With other teachers the balance was lost and mucking around and denial of teacher control gained the upper hand. The children did not see themselves as unreasonable when this happened though they were disturbed by the fact that work was not being done and that the teacher was not in control. Their conversations with me involved endless attempts to describe, explain, negate and resolve the problems their various teachers presented them with. There is no simple way of summarising the many points the children made. Rather I should reiterate that they showed a degree of sympathy, tolerance and acceptance for their teachers which might well have startled some of these teachers had they known of it. They possessed a remarkable capacity to switch ground rules where they deemed it worthwhile to do so, and they showed a remarkable capacity to reconsider earlier judgments in the light of the perceived present.

Reflections on the Interactive Effect Between the Research Project and Life in the Classroom

Generally my presence in the library, interviewing the children, or my presence in the staff room or the classroom did not seem to be viewed as a problem by the teachers. Several times during the year the teachers also sat down to talk to me about what they were doing. This they did, not because I asked them to do so, but because they knew I was interested in their classroom and would be both a willing and an informed listener. The following field notes were made after I had been cornered in the staff room first by Mr Droop and then by Mr Bell.

> Mr Droop has taken over the classroom again. Mr Bell was becoming utterly exhausted by demands of being a headmaster as well as a teacher. He felt he was becoming ineffective as both, rather than effective as one or the other. He feels the system is crushing him and crushing his wish to be an effective person. He is going to explain this to the kids. Mr Droop lectured me at length on the nature of interaction in open classrooms. He says the teachers should use whichever style of teaching is appropriate at the time, that individual, small group and large group work should be possible. He is very willing to succeed. Both mentioned their perception of my function as 'a counsellor' who could help the children clarify their views. By talking to me, Mr Droop said, the children were then more able to talk to him. Mr Bell felt that my function was also to help him clarify his own thoughts. What therefore would be happening if I wasn't there? *Would there more often be a stalemate of non-communication because neither parties had time or opportunity (or know-how) to clarify where they were at?*

That question is, of course, unanswerable. Perhaps if I had not been there, someone else would have been used to help the teachers and the pupils clarify to themselves what they thought. Reality is continually under revision. When there are as many problems as there were in this classroom, considerable revision and negotiation is required by all parties. The attempt to discover the rules whereby each party can act competently will be continued until a satisfactory pattern has been found. Much of this discovery took place within the classroom. But classrooms are busy places. The opportunity to remove oneself from the situation and to use talk to clarify what has happened and to find some way of construing events so that they make sense speeds up the process whereby competent action can be engaged in. Clearly Mr Droop and Mr Bell saw the children emerging from the interview situation as more competent people. They ascribed to me the role of counsellor though rarely did I give counsel. I often asked however for points of clarification, because I too wanted to 'understand' what was going on.

In the process of clarifying their thinking with me, the children displayed a somewhat surprising degree of linguistic competence in terms of vocabulary, style and analytic muscle.* Though Mr Droop claimed that they were able to talk to him more easily after they had talked to me, it was clear that in the day-to-day classroom activities they did not display the same linguistic competence that they did with me. Rather they came over as disruptive, disturbed children who lacked an understanding of classroom procedure. There are several reasons, I think, for this difference.

First, what is *possible* in the interview is not possible in the classroom. The teacher's agenda, based on curriculum material to be taught, has first priority. While I spent hours and hours with the children, teachers are really only free to spend a small percentage of their time analysing interpersonal problems. The lesson must go on, otherwise the teacher is not really doing his job.

Second, what is *appropriate* in the interview is not appropriate in the classroom. Free-ranging discussion, skipping from one topic to another until the children settle on the problem they want to talk about, and then set about analysing it, is clearly not the way lessons are conducted. The children would probably become frustrated if 'lesson matter' was as vague in purpose as some of our conversations were.

Third, the *role* the children played in relation to me was influenced by the fact that they chose when and how long our conversations would be and what they would be about. Further, they were usually able to stay until the conversation came to a natural conclusion. Only rarely did my time constraints prevent a natural finishing off of the conversation. Given this element of choice on their part, their problems and their thinking through of these problems were occasionally chosen as appropriate topics of conversation. Sometimes, in contrast, they simply chatted to each other and to me, using the library as a venue for the carrying out of their own agendas. Further, the interactional style was influenced by my agenda only in so far as I wanted to understand what they thought. Other than that there was no adult agenda or purpose to influence or shape the patterns of interaction.

* Novick and Waters make a similar observation based on their interviews with and observations of children in lower primary classrooms; they felt that 'relatively more complex language was being elicited by the interview' (1977, p.6).

On occasion, when I went into the classroom the children and/or the teachers inveigled me into helping out with the teacher's agenda. On one occasion this was embarrassing. Mr Droop was testing the children to find out just how deficient they were in their basic skills. I walked into the classroom to loud cries of, 'Hey Bronwyn, come and help us with this stupid test will you.' As far as they were concerned, testing did not belong in open classrooms and any form of disruption was legitimate. Needless to say, I beat a hasty retreat. This incident was fortunately an exception. Otherwise my welcome would have worn out fairly rapidly. On other occasions I felt embarrassed because the analysis the teachers made of their situations sometimes glossed over the more negative aspects of their interactions with the children. In the adult world, maintenance of face with each other is awkward when one knows too much of the seamier side of the other's life. On some occasions I experienced a feeling of awkwardness as I listened support-ively and said nothing about what I knew (though I did on occasion say what I thought, if it seemed beneficial to both teacher and pupil to do so).

It would seem then that the effect of my presence was a facilitation of the process of self-reflection on the part of the participants, both teachers and pupils, simply because I was there and willing to listen. Through talk they were able to make sense or partial sense of what was happening to them. Clearly I was not the only person they talked to, and if I had not been there, though there may have been less oppor-tunity for on-the-spot analysis of classroom process, there would still have been some talk and some analysis, since the drive to understand was not *created* by my presence.

6
Conclusion: The Double World of Childhood

In arriving at the conclusion I find myself reflecting upon the fact that something essential in the children's world is, so far, missing from my analysis of their accounts. In seeking to arrive at some form of closure, in searching for the rational elements in their perception of the situation, I have *under*emphasised the fluidity and creativity of their world. In a sense I have stripped their accounts of inconsistencies, thereby idealising their perspective. This process has been satisfying because it emphasises a neglected aspect of the children's world. The re-emphasis reveals that children of primary school age are more perceptive and more complex than we generally give them credit for. It further demonstrates that the models they have of the world are suitable, given their agendas and their roles, i.e., the world makes best sense to them with their templates, though they know that they will eventually *be* adults and adopt adult templates, adult scripts. At the same time, in not yet being adults, they have obligations related to the moral order of the culture of childhood. Correct or 'moral' behaviour from their perspective does not involve allegiance to the adult moral order, for that is to become an outsider, even a traitor, to their own culture. This re-emphasis, via the children's perspective, on the coherence and rationality of their position is very important. Nevertheless, in this concluding chapter I wish to refocus slightly, to return to that element of the children's talk that I compared to jazz:

> Extemporise. Like jazz. Find a time, find a theme, get lost in it,
> leave it if it doesn't work, play with it a little, no lasting pattern is
> necessary, best of all, find music that makes you run hot, high, takes
> you outside of time and place but don't worry if you don't see it
> again . . . . (present volume, p. 17)

Or which Silvers refers to as the timeless and emergent quality of children's play:

> One's purpose is successively defined by what you discover
> potentially to be, yet all the while you do not wait for or expect
> another potential. (1979, p.19)

The element of the children's world which most clearly illustrates
this fluidity is their sense of humour. Often in the conversations I had
with them, fun was the dominant element, as their minds played with
the possibilities in what was being said (cf. Woods, 1976). In the
following transcript, for example, Roddie capitalises in a humorous way
on the fact that Roy and I suffer a communication breakdown:

Transcript 6.1: Roy, Roddie and Warwick

1	*Roy:*	My two fastest cousins are coming up here to race.	1-11 Confusion. I want information which Roy doesn't have.
2	*B.D.:*	Why?	
3	*Roy:*	Yeah.	
4	*B.D.:*	That's good. Why are they racing?	
5	*Roy:*	A race.	
6	*B.D.:*	Which race?	
7	*Roy:*	Hundred metre race.	
8	*B.D.:*	What for the school or what?	
9	*Roy:*	For our school.	
10	*B.D.:*	Well, is it an interschool carnival, are the schools all competing against each other?	
11	*Roy:*	Yeah.	
12	*Roddie:*	I thought you meant a racing car.	12 Roddie capitalises on the sense of confusion.
13	*Warwick:*	So did I.	13 Warwick joins in.
14	*Roy:*	You're nuts.	
15	*Roddie:*	Well you said 'coming up for a race'.	
16	*Roy:*	I got a boxer cousin coming too.	
17	*B.D.:*	A boxer cousin?	
18	*Roy:*	Yeah.	
19	*B.D.:*	Is he very good?	
20	*Roddie:*	Has he got a short	20 Roddie continues the theme

tail? (*everyone laughs*)

21 *Roy:* He'll box you. He's got about ten cups.

22 *Roddie:* Who is he, Mohammed Ali or something?

23 *Roy:* Yep. (*everyone laughs*)

24 *Roddie:* Tell us another one! Tell us another one!

of misunderstanding.

21 Roy is still taking his information seriously.

22 A black boxer with ten cups — who else could he be?

23 Roy likes the allusion and joins the fun.

24 Roy is now accused of lying, though in a chiding and humorous way.

In another conversation humour is used to resolve two conflicting statements about a previous teacher they had all liked, Mr Chalmers:

Transcript 6.2: Garry, Roy and Warwick

1 *Garry:* He used to be a real good teacher.

2 *Roy:* (*laughing*) You said 'Gee he got on my goat' and now you say, 'He's a real good teacher'.

3 *B.D.:* (*teasing*) He's silly isn't he? Can't make up your mind?
(*General conversation, everyone talking at once, about the fact that teachers can be both cranky and nice.*)

4 *B.D.:* Well I reckon all teachers might get a bit cranky with all kids they have to look after all the time.

5 *Roy:* Sometimes.

6 *Warwick:* (*mumbles*) All the time.

7 *B.D.:* Do you think you might get cranky if you had to look after thirty or thirty-five kids all the time?

8 *Roy:* No I wouldn't.

9 *Garry:* I wouldn't.

10 *B.D.:* What would you do?

11 *Roy:* (*laughing*) I'd be happy

and give them the cane.
(*everyone laughs*)

The children's dual membership in childhood and adult cultures can be an endless source of fun-making. As Koestler points out, that which is funny involves the 'bisociation' of two frames of reference ('matrices of thought'). In the 'normal' adult world there is usually only one frame of reference operable at any one time:

> Drifting from one matrix to another characterises the dream and related states; in the routines of disciplined thinking only one matrix is active at a time. (1966, p.39)

However,

> When two independent matrices of perception or reasoning interact with each other the result . . . is either a *collision* ending in laughter, or their *fusion* in a new intellectual synthesis, or their *confrontation* in an aesthetic experience. The bisociative patterns found in any domain of creative activity are tri-valent; that is to say, the same pair of matrices can produce comic, tragic, or intellectually challenging effects. (1966, p.39)

And the children are ideally situated to constantly provide these collisions, fusions and confrontations through bisociation of the different orders in which they interact. They switched easily from talk in one framework to talk in another. They held both their framework and the adult framework open most of the time and wherever opportunity presented itself collided the two frames to create a funny situation. When humour was not produced, the result for me was frustrating because of an apparent lack of order and purpose in the talk. But humour was often the result. Where humour does not result the children can be seen to be mixing frames of reference, stretching the boundaries of each, in an ongoing play with words and ideas which might eventually produce something worthwhile. Certainly in replaying the tapes, which they often did, they would listen for the funny bits, warning each other when the funny bits were coming up and laughing afresh as they listened to them. Because their minds are not tied to any one framework at any one time (as is usually the case with adults) every situation is elastic and endlessly potentially productive.

A game that emerged out of my own children's play is worth describing in detail because it creatively brings together the different frameworks operable in the children's world to create a humorous situation. The game was a variation on the theme of 'mothers and fathers'. It was played repeatedly over a long period of time and led to gales of uncontrollable laughter every time it was played. I personally found the game worrying when I first heard it because I made a psycho-analytic interpretation of it, i.e., I thought they had a problem they were trying to resolve relating to their early childhood. When I suggested my interpretation to the children they unanimously declared that it had nothing to do with me or their deceased father. The purpose of the game was to have fun and nothing else. It took quite a long time for them to convince me that I needn't worry, and that I should simply accept their view of what they were doing. But first the game:

The children decide who is to have turns at being mother, father and baby. (Everyone eventually has several turns at each.) The dialogue, with variations, is as follows:

Mother: Now I'm going out, you look after Junior, and be nice to him.

Father: OK

(*Mother walks out. Baby plays up, crawling over father, pulling his hair, his nose, his ears, generally making father uncomfortable.*)

Father: (*repeatedly asks baby to stop but baby innocently, not recognising father's discomfort, goes on doing the same thing*) Now Junior stop that! If you don't stop I'll have to smack your bottom!

Junior: (*either winges and plays up more or says*) If you do, mummy will get you.

Father: (*bashing up baby horribly, shouts*) You horrid little boy, you horrible stupid little twerp! (*etc.*)

Mother: (*walks in and says*) What have you done to my little baby, you beastly father. I'll teach you not to do that again. (*Bang, biff, smack, wop, wack, i.e., mother bashes father while baby innocently continues to crawl over them both.*)

At this point all three would be in a tangled heap on the floor, howling with laughter to such an extent that they could no longer beat each other up. When they had recovered sufficiently they would renegotiate roles. Baby was the favourite and mother next. No one wanted to be the father.

From the children's point of view, as they explained it to me, there were several humorous aspects to this game. First, baby didn't know he was being naughty, but was none the less annoying the father. Second, the father is not in the wrong, really, but he gets in trouble anyway. Third, mothers do not usually beat up fathers so it is funny to have the roles reversed. Fourth, the children are not allowed to bash each other up (according to my rules), but the game allowed them legitimately to do so.

In such a game the children are combining the rules of their culture, the rules of adult culture (with a twist) and the rules of adult-child interaction: 1 From their own culture is the love of fighting and physically romping around. There is an expression of the spontaneous and exploratory nature of childhood behaviour (in baby) which adults can find so difficult. 2 From the adult culture comes the responsibility for looking after children, agreeing on how this is to be done, and the consequent difficulties and conflicts that arise. Indirectly from adult culture via comedy TV and comic strips, comes the idea of the role switch where father is little and weak and puny and henpecked and the mother is big and fat and domineering. 3 From the rules for interaction between adults and children there is a play on the innocent (yet knowing) child who creates mayhem in the adult world.

The laughter arose through the *tri*sociation of these worlds, or frames of reference. They have collided the different agendas, roles and realities in which they habitually participate. They have used their knowledge of the adult world (of which they are partial members) their knowledge of their own world (of which they are full members) and their knowledge of the interactive patterns between these worlds, to create an explosively funny situation. They cannot *be* adults but they can play at being adults and use the adult world as a source of fun. Their entertainment is about and from the adult culture. It is at the same time an indulgence in favourite elements of their own culture and an exploitation of their side of the rules of adult-child interaction.

This fluidity of movement between frames of reference is not only creative in a humorous sense but also in an aesthetic sense. The essence of much poetry for instance derives from ambiguity which calls up two different images at the same time or which combines, unexpectedly, images which are not usually associated with each other.

In the following poems, for example, the children use the talents they bring to their talk in the more disciplined form of poetry. These poems are evocative, perhaps more so for the Australian reader, of the dry heat of summer and the fears that dryness brings of death and drought, and of the contrasting beauty of water and rain.

Dry ground scents the air
Dry trees everywhere
Little water stains the ground
Which stands there bare and brown
Brown grass, dry sky, desert winds, desolate plains
Dry dusty rocks lie dead
Tumbleweeds sweep by.

Catherine

Deep under the sea where the fish are green
and desolate coral lie

the octopus swims wild and free
there's a flutter of fish
as a big grey shark goes by
and the life in the sea dies.
                                    Catherine

Part of the sun came down
It was hotter than fire
Everything was burning
And suddenly rain came down
Flowers bloomed, animals were free
That night everyone thanked God for the rain.
                                    Suzie

The nights were cold, the sprinklers were on.
In the morning there were icicles hanging from the trees.
                                    Linda

Along with these creative uses of the double world of childhood I
could include endless pages of conversation where the children switch
rapidly and continuously from one frame of reference to another in
an unstructured and apparently aimless fashion. Occasionally they
found their own aimlessness annoying and said, 'Come on let's talk!
What will we talk about?', which sometimes led to a discussion about
some aspect of their lives and on other occasions simply called forth
comments such as, 'Right, we'll talk, yap, yap, yap, yap, yap, yap.'

This fluidity and drifting purposelessness is important for several
reasons. First, as I have demonstrated, it lends itself to creative acts of a
humorous or aesthetic kind. Second, it allows them to encompass the
various incompatible elements of their lives without needing all the
inconsistencies and wrinkles ironed out in one readily verbalised
rational line of thought. Third, it allows exploration of possibilities in
language and thought beyond the rules of the cultures in which they
participate, and a consequent appreciation of the enigmatic qualities
of many of the episodes in which we all take part.

In looking at children from their own perspective several implications
emerge for the adults who interact with them. Children are very willing
to learn (from each adult that they have to interact with) the particular
adult-child rules of interaction adhered to by that adult. They are also
interested to learn what that adult has to tell them about the adult
world. At the same time, however, they prefer it if the adult can be
sensitive to the adult-child rules they have already gone to some trouble
to learn *and* can be sensitive to the fact that their membership in the

culture of childhood is a serious membership and involves adherence to rules and patterns of interaction not operable in adult culture. Let me end with one final example of a teacher greatly admired by Jacob for his ability to switch into the pupils' framework. As light punishment Jacob had been asked by this teacher to write out ten times that he must not talk. Jacob wrote his lines hurriedly and in his worst possible writing. The teacher wrote across the page in perfect handwriting, 'Jacob your writing is 'orrible (just like your face, yuk, yuk)' and signed his name with a beautiful flourish. Jacob's comment was, 'He's great. He really knows how to chop people.' The teacher had corrected Jacob, shown himself very correct on the point at issue, made a joking insult (using the 'yuk yuk' to ensure it was recognised as a joke) and displayed at the same time a capacity to play the pupils' game of chopping each other up. In other words he had pursued his central purpose of teaching (in this case, how to write properly) and had at the same time revealed a knowledge about and acceptance of the pupil's perspective in which neat writing, especially the writing of lines, is an awful bore, and where being artfully chopped up is infinitely preferable to being punished. . . .

Teachers who are aware of the children's perspective will not be unduly upset by the breaking of adult rules since they will perceive the code the children are following. They will recognise the responsibility they have for making the rules of interaction with them explicit and clear and the responsibility for making the dimensions of their own adult culture, encapsulated in the curriculum, clear to the children. At the same time they will not underestimate the extent of the children's knowledge of life in the classroom. They will understand the switches the children make from one interpretive framework to another and will appreciate the potential humour in these switches. In understanding the balance between the two worlds they will be able to maintain the official adult line in the classroom as the central purpose of schooling, at the same time capitalising on their knowledge of childhood culture and the creativity and fluidity of the children's minds, to pursue their central purpose of teaching the children.

Further Research

The major significance of this study for me is that children do have a culture of their own, and if we are able to listen we will find that the children are very willing to teach that cultural knowledge to us. And in understanding and appreciating children's culture we are more able to teach them from our culture, appreciating that it is an *alternative* view we are presenting them with, rather than the only or 'correct' view.

The information I have presented here on children's culture can be used as background for further studies which ask more specific questions. Those questions might relate to minority group children (for example deaf or autistic children), to adult-child interaction in a variety of settings, or even to the parallels we might find between children's interpretive frameworks and the related coping strategies and the frameworks and strategies of adults who find themselves in similarly powerless situations.

Some of the questions to which I and my students have begun addressing ourselves are as follows:

— given that children wish the classroom to make sense and to be predictable, what work do *they* do towards the construction and negotiation of the social reality of the classroom? (Davies, forthcoming)
— given the way in which children balance their own and their teacher's agendas what sense do they make of teacher agendas which are intended to influence their own agendas, e.g. religious teaching?
— given the capacity of children to participate in adult and childhood cultures, and to make creative use of this dual membership, what implications does this have for the teaching of art to children? And further can this art work be analysed as an extension of their verbal communications and explorations?
— given the parallels occasionally observed throughout this study between children's coping strategies and the coping strategies of adults who find themselves in relatively powerless positions, what can we learn through interviewing women in the work force about their coping strategies when confronted by a system which cannot or will not give any credibility to their (woman's) perspective?
— given the recommendations that teachers take the pupils' perspective into account, how can teachers in training (or retraining) learn to understand this perspective and incorporate it into their teaching?

Apart from the research implications I find the implications of this study reaching into many aspects of my life. My interactions both with my own children and with other children, and with my students, have benefited from a capacity on my part to cue into the interpretive frameworks they bring to their talk with me. I can both enjoy sharing their perspective and feel more certain about what it is I want to share with them from mine. As well I feel more able to make sense of the frustrations I experience in the face of authorities who do not or cannot take me into account. It seems, then, that listening to children, *listening* to those who we usually assume have nothing to add to our understanding of the social world can have a powerful effect on our ability to act more effectively as social beings in a complex and often unjust social world.

Appendix 1
Unfolding Perceptions
of the Research Act

In this appendix I wish to examine the second level of the research act, that is, the experience of moving *outside* the conversations I had with the children, and analysing them in such a way that they reflected the intended meanings of the children *and* made sense to others who had not experienced the particular We-relationships in which these intended meanings were expressed. This second level involved a variety of inter-actions with others, e.g., the reading of the written work of others whose work I turned to as potentially useful in aiding my analysis; conversations with friends and colleagues (spoken and written) about what it was I was trying to do, and conversation with my own children about ideas arising from my analysis. Some of these interactions took me a long way away from the first level of the research act. My role became one of theorist sorting out the meanings of the words I wanted to use, i.e., discovering the appropriate language with which to share my ideas so that my meaning was not mistaken by my (potential) new audience. The research act is usually reconstrued not in its emergent stages, but as a final project which was planned and carried out on the basis of these plans. Though it may take a great deal of work and effort to present research findings in this way, it is part of a long and revered tradition that personal qualms must be put aside and work presented as a rationally planned project with anticipated outcomes.

In my own endeavours I went on perceiving my project as emergent, perhaps longer than others, partly because I lacked a mentor who could 'help' me towards closure in terms of my understanding of the direction I was taking. There were so many ways in which I could have attended to my conversations with the children. Only in its final stages with its final form clearly visible has it met with the eye of the editor and thus with the eye of someone who has any idea of its final possibilities, out-side of what I myself have produced. I, myself, that is, in conjunction with the authors whose work I have read, the friends, children and students I have talked to, and the tapes and transcripts of tapes resulting from my study.

The interaction between my reading of the work of others and my interpretation of my own data went on in a cyclic fashion over the year, my reading influencing my interpretation of what the children said, and my understanding of what the children said influencing my reading of the work of others. My earlier reading took me into phenomenology, symbolic interactionism and ethnomethodology. Later reading led me to Harré and Secord's ethogenic paradigm which is where I have rested. I draw none the less on the earlier literature where I think it helpful to do so. Much of the literature is useful in helping me to cast my understandings in a form comprehensible to others by providing constructs which facilitate the organisation and expression of ideas. This is not to say the ideas are derived from others, rather, they interact with earlier ideas in a way that seems fruitful. This process of revision, clarification and extension of ideas in interaction with the ideas of others is, I think, potentially endless.

What follows are excerpts from notes written during the second level of the research act. I start with notes made on my second day in school, before I had talked to the children and after I had observed them in the classroom. These first notes illustrate early formulations of questions along with a recognised anxiety that the questions would seem absurd to teachers within the framework of school and classroom. Subsequent notes are taken from the period after I had finished talking to the children. A different sort of influence is evident in these notes as they become more and more concerned with theory rather than data, and as I struggle to say what process I am engaged in, in my analysis of the tapes. These notes illustrate the powerful influence of the written work of others, the stimulating influence of the work of students and friends, and the possibilities of defining and redefining again and again what it is one is after.

Notes on first two days of observations in classroom: impressions created by my first contact with the school and the children

Day 1 Wednesday, 11 February 1976

Observation Notes
Went to Mr Bell's class first (5th grade). He was busy so a prac. teacher and a replacement teacher (Mr Droop) were running his class. The classroom is made up of children who (or whose parents) have chosen to be in an open-plan classroom (OP) as opposed to a teacher directed (TD) classroom. The first few minutes of the day were to consist of some TD learning on 'the characteristics of fish'. The children were noisy and

unsettled and two boys in particular resented the directed learning and indicated this by disruptive behaviour as well as vocal complaints at TD learning. When the TD lesson was over the children went off to do their own things. Chosen activities were: geometry, music, cars, number work, reading. The music I observed and found chaotic: the boys were disrupting attempts on the part of girls to make music in time to a pop record. Settled down to talk to boys drawing cars. (These included the disruptive pair.) They were tracing or drawing and colouring the cars from a book and chatted about such matters as independent suspension, jet engines, world speed records, automatic gears, etc. The fear the replacement teacher had expressed to them about wasting time drawing pretty drawings seemed to be unfounded. Also his direction to them to 'find out how engines work' was unrealistic in view of the limited reading ability of the children and the complex diagrams in the book they were using.

Thought 1
It is difficult, if not impossible, for a new teacher to rely on anything but firmly established views of the world in his initial teaching interactions with children. Beliefs about 'time-wasting', for example, are part of one's thinking as usual.

Thought 2
'Difficult' children were making a simple protest against lesson structure.

Day 2 Thursday, 12 February

Stayed only in 2nd grade classroom for an hour . . . a directed singing lesson and then a directed 'creative writing' lesson. Not much to report except some descriptions/explanations volunteered by one of the teachers: first, one particular boy is difficult because he comes from a one-parent home, he lives with his mother and she doesn't particularly want him. He doesn't display normal boyish characteristics of aggression; second, the boys are more attractive than the girls.

Thought
One can feel the school's definitions of reality bearing down or taking over. Questions which I had in mind to ask the children become more distant as the legitimate school interactions between teachers and pupils impinge on my consciousness. 'They' would consider that questions I wish to ask are a bit pointless. The teachers' world seems to be filled with taken-for-granted formulae which are workable and generally unquestioned in the teaching-learning situation. The world of the

teacher is predictable and my ideas, not part of the formulation of this predictable world, would not mean anything.

Questions raised on reading Garfinkel: the relation between his work and my own (December 1977)

My own study might be said to be exploratory. Garfinkel's studies also were exploratory but in a different sense. He predicted how people should react if their taken-for-granted worlds were disrupted. He then had his students disrupt the world of others and examine their own responses and the responses of their 'subjects'. This mode of approach required that Garfinkel could predict which aspects of the world were taken for granted. He was facilitated in this by the fact that his subjects shared his taken-for-granted world. Generally we assume that children share our taken-for-granted world. In large part this is indeed the case. As Schutz says:

> All interpretation of this world is based on a stock of previous experiences of it, our own or those handed down to us by parents or teachers; these experiences in the form of 'knowledge at hand' function as a scheme of reference. (1973, p.7)

Where children do not share the adult scheme of reference, adults tend to assume simply incomplete knowledge due to incomplete socialisation. My hypothesis is however that their taken-for-granted world differs from ours not only in quantity but in quality. This is so for fairly obvious reasons. According to Natanson in his introduction to Schutz;

> The typifications which comprise the stock of knowledge are generated out of a social structure. Here as everywhere, knowledge is socially rooted, socially distributed, and socially informed. Yet its individuated expression depends on the unique placement of the individual in the social world. (1973, p.XXIX)

From the child's point of view adults 'know' about the world and they (children) don't. Adults have control over the world and they don't. Adults assume responsibilities that children are not expected to assume. Adults have essential knowledge which they only share in small part with children, i.e., all sorts of explanations are not given; a select few are given in school and sometimes at home. Yet they cannot function in a vacuum. Quite naturally from their own particular positions in the world they make sense of what they see. This lack of access to adult meanings has been described by Holt (1975) as a plot by adults (albeit unwitting) to keep children in the bondage of childhood. What I propose is different: what is critical from the point of view of this study is that children, notwithstanding the situation they are in, do make sense of the world they live in. They develop complex sets of understanding and a workable knowledge of this world. What then are the basic elements of their world *as they perceive it?* This is the substantive question addressed in this study. Like Garfinkel I have used disruptions in the everyday world to detect what that taken-for-granted world is. I have not had to create these disruptions, however, since they occurred often, quite naturally in the time I spent with the children. Old teachers left and new teachers came, new teachers broke old rules and even old teachers broke their own rules; similarly with friends and other children, frictions occurred, and finally I broke rules occasionally and unwittingly because I did not understand their world. Just by being there and by defining myself as a person who could be talked to, I was instantly told about these disruptions when they occurred. Even though I had started with the premise that I wished to explore their assumptions about the nature of the world I was often startled, shocked and irritated at what I found. There were considerable differences in what I would accept and take for granted without comment and what they would accept. They saw sense where I could see no sense. They enjoyed conversations which irritated me intensely. And so on. What are the essential differences then between my world (the adult world) and the world of these children? What is the nature of reality? What will count as given? What will need to be questioned? What is cause for anger? for laughter? for grief? What does it mean to be faithful? to have friends? even to like someone? How do we read these things in other people? and how do we let other people know these things?

This range of questions that I wish to ask of the children's world is broader than that which Garfinkel has considered proper to matters of ethnomethodological interest. Partly they are broader because there is a 'cross cultural' dimension to the questions. There is less that I can assume about their world than Garfinkel could assume about his adult population. He understood their frame of reference and wanted to discover how that frame of reference was used in the everyday world of his subjects to achieve competent interactions and to make the world appear sensible. In his earlier work he merely guessed at the frame of reference and learned as he went along, getting his students to break rule after rule in everyday settings. But I could not even guess at the frame of reference of these children. I had to immerse myself in novels written about children, recall my own childhood, cross-question my own children at every point of the day — talk endlessly to the children of the study before I could begin to understand reality as perceived by them.

Close analysis of the conversations I had with them will reveal this growing awareness on my part. It will also reveal some answers to the questions posed. It will reveal something too of the problems of communication across groups of children where taken-for-granted worlds are not shared. . . .

Notes made at the Open University Ethnography Conference (January 1978): the problems of paradigmatic membership versus reflexivity and freedom

At several points the critical role for the ethnographer of the *reflexive* relation between theory and research was mentioned. It was felt this reflexivity was the critical element which allowed theoretical positions to be taken into account, i.e., a reflexive relationship between the theory and the data allows understandings gained from one to influence the other. The theory must not simply impose its structure on the data. There must be room for reciprocal influence and development from theory to data and vice versa. The question was asked as to whether one needed to 'belong' to one paradigm or another and generally the feeling was no. Martyn and David especially noted the importance of drawing insights from a variety of paradigmatic or theoretical positions. A critical point was made here though – I think by Roger – that the Marxist paradigm will not allow the same relation between theory and research that the ethnographers want. For the Marxists the theory dictates the meaning of the data and there is no room for the reverse. So you can't be in the Marxist paradigm and do what the ethnographers want to do. Similarly I think with the ethnomethodologists: they will not have it that their position can slot into the symbolic interactionist position because they want to insist that one can assume nothing about the society, one can only examine the process. So Roger's point was valid – the ethnographer draws on the Marxist and ethnomethodological insights but ignores what they would hold as fairly basic tenets, so you do have to declare your position as a symbolic interactionist because the reflexive act is the basic tenet of being a symbolic interactionist.

David (I think) mentioned the fact that Marx and Engels note at the end that they are not really deterministic though they argue that way because of the prevailing philosophy.

If this point is extended it could be that the Marxists and the ethnomethodologists are doing the same thing without realising it – making 'incorrigible propositions' out of elements in their philosophy which are purely reactions against the prevailing philosophy.

These points need following up.

Notes made on the conflict between two particular paradigms:
ethnomethodology and symbolic interactionism (February 1978)

As a consequence of turning my attention to the ethnomethodological
literature I became enbroiled in the controversies between the ethnomethodologists and the interactionists. The problems/controversies
were not originally mine and yet became mine as I tried to sort out just
what each of them was saying and what their critical points of difference were. I wanted to draw on both paradigms and yet seemingly
could not do so if they contradicted each other and (more importantly)
if one camp so vehemently rejected any conflation/confusion or fusion
with the other (as illustrated in Zimmerman and Wieder, 1971).

The analysis of my data (currently ongoing) has been and is being
influenced by theorists who live in somewhat antagonistic traditions.
More typically, the competent researcher selects the most suitable
theory for his data such that theory and data are mutually supportive.
The phenomenological tradition (as in Berger) has strongly influenced
my thinking however such that I remain interested in the *process*
whereby I came to see my data as meaningful. My suspicion was that
to follow the usual pattern would be to render the data less meaningful.
So I have not rejected any of the influences out of hand but have self-
consciously monitored their influence.

One of my first tasks was to find out in some definitive way what
each of the theories was and how they differed from each other, e.g.,
what *is* symbolic interactionism and what *is* ethnomethodology? How
do they differ? I wrote a paper seeking to explore then illustrate this
difference. In retrospect I can see several processes under way:

1 (a) reification of the labels, related to the (b) assumption that they
    were coherent bodies of knowledge which were identifiable as such.
2 (a) attempt to say which was superior. (b) being influenced by the
    fact that my data collection broke symbolic interactionist rules of
    data collection (e.g., no triangulation), I was moved to identify with
    the ethnomethodologists, and argue that their position was superior.

Further reading leads me to the notion that these labels should not
lead to an assumption that there is *a* symbolic interactionism or *an*
ethnomethodology. There are many of each. Their methods and
theoretical assumptions vary enormously. Even their statements as to
what symbolic interactionism or ethnomethodology is vary from one
author to another. Ideally then I should talk about various authors or
even various pieces of research and the relevance of each of these
to my work. The danger here of course is that the product is filled
with such a diversity of detail that the reader finds it incomprehensible.
In response to this sense of over-complexity I immediately began to

structure the information so that it made easier sense. In order to do this I reverted to the known terms 'symbolic interaction' and 'ethnomethodology'. And I was in danger of being back where I started. The terms, once in usage, seem to have a coercive life of their own. . . . My own position (at the moment) in relation to this conflict is that I consider the ethnomethodological interest in the process whereby the world is rendered into a meaningful place as central to my own concerns. I am not prepared to withhold my subsequent observations and analyses of the structures made visible in the accounting process since I consider that they are too important. This places me, I suppose, in the camp of those symbolic interactionists who have been influenced by ethnomethodology, if there is such a camp. Though in many ways I prefer not to label myself in this way because of the coercive nature of labels. It none the less provides something of a frame from which the reader can make sense of my data. It also saves me from the possibility of erroneous assumptions being made about the theoretical stance I am taking and consequent judgments made about my failure to do that which I was not setting out to do anyway. These points of difference, then, must be aired. Ultimately, I must view them as less important than the areas of overlap or similarity, since I believe my work to be a coherent whole stemming from these different theories.

Notes made on the impossibility of freeing oneself from assumptions attached to one theory or another. (August 1978)

My research question was simply 'how do children perceive or construe their social world?' The reason I asked this question was that it was logically prior to my original interest in how Aboriginal children perceive the world. I could not ask how Aboriginal children construed reality if I knew nothing about how the supposed contrast groups perceived the world. I was influenced by the phenomenological literature which suggested that each person will construct his or her reality differently according to his/her vantage point along with the view that adults have erroneously studied children from their own perspective, thus missing what is essential in the child's world. Piaget (see, for example, 1977) asks children about constructs which are of great interest to him (conservation, etc.) and does not often ask them about the world with which they are familiar (an obvious exception being the work on the rules of children's games).

In my attempts to make sense of what the children say, I am often prompted to ask more specific questions. Because the teachers differed in important ways I can ask what sense the children made of these differences. Since the children talked often about their friends I can ask what is peculiar to friendship as these children perceive it. As I note that most of the children who came to the interviews were working-class I can perhaps make statements about working-class children's language. And so on. Not only what the children say, but each literature I read prompts me to ask further contrastive questions of my data. How are children different from adults? How are these 10- and 11-year-old children different from older or younger children? How are the Aboriginal children different from the working-class children of my sample? And so forth. Yet my study was explicitly ignoring these questions in its inception, hoping to be open-minded and exploratory. If I note age, socio-economic status, sex, race of the children, it is more by way of making the data available for later contrastive work, rather than to say that these variables are significant.

Many researchers, especially in education, have started by assuming that these variables are important only to find after many years that the variables may well be misleading (see Robinson's 1978 analysis of Bernstein's use of class as a significant variable). That most of the children in my study could be classified as working-class and yet seem unhampered by any restrictions in their linguistic usage may be of interest to Robinson and it is incidentally of interest to me. Yet to claim that this was an interest I set out with is to misconstrue my purpose and to make my data less than adequate for the purpose.

Ethnomethodology v. symbolic interaction (September 1978)

Back to the ethnomethodologists and symbolic interaction. Mehan and Wood (1975) claim that each ethnomethodologist styles himself in contrast to someone else. They claim it is the essence of ethnomethodology to do so. The symbolic interactionists, according to Rose (1962), style themselves in contrast to the behaviourists and positivists. They say, in essence, this is what we are like, see, we are not like them in *these* critical ways. It does not make *much* sense then to contrast people with *each other* who are busily defining themselves in contrast to someone else, though the ethnomethodologists contrast themselves on occasion with the symbolic interactionists. The symbolic interactionists are willing to shift ground, however, and agree with the ethnomethodologists – so the distinction becomes unimportant to the symbolic interactionists but remains for some ethnomethodologists a critical defining feature. Schemes which I turned to, then, to aid me in conceptualising the children's reality construction and putting those conceptions into a recognisable and acceptable form presented their own sets of dilemmas and contrasts. Should one identify with the one theoretical stance and limit oneself to the conceptual tools within the single model? Is it necessary to show why this one group of conceptual tools is better than another? In process of exploring other conceptual systems some of it seems useful and yet internal conflicts arise if one's system incorporates a paradigm which in its conception used other paradigms to contrastively define itself. (It is easier, as Mehan and Wood point out, to say what one is not rather than what one is.) Whichever set(s) of conceptual tools/paradigms I decide to use, I will be forced in part to *contrastively* define these, i.e., to say what they are not as well as what they are. This is built, I think, into our language. Though we might assume that words carry their own meanings, they do not make sense (at least experientially) unless we know something to contrast them with. The colour red, for instance, is only recognisable as one colour amongst others. If there were no other colours it would not make sense to say something was red − since everything would be red.* So with the analysis of the children's construction of reality one uses words which imply contrast. By the very use of the word *children* one implies a contrast with adults even though in the final event I may wish to claim that it is people I am talking about and not just one of the sub-groups of people called children. There are discernible parallels in the children's attempts to make sense of classroom conflict with scientists' attempts to make sense of conflicting data, for instance. The significant variable may be conflict rather than age. Every such choice of category label carries with it these implied categories. It would be tedious − and in the final event unhelpful to the job at hand to stop and spell them all out − though it may be necessary to point to significant choices on occasion.

Note: I have stated what I do want to do then, by contrasting it with what I don't want to do, i.e., make contrastive statements.

Of course, each choice of words, child v. person, boy/girl v. child, person v. member v. actor v. subject, indicates a choice to go along with a particular paradigm, unless of course I invent my own new term and set out the beliefs attached to that term. As C. Wright Mills states:

> The thinker is 'circumscribed' by his audience, because, in order to communicate, to be understood, he must 'give' symbols such meanings that they call out the same responses to his audience as they do in himself. The process of 'externalising' his thought in language is thus, by virtue of the commonness essential to meaning, under the control of the audience. Socialisation is accompanied by

---

* According to Mead, all things and all action are 'in relation' to something or someone else. Food exists only in so far as there is someone to devour it as a nutritive substance: 'If an animal that can digest grass, such as an ox, comes into the world, then grass becomes food. That object did not exist before, that is, grass as food.' (1934, p.129)

revision of meaning. Seldom do identical interpretations obtain. Writings get reinterpreted as they are diffused across audiences with different nuances of meanings. We call the tendency to telescope (by variations of interpretation) the meaning of concepts into a given set of social habits, ethnocentrism of meanings. Functionally, i.e., as far as communication obtains, the reader is a factor determining what the thinker writes. (1972, p.62)

In relation to this contrastive tendency it is my intention in the theoretical discussion to discuss some of these apparent opposites or contradictory elements encountered in the paradigms I intend to use. As part of the general attempt to resist being trapped into either one or the other there are times when I opt for both being true, though apparently excluding each other, at least in their final conception. Though it may generally be an incorrigible proposition of Western thought that opposites cannot both be true, I wish to argue that this leads on occasion to over-simplification, even misrepresentation of the data. Many things can be true at one time. Any act has many meanings. When I select particular meanings to create my own pattern of inter-pretation, this is not meant to exclude other interpretations, but to draw attention to something which strikes me as being of value.

Notes made on reading a student's paper on friendship (November 1978)

An empirical study which set out to verify my notion that friendship in childhood is closely related to the children's experience of vulnerability and isolation. Reflections on the continuing influences of the ongoing world on the research act

Processes involved here are interesting.

1 I noted or listed the statements on friendship made by the children interviewed by my student.
2 His analysis seemed somehow inadequate so I looked for something else.
3 I recognised several remarks by children which introduced a new element into the picture over and above isolation/vulnerability and proximity. This was the 'family' function of the boys' groups and the 'rule' function of the girls' groups. This then led to hypothesising about the different kinds of conflicts I had observed but had been unable to explain, between the boys and girls of my own study. The new element in the student's work seemed adequate to explain an aspect of my own work that I had been vaguely bothered by for

some time.

A theory has arisen because isolated observations which didn't fit together could be assembled in a satisfying way so that most of the variance could be accounted for.

The next step is to search through the data for support for the theory.

This step is now critical. I can hunt selectively for support.

I thereby reify the theory. I claim to have proved myself correct.

OR I can go through the same process with my own data. Jot down everything they have said on friendship and see whether the theory still fits or whether it is a bit shaky. If it's shaky it may do as a partial explanation or I may throw it away. Even though I throw it away it may have been important in helping me conceptualise and categorise the different statements made by the kids.

Further, I am prompted to write this process down because I am reading Johanna's paper which is discussing the relation between empirical data and theory, stating that the theory is either a description or an expression of the facts. I was prompted then to examine my own theorising more closely. Definitely one does not simply describe – one goes intuitively beyond all the time.

Another important distinction here – does one intuit beyond on the basis of knowledge of someone else's intuitions OR does one intuit and then look for confirmation in others' intuiting?

Step 1 Reading in area.

Step 2 Observation of the world (data).

Step 3 Moment of intuition or explanation (intuitive because it draws on 1 and 2 to make a coherent idea).

Step 4 Return to 1 to hunt out the parallels in others and thereby gain higher credibility for own intuition.

Step 5 Write up stating ideas from others as prior which in one sense they are and which in another sense they are not.

It seems to me it would be more academically honest to write one's own idea first and in brackets write, cf. Kuhn or cf. X, i.e., my idea is acknowledged as comparable to that of Kuhn or X, but does not rely on it for support. The idea in itself should be sound enough and well enough documented to stand on its own legs. It is useful to the reader, however, to provide a frame or guide to other writers who have had the same intuitions or built the same theories.

Notes made to Johanna on reading a draft of her thesis (a Marxist analysis of the family): the need for a reference group and the dangers of this need (December 1978)

In pages 3 and 4 are you relying too heavily on reference to others' ideas? Are you straining to fit in with a particular paradigm or combination of paradigms? Why not just say this is the way I'm doing it then in brackets where necessary (cf. Marx or cf. Willer and Willer)?

I have been very conscious of this process in myself. There was one stage when as I worked through Garfinkel I felt I wasn't going to be able to take the institution into account, i.e., because he doesn't. This worried me. I knew I wanted to and yet how could I fly in the face of the man who was the main inspiration behind the ethnomethodological enterprise? I knew I would have to take the institution into account and felt I would have to be apologetic and self-justificatory when I did. Then one day I read the introduction to Hammersley and Woods's *Process of Schooling* and a great light dawned in my mind. Hammersley and Woods have included work from several different perspectives (including the ethnomethodological) in their book and they say in their introduction that they wish to have a view which encompasses all of these:

> Our position recognises both the autonomy of the moment and the range of choices open to the actor in any situation, *and* the existence and influence of social structures which not only constrain but also make possible particular activities. It is concerned with the analysis of micro-situations such as pieces of conversation, and with the macro-societal context in which they occur. It is interested in the thoughts, values and feelings of the actor as an individual and in the structure and operation of collectivities of various kinds. It recognises actors' accounts but also the necessity for analytic concepts. It realises the political nature of all interaction but is also aware of the routine everyday character of much interaction and the underlying understandings which envelop and cross-cut conflicting groups. (1976, p.7)

The power of those words was such that I no longer felt bound by any paradigm which emphasised any *one* of the points mentioned to the exclusion of any others. Of course there was also the comforting knowledge that there was some group of (respectable) people in the world who would support me in this view. So the adopting of a position (even an eclectic one) is a two-way process. You look for a position which most closely resembles what you want and you feel good if you find someone who does in fact closely approximate what you want. The danger at that point is that you reduce your own perspective to a mere echo of the respectable people who have foreshadowed you. This is to do yourself a disservice and to make your own statements less clear. Ultimately I think it is impossible to separate out clearly who is influencing whom, how much and when. I think some authors are too arrogant when they make no reference to the work of others. Arrogant, and also irritating because they provide no easy frame of reference for the reader to draw on in the attempt to understand what they are saying. But it is possible to go too far – and thesis students do this – and become utterly enslaved by the words of the masters.

Notes on reading Glaser and Strauss: the importance of acknowledging the various sources of my thought (January 1979)

These authors stress the importance of comparative data for the move (which they see as essential) from substantive to grounded formal theory. In my case I wish to move from how *this* group of children sees the world and makes sense of it to the mode in which children in general tackle the problems they encounter. Comparative sources of data which I used were:

1 novels about children and for children;
2 other research dealing with children;
3 other treatises on research;
4 most important, conversation with my own children;
5 memories of my own childhood.

These inputs at various times – some at the time of data collection (esp.4) and some after helped me to 'understand' my data and to clarify the position I wished to take. In my write-up to date I have ignored these sources of input. I should pay attention to acknowledging these sources – especially for example regarding the importance of friendship.

Notes made on the problem of social order (January 1979)

Along with Harré and Secord, I am not so committed to the assumption of orderliness and rationality either in pre-existing form or in process of creating form. I do not wish to assume that an orderly world *exists* to be apprehended. Nor do I wish to assume it doesn't. Often the world one apprehends appears not to make sense. In an important phenomenological sense, then, it does not always make sense (have order). Nor in my experience am I (or others) always rational or orderly in my choices of action (again phenomenologically speaking). I recognise on the other hand a strong drive to render (or perceive) things as orderly and meaningful. On whether there is or is not an external structure then I must remain agnostic. Yet I share with the symbolic interactionists an interest in the roles and structures which people experience. I share with the ethnomethodologists an interest in the work that goes into the rendition to oneself of the world as orderly. This is a phenomenological stance. The world is or is not orderly as it is experienced. It is at the same time coercive (external) and modifiable. In my research, I have sought to learn the meanings of a specific group of people. On occasion I assume they had these meanings before I did my research. On other occasions I see it as emerging out of the research situation itself or my subsequent analysis. (To have admitted this is to have failed according to a strong symbolic interactionist tradition of the discoverable nature of the subject's world if only researched correctly. In contrast it is to have opened up an area of interest to the ethnomethodologist: the methodology used by the researcher to construct coherent meanings from an incoherent body of data.) In sum then I maintain the phenomenological position on pre-existing external structure – it is there in so far as it is experienced as being there, and it is not, where it is experienced as not.

Notes made on the problem of making a final statement about the research act (June 1979)

As Mehan and Wood note, the final moment of understanding may well come to the researcher long after the manuscript has been sent to the publishers. The changing nature of the study, evidenced by the different questions asked at different points in time, must lose its state of fluidity and achieve an apparent stasis or closure (which is satisfying at the time of writing) in order to be rendered into a publishable form.

At this point, I have chosen to cast the work within the ethogenic framework. Further insights and extensions of the ideas presented here must wait for their expression in later research projects. Ideas which seemed central at some earlier point and yet which have been dropped in the current thinking though may appear in further work or they may vanish altogether.

Appendix 2
Analysis of the Interaction between Language and Experience in the Making of Accounts

'. . . language marks the co-ordinates of my life in society and fills that life with meaningful objects.'

(Berger and Luckmann, 1967, p.36)

The medium which allows people to move into We-relationships where each other's perspective is known, the medium through which one can tell that knowing to someone else is, of course, language. It is language that traps us into old ways of perceiving and it is language that facilitates the perception (emergence) of something new. Each level of the research act (the first, where the children and I talk to each other, and the second, where I analyse or make sense of our talk) involves the rendering of experience into words. The relationship between the words spoken and the experience described or analysed is an extraordinarily complex one. Sometimes the words create the experience by bringing together isolated fragments of experience which had no coherence in their original form, and on other occasions words can appear to destroy the original experience by construing it in ways too different from the original experience.

In writing this book, my constant struggle has been to find the precise words which capture my meaning. I have been both dominated and inspired by the words written by others, by the words I have written down myself, and by the words, spoken and transcribed, that formed the substance of my conversations with the children. Written words can have a coercive life of their own, and can be more difficult to negotiate with than spoken words. What I wish to do here is examine briefly some insights I have gained from a reading of the phenomenological and the socio-linguistic literature on the way in which language and experience interact.

Without the structure and meaning provided in large part by

language we would exist in a state of anomie or normlessness. Through the process of socialisation the structures and meanings shared by adults within a particular cultural group and encapsulated in their language are passed on to their children. To the extent that these meanings are reified and passed on as unquestionable they may be experienced by the child as external and inevitable. At times, however, that very externality and inevitability interferes with understanding; indeed the experience of oneself in the social world of meanings is sufficiently complex that it requires an ongoing process of coming to know (through socialisation or negotiation). It is through talk that we can come to know ourselves in relation to others, and to society. In this sense talk is creative activity. This creative element of conversation arises from the reciprocal access we gain to each other's consciousness through conversation.

Our subjective experiences become both subjectively and objectively known through language. Through talk with others our experiences are crystallised, made clearer, and thereby made more stable. The external facticity of words allows me, once outside the conversation or face-to-face interactions, to know those things of myself that were verbalised during the conversation (cf. Berger and Luckmann, 1967, pp. 52–3).

At the same time that language is experienced as *creative* in allowing us to come to know ourselves and our own experiences more fully it can also be experienced as *coercive* in so far as the negotiated knowledge takes on an external facticity which may be experienced as unchangeable. Further, the particular words available within a particular cultural group will mean that there are certain limitations to the verbal renderings of experience:

> As a sign system, language has the quality of objectivity. I encounter language as a facticity external to myself and it is coercive in its effect on me. Language forces me into its patterns. . . . Language provides me with a ready-made possibility for the ongoing objectification of my unfolding experience. . . . Language also typifies experiences, allowing me to subsume them under broad categories in terms of which they have meaning not only to myself but also to my fellow men. As it typifies, it also anonymises experiences, for the typified experience can, in principle, be duplicated by anyone falling into the category in question. For instance, I have a quarrel with my mother-in-law. This concrete and subjectively unique experience is typified linguistically under the category of 'mother-in-law trouble'. (Berger and Luckmann, 1967, pp.53-4)

Because this category exists in Western parlance Berger and Luckmann can think in this way about particular quarrels, thereby in a sense rendering them less problematic, because everyone is bound to have such quarrels sooner or later in this society. In a way, thinking about the quarrel can sometimes cease where such labels are handy. Where a category is strongly maintained in a social group, certain behaviours are not problematic and need not have any kind of creative thinking applied to them.

Each individual, too, may be limited by the words he knows and the meanings he has learned to attach to these. Many people, particularly when they are writing, do not feel fully in control of the medium of language because the words they use seem to take on a life of their own and to create their meanings for them. In struggling to find the words to express our meaning we may well find ourselves saying only more or less what we intended. (Many personal quarrels take on a more-than-intended heat through careless or uninformed use of words.)

The way in which we label topics or events has implications for the location of that topic or event in relation to the rest of the world. In changing the label we change a complex series of relationships between the thing labelled and the context of that thing. To label is also to locate something within a wider framework:

> To name, then, is not only to indicate; it is to identify an object as some kind of object. An act of identification requires that the thing referred to be placed within a category. Borrowing from the language of logic, we may say that any particular object that is referred to is a member of a general class, a representative of that class. An orange is a member of a class called oranges; but note that this class itself receives its placement, or definition, only by virtue of its relationships with other classes. These relationships are of quite a systematic sort. Thus oranges may be defined in relation to such classes as fruits, foods, tropical growths, tree products and moderately priced objects. Defining any class, then, means relating it to systematically associated classes. (Strauss, 1972, p.72)

Strauss goes on to quote Burke (1945):

> To tell what a thing is, you place it in terms of something else. This idea of locating, or placing, is implicit in our very word for definition itself: to *define* or *determine* a thing is to mark its boundaries. (Burke, 1945, p.24)

Through words, then, we come to know ourselves in relation to the external world. We come to see ourselves as objective beings in an objective world. What happens, then, to external facts presented to us via language when placed under the strain of new and contradictory experiences? Verbalising, in fact, may not necessarily mean that any *final* form of understanding has been reached. The cyclic process whereby action and words about action interact with each other is described by Strauss. New experiences require new labellings. New labellings can cause us to experience (or attend to) things differently:

> The naming or identifying of things is then, a continual problem, never really over and done with. By 'continual' I do not mean 'continuous' – one can lie in a hammock contentedly watching the moon rise and raising no questions about it, the world or oneself. Nevertheless, some portion of one's classificatory terminology, the symbolic screen through which the world is ordered and organised, is constantly under strain – or just has been – or will be. George H. Mead (who asserted that classifications are really hypotheses) would say it necessarily must be, from the very nature of action which brings in its train the reconstruction of past experiences and the arising of new objects. (1972, p.74)

People do, however, arrive at formulations and understandings which they regard as final or complete. It is a rare philosopher, and perhaps even rarer man-in-the-street who keeps everything open to question. Relief from tensions relating to doubt are eased with certainty, and habits of thought set in wherever we do not vigilantly guard ourselves against them. Whatever we regard as non-problematic, slips into the 'background' as a set of taken-for-granted expectancies on the basis of which we can organise our day-to-day activities. Taken for granted or tacit knowledge requires no mental energy or conscious attention. It helps in our interactions with others to be able to assume that many things can be 'taken as read'. This frees us to attend to the problem or project at hand.

> By providing a stable background in which human activity may proceed with a minimum of decision-making most of the time, it frees energy for such decisions as may be necessary on certain occasions. In other words, the background of habitualized activity opens up a foreground for deliberation and innovation. (Berger and Luckmann, 1967, p.71)

The positive function of the taken-for-granted, the provision of a stable, predictable basis for competent action, may lead people to cling to certain habitual explanations even when events conspire to indicate the need for some reconstruction and redefinition.

Some of the strains on our understanding of the world arise from the tension between our belief that we ought to be consistent,* and our

---

* This need for consistency would seem to be, from my experience, stronger for those influenced by Western rather than Eastern philosophy, and stronger for males than females.

experiences in a world which makes inconsistent and complex demands on us. C. Wright Mills, quoting from Gerth and Mills, gives the following example which illustrates that our actions may stem from incompatible demands and that language will not necessarily serve to provide a coherent pattern of meaning to the inconsistent action.

> A skilled compositor employed by a reactionary newspaper, for example, may for the sake of making a living and holding his job conform to the demands of employer discipline. In his heart, and outside the shop, he may be a radical agitator. Many German socialists allowed themselves to become perfectly disciplined soldiers under the Kaiser's flag — despite the fact that their subjective values were those of revolutionary Marxism. It is a long way from symbols to conduct and back again, and not all integration is based on symbols. (1970, p.48)

Mills goes on:

> To emphasise such conflict of value is not to deny 'the force of rational consistencies'. The discrepancy between word and deed is often characteristic, but so is the striving for consistency. (1970, p.49)

This point is relevant to the inconsistencies in some of the children's talk. There is a striving towards consistency, yet consistency, given the complex demands of any situation is not always possible. No one explanation seems of itself satisfactory. Multiple explanations, containing contradictions sometimes emerged in their talk.

Where for the sake of consistency the contradictory elements of an experience are ignored we may develop a view of the world which is not particularly useful, due to its inelasticity. Britton makes the following point about people who are unable to incorporate their ongoing experience into the way they see the world:

> As we talk about events — present, past or imagined — we shape them in the light of, and incorporate them into, the body of our experience, the total. We may of course fail in our attempt to adjust the corpus and digest the new event: life does sometimes make irreconcilable demands upon all of us. To preserve the order, harmony, unity of our represented world we may ignore the recalcitrant event (or aspect of events); or we may, over a period of time, continue the effort to come to terms with it. Those who too readily ignore disturbing aspects of experience are destined to operate in the actual world by means of a represented world that grows less and less like it: and so the fool has his paradise. (Britton, 1972, p.246)

Clear and consistent accounts may be impeded, then, sheerly through the complexity of the action. Harré and Secord (1972, p.12) suggest that when episodes or events are enigmatic we draw on explanations and understandings arrived at in clear episodes to make sense of that which is not readily and of itself explicable. Harré and Secord claim, in fact, that most episodes are enigmatic, i.e., they have no clear set of rules and no clear causal structure.

Action is sufficiently complex, then, that words, however incisive, external, and inevitable they may seem, can make no final rendition of the actions possible. Some matters, Robinson points out (1978, p.21), 'require more than patterns of words to understand'. We may act in ways which seem (are) significant and yet are not *necessarily* renderable into words. In accounts, we are relying, by and large, on the words (along with tone of voice and other aspects of conversation which are not captured in the words themselves) as if all action could be accounted for verbally.

What we say is an attempt to approximate most closely what we perceive, though we may not have the words or the conceptual tools to do this as well as we might like. Thus there may always be a certain sense of dissatisfaction accompanying some of the explanations we have made or have had made to us. Where this dissatisfaction precludes closure we will generally await some further information which can be shaped into a sensible or meaningful pattern. The pattern we finally accept may well be an '*idealised*' pattern, stripped of the inconsistencies which prevent closure. Idealisation, according to Mehan (1974, p.127) 'is a feature of the accounting process'. Mehan quotes the explanation Garfinkel gives of this phenomenon in his description of the documentary method:

> The documentary method consists essentially in the retrospective prospective reading of a present occurrence so as to maintain the constancy of the object as a sensible thing through temporal and circumstantial alterations in its actual appearances. . . . The documentary method occurs as a feature of situations of incomplete information in which effective actions nevertheless must be taken, matters of fact decided, and interpretations made. The method would seem to be an intimate part of a social process wherein a body of knowledge must be assembled and made available for legitimate use despite the fact that the situations it purports to describe (1) are, in the calculatable sense of the term, unknown; (2) are in their actual and intended logical structures essentially vague; (3) are modified, elaborated, extended if not indeed created by the fact and manner of being addressed. (1959, p.128)

Closure may occur some time after an episode or event has passed.

At the time of the event, no explanation may seem necessary. The following account of a balloon voyage nicely illustrates a considerable time lapse between action and explanation:

> Now, months later, each of us recalls certain moments during the aftermath.
>
> There was my sadness that the voyage was done, a feeling I hadn't anticipated and can't quite explain. Maxie vividly remembers the mayor of Evreux giving a speech of welcome from a balcony.
>
> And there was Larry feeling what each of us sensed: an absolutely genuine joy, a shared joy, in our adventure. Frankly, until we landed, I never understood fully what had motivated me, the real reason for trying what had ended in grief for so many before us. People may not have been able to picture themselves in a spacecraft to the moon or beyond, but they can see themselves in the balloon. They can feel with us that when mankind stops crossing frontiers or achieving new goals, it stagnates and moves backward instead of forward. That moving forward was, for me, the long hidden motive of our voyage. (Abruzzo *et al.*, 1978, pp.881-2)

What the author has produced is a formulation which most satisfies him at the time of writing concerning the flash he had after the event about what had motivated him in the beginning. That he did not '*know*' in the beginning what motivated him is one of the fascinating and enigmatic aspects of the process we engage in when we try to understand what we do.

We cannot know if Abruzzo's motives were what he said. We can know, however, (which seems to me more significant) that:

1 Motives are very often clearer after the event.

2 At the point of involvement we are driven forward without necessarily formulating in words what is driving us forward.

3 Even if we do make explanations at the time we may reject them in favour of superior explanations at some future time.

4 Some explanations have a peculiarly satisfying nature which is exciting to the person who makes the explanation. (This excitement may be due to the fact that the explanation we have found fits the available information in a way which transcends any possible negative or mundane interpretations.)

5 This interpretation is experienced as more 'real' than any other explanation.

6 It was in writing, *in putting into words*, the description of his balloon voyage, that the author *discovered* his motive, i.e., in attempting to communicate with others.

To conclude this section on the relationship between language and experience one must note the profound importance of the particular listener to whom the person is making the account and of the particular context about which and in which the account is made. Through time we change our perceptions of what we are and what the meanings of our experiences are. Similarly as we move from one person to another, and one context to another we attend to different aspects of our experience. We may see differently because we take into account what the listener understands and what meanings he imputes. Similarly, each context has its own relevant conceptual framework, or script. Each situation, along with the people in that situation, provides possible ways of being and possible ways of seeing the world. Each relationship provides a framework, which makes possible the expression of one's experience in a particular way. Thoughts which seemed important in one context may be lost in another, and only regained when certain elements of the particular framework, relevant to that context, are reviewed. Words may be coercive and external and unquestionable, but they give us the power to endlessly define and redefine our experience and to see it anew through the eyes of those others with whom we share our experience. This stimulation from the other is not a negation of our own experience. The other facilitates the ongoing negotiation necessary for our knowledge of who we are in relation to the rest of the world. Some others will facilitate more *satisfying* perceptions than others. Some others will cause us to pause and question some taken-for-granted elements of our world. Some others will serve to confirm by being part of the tacit background knowledge from which we view the world.

The unstructured interview is potentially all of these things. In the conversations I had with the children I prompted them to look freshly at the classroom situation and at their interactions with each other. I did this simply by being a questioning stranger. That they found this a satisfying process is indicated by the enthusiasm with which they constantly returned to the interview situation; a situation in which they both discovered and confirmed the world they knew.

Bibliography

Abruzzo, B. L. *et al.* (1978), '"Double Eagle II" has landed!', *National Geographic*, 154, pp. 859-82.

Aries, P. (1962), *Centuries of Childhood* (Harmondsworth, Penguin).

Baker, C. (1980), 'An Interpretive Approach to the Study of Adolescent Socialisation and Identity' (PhD thesis, University of Toronto).

Berger, P. L. (1966), *Invitation to Sociology* (Harmondsworth, Penguin). First published by Doubleday, 1963.

Berger, P. and Luckmann, T. (1967), *The Social Construction of Reality* (Harmondsworth, Penguin).

Berlak, A. and Berlak, H. (1975), 'The dilemmas of schooling: an application and interpretation of G. H. Mead's Social Behaviourism', *ERIC*, ed. 108 986

Blom, J. P. and Gumperz, J. J. (1972), 'Social Meaning in Linguistic Structure: Code Switching in Norway', in Gumperz, J. J. and Hymes, D. (eds), *Directions in Sociolinguistics* (New York, Holt, Rinehart & Winston).

Britton, J. (1972), 'What's the Use? A Schematic Account of Language Functions', in Cashdan, A. *et al.* (eds), *Language in Education* (London, Routledge & Kegan Paul).

Bruner, J. S. (1974), *The Relevance of Education* (Harmondsworth, Penguin). First published by George Allen & Unwin, 1972.

Bullivant, B. (1973), *Educating the Immigrant Child* (Sydney, Angus & Robertson).

Burke, K. (1945), *A Grammar of Motives* (New York, Prentice-Hall).

Byers, P. and Byers, H. (1972), 'Nonverbal Communication and the Education of Children', in Cazden, C. B., John, V. P. and Hymes, D. (eds), *Functions of Language in the Classroom* (New York, Teachers College Press).

Cicourel, A. V. (1973), *Cognitive Sociology* (Harmondsworth, Penguin).

Cicourel, A. V. and Boese, R. J. (1972), 'Sign Language Acquisition and the Teaching of Deaf Children' in Cazden, C. B., John, V. P. and Hymes, D. (eds), *Functions of Language in the Classroom* (New York, Teachers College Press).

Cook-Gumperz, J. (1975), 'The Child as Practical Reasoner', in Sanches, M. and Blount, B. C. (eds), *Sociocultural Dimensions of Language Use* (New York, Academic Press).

Cooley, C. H. (1972), 'Looking-glass Self' in Manis, J. G. and Meltzer, B. N. (eds), *Symbolic Interaction* (Boston, Allyn & Bacon).

Corrigan, P. (1979), *Schooling the Smash Street Kids* (London, Macmillan).

Cottle, T. (1967), *Time's Children* (Boston, Little, Brown).

Cusick, P. A. (1973), *Inside High School: The Student's World* (New York, Holt, Rinehart & Winston).

Damon, W. (1977), *The Social World of the Child* (San Francisco, Jossey-Bass).

Davies, B. (forthcoming), 'The role pupils play in the social construction of classroom order', *British Journal of Sociology of Education.*

Denzin, N. K. (1977), *Childhood Socialisation* (San Francisco, Jossey-Bass).

Dumont, R. V. and Wax, M. L. (1971), 'Cherokee School Society and the Intercultural Classroom', in Cosin, B. R. *et al.* (eds), *School and Society* (London, Routledge & Kegan Paul).

Dunkle, M. and the Children's Panel (eds) (1979), *Our World* (Melbourne, McPhee Gribble).

Edwards, A. D. and Furlong, V. J. (1978), *The Language of Teaching* (London, Heinemann).

Erikson, E. H. (1965), *Childhood and Society* (Harmondsworth, Penguin). First published by Imago, 1951.

Freud, S. (1963), trans. J. Strachey, *An Outline of Psycho-Analysis* (London, Hogarth Press).

Furlong, V. J. (1976), 'Interaction Sets in the Classroom: Towards a Study of Pupil Knowledge', in Hammersley, M. and Woods, P. (eds), *The Process of Schooling* (London, Routledge & Kegan Paul).

Garfinkel, H. (1959), 'Aspects of the Problem of Common Sense Knowledge of Social Structures', *Transactions of the Fourth World Congress of Sociology* (Belgium, International Sociological Association).

Garfinkel, H. (1967), *Studies in Ethnomethodology* (New York, Prentice-Hall).

Glaser, B. and Strauss, A. (1967), *The Discovery of Grounded Theory* (Chicago, Aldine).

Goffman, E. (1968a), *Asylums* (Harmondsworth, Penguin). First published by Anchor Books, Doubleday, 1961.

Goffman, E. (1968b), *Stigma* (Harmondsworth, Penguin).

Goffman, E. (1971), *Presentation of Self in Everyday Life* (Harmondsworth, Penguin).

Goffman, E. (1975), *Frame Analysis* (Harmondsworth, Penguin). First published by Harper & Row, 1974.

Goodnow, J. (1976), 'The Nature of Intelligent Behaviour: Questions Raised by Cross-cultural Studies', in Resnick, L. (ed.), *The Nature of Intelligence* (New York, Erlbaum).

Gouldner, A. (1960), 'The Norm of Reciprocity: A Preliminary Statement', *American Sociological Review*, 25, 2, pp. 161-78.

Gracey, H. (1975), 'Learning the Student Role: Kindergarten as Academic Boot Camp', in Stub, H. R. (ed.), *The Sociology of Education: a Sourcebook* (Homewood, Dorsey Press).

Griffin, P. and Mehan, H. (forthcoming), 'Sense and Ritual in Classroom Discourse', to appear in Florian Coulmas (ed.), *Conversational Routine: Explorations in Standardised Communication Situations and Pre-patterned Speech*, Janua Linguarum (The Hague, Mouton).

Hammersley, M. (1977), 'School Learning: Cultural Resources Required by Pupils to Answer a Teacher's Question', in Woods, P. and Hammersley, M. (eds), *School Experience* (London, Croom Helm).

Hammersley, M. (1976), 'The Mobilisation of Pupil Attention', in Hammersley, M. and Woods, P. (eds), *The Process of Schooling* (London, Routledge & Kegan Paul).

Hammersley, M. and Woods, P. (eds) (1976), *The Process of Schooling* (London, Routledge & Kegan Paul).

Hargreaves, D. (1975), *Interpersonal Relations and Education* (London, Routledge & Kegan Paul).

Hargreaves, D., Hestor, S. and Mellor, F. (1975), *Deviance in Classrooms* (London, Routledge & Kegan Paul).

Harré, R. (1979), *Social Being* (Oxford, Blackwell).

Harré, R. and Secord, P. F. (1972), *The Explanation of Social Behaviour* (Oxford, Blackwell).

Hartley, L. P. (1963), *The Shrimp and the Anemone* (London, Faber & Faber).

Henry, J. (1965), *Culture Against Man* (New York, Vintage Books).

Henry, J. (1968), 'Docility, or Giving the Teacher What She Wants', in Bell, R. R. and Stub, H. R. (eds), *The Sociology of Education* (Homewood, Ill., Dorsey Press).

Holt, J. (1969), *How Children Fail* (Harmondsworth, Penguin). First published by Pitman, 1965.

Holt, J. (1975), *Escape from Childhood* (Harmondsworth, Penguin). First published by E. P. Dutton, 1974.

Homans, G. C. (1951), *The Human Group* (London, Routledge & Kegan Paul).

Hunter, E. (1977), *The Blackboard Jungle* (London, New English Library).

Jackson, P. W. (1968), *Life in Classrooms* (New York, Holt Rinehart & Winston).

James, W. (1978), *Pragmatism and the Meaning of Truth* (Cambridge, Mass., Harvard University Press).

Kesey, K. (1962), *One Flew Over the Cuckoo's Nest* (London, Methuen).

Kitwood, T. (1980), *Disclosures to a Stranger* (London, Routledge & Kegan Paul).

Kochman, T. (1972), 'Black American Speech Events and a Language Program for the Classroom', in Cazden, C. B., John, V. P. and Hymes, D. (eds), *Functions of Language in the Classroom* (New York, Teachers College Press).

Koestler, A. (1966), *The Act of Creation* (London, Pan Books).

Kohlberg, L. (1969), 'Stage and Sequence: The Cognitive-developmental Approach to Socialization', in Goslin, D. (ed.), *Handbook of Socialization Theory and Research* (Chicago, Rand McNally).

Laing, R. D. (1972), *Knots* (Harmondsworth, Penguin). First published by Tavistock, 1970.

Lambart, A. M. (1976), 'The Sisterhood', in Hammersley, M. and Woods, P. (eds), *The Process of Schooling* (London, Routledge & Kegan Paul).

Leiter, K. C. W. (1976), 'Ad Hocing in the Schools', in Hammersley, M. and Woods, P. (eds), *The Process of Schooling* (London, Routledge & Kegan Paul).

Mackay, R. W. (1974), 'Conceptions of Children and Models of Socialization', in Turner, R. (ed.), *Ethnomethodology* (Harmondsworth, Penguin).

Mackay, R. (1977-8), 'Children's Intellectual Rights', *Interchange*, vol. 8, 1-2, pp. 109-18.

Malcolm, I. G. (1977), 'Developing Concepts and Terminology for the Description of Aboriginal Children's Classroom Communication', unpublished paper given at the Ninth Annual Conference of the Linguistic Society of Australia (Melbourne).

Malcolm, I. G. (1978), 'The West Australian Aboriginal Child and Classroom Interaction: A Sociolinguistic Approach', unpublished paper presented to the Fifth AILA congress (Montreal).

Marsh, P., Rosser, E. and Harré R. (1978), *The Rules of Disorder* (London, Routledge & Kegan Paul).

McHugh, P. (1968), *Defining the Situation* (Indianapolis, Bobbs-Merrill).

McKeich, R. (1974), 'The Construction of a Part-Aboriginal World', paper presented to the Australian Institute of Aboriginal Studies Biennial Conference (Canberra).

Mead, G. H. (1934), *Mind, Self and Society* (University of Chicago Press).

Mehan, H. (1974), 'Accomplishing Classroom Lessons', in Cicourel, A. V. *et al.* (eds), *Language Use and School Performance* (New York, Academic Press).

Mehan, H. (1979a), *Learning Lessons* (Cambridge, Mass., Harvard University Press).

Mehan, H. (1979b), 'The Competent Student', unpublished paper (University of California, San Diego). Currently being circulated as a Working Paper in Sociolinguistics SED1, Austin, Texas. Forthcoming in a book edited by C. Cazden.

Mehan, H. and Wood, H. (1975), *The Reality of Ethnomethodology* (New York, Wiley).

Meyenn, R. J. (1980), 'School Girls' Peer Groups', in Woods, P. (ed.), *Pupil Strategies: Explorations in the Sociology of the School* (London, Croom Helm).

Miller, C. M. L. and Parlett, M. (1976), 'Cue-consciousness', in Hammersley, M. and Woods, P. (eds), *The Process of Schooling* (London, Routledge & Kegan Paul).

Mills, C. Wright (1970), *The Sociological Imagination* (Harmondsworth, Penguin). First published by Oxford University Press, 1959.

Mills, C. Wright (1972), 'Language, Logic and Culture', in Cashdan, A. *et al.* (eds), *Language in Education* (London, Routledge & Kegan Paul).

Morgan, J., O'Neill, C. and Harré, R. (1979), *Nicknames, Their Origins and Social Consequences* (London, Routledge & Kegan Paul).

Newcombe, T. M., Turner, R. H. and Converse, P. E. (1965), *Social Psychology* (London, Routledge & Kegan Paul).

Novick, D. and Waters, D. (1977), *Talking in School* (Adelaide, Publications Branch, Education Department of South Australia).

Opie, I. and Opie, P. (1959), *The Lore and Language of School Children* (London, Oxford University Press).

Parsons, T. (1959), 'The School as a Social System', *Harvard Educational Review*, 29, pp. 297-318.

Piaget, J. (1977), *The Moral Judgment of the Child* (Harmondsworth, Penguin). First published by Routledge & Kegan Paul, 1932.

Robinson, P. (1978), *Language Management in Education* (Sydney, George Allen & Unwin).

Rose, A. M. (1962), 'A Systematic Summary of Symbolic Interaction Theory', in Rose, A. M. (ed.), *Human Behaviour and Social Processes* (London, Routledge & Kegan Paul).

Rosser, E. and Harré, R. (1976), 'The Meaning of Trouble', in Hammersley, M. and Woods, P. (eds), *The Process of Schooling* (London, Routledge & Kegan Paul).

Schegloff, E. A. (1972), 'Notes on a Conversational Practice: Formulating Place', in Sudnow, D. (ed.), *Studies in Social Interaction* (New York, Free Press).

Schutz, A. (1971), 'The Stranger', in Cosin, B. R. *et al.* (eds), *School and Society* (London, Routledge & Kegan Paul).

Schutz, A. (1972), *The Phenomenology of the Social World* (London, Heinemann).

Schutz, A. (1973), *Collected Papers, vol. 1, The Problem of Social Reality* (The Hague, Martinus Nijhoff).

Sharp, R. and Green, A. (1975), *Education and Social Control* (London, Routledge & Kegan Paul).

Shields, M. M. (1978), 'The Child as Psychologist: Construing the Social World', in Lock, A. (ed.), *Action, Gesture and Symbol* (London, Academic Press).

Silvers, R. (1977a), 'Appearances: A Videographic Study of Children's Culture', in Woods, P. and Hammersley, M. (eds), *School Experience* (London, Croom Helm).

Silvers, R. (1977b), 'The First Day', *Educational Courier*, April.

Silvers, R. (1979), 'Understanding Phenomenological Inquiry', paper presented as an address to the Ontario Psychological Association, 10 February 1979 (Toronto).

Speier, M. (1976), 'The Child as Conversationalist', in Hammersley, M. and Woods, P. (eds), *The Process of Schooling* (London, Routledge & Kegan Paul).

Strauss, A. L. (1972), 'Language and Identity', in Cashdan, A. *et al.* (eds), *Language in Education* (London, Routledge & Kegan Paul).

Turner, I. (1969), *Cinderella Dressed in Yella* (Melbourne, Heinemann Educational).

Werthman, C. (1971), 'Delinquents in Schools', in Cosin, B. R. *et al.* (eds), *School and Society* (London, Routledge & Kegan Paul).

Willans, G. and Searle R. (1973), *Down with Skool!* (London, Collins). First published by Max Parrish, 1958.

Willis, P. (1977), *Learning to Labour* (Westmead, Saxon House).

Woods, P. (1976), 'Having a Laugh: An Antidote to Schooling', in Hammersley, M. and Woods, P. (eds), *The Process of Schooling* (London, Routledge & Kegan Paul).

Woods, P. (1979), *The Divided School* (London, Routledge & Kegan Paul).

Woods, P. (1980), *Pupil Strategies: Explorations in the Sociology of the School* (London, Croom Helm).

Zimmerman, D. H. and Wieder, D. L. (1971), 'Ethnomethodology and the Problem of Social Order', in Douglas, J. (ed.), *Understanding Everyday Life* (London, Routledge & Kegan Paul).

Name Index

Subject Index